Heart Healthy Cookbook for Beginners

Low-Fat Easy Recipes, Low-Sodium Wholesome Snacks with a Comprehensive 60-Day Meal Plan for a Balanced Lifestyle, Plus Hearty Beverages

By Alison Grace

Copyright and Disclaimer

Copyright © 2024 by Alison Grace

Publisher: Alison Grace

Disclaimer:
The information provided in this book is for educational and informational purposes only and is not intended as medical advice. The content is not meant to replace the advice of your healthcare provider. Always seek the advice of your physician or other qualified health providers with any questions you may have regarding a medical condition.
The author and publisher of this book are not responsible for any specific health or allergy needs that may require medical supervision and are not liable for any damages or negative consequences from any treatment, action, application, or preparation to any person reading or following the information in this book. References are provided for informational purposes only and do not constitute endorsement of any websites or other sources.
Use of the recipes and advice contained in this book is at the sole choice and risk of the reader.

First Edition: 2024

TABLE OF CONTENTS

Introduction..**5**

    How Diet Shapes Heart Health 5

    Balancing Cholesterol and Blood Pressure 6

    Best Cooking Methods for Heart Health................................6

Chapter 1: Breakfast..**8**

    Easy and Nutritious Breakfast Recipes 8

    High-Fiber Breakfast Options................................10

    Heart-Healthy Smoothies 13

Chapter 2: Snacks and Appetizers................................**15**

    Heart-Boosting Snacks................................15

    Simple and Tasty Appetizers................................18

    Low-Sodium Snack Options................................20

Chapter 3: Salads **23**

    Leafy Greens and Vegetable Salads................................23

    Protein-Packed Salads................................26

    Fruit Salads................................29

Chapter 4: Grains, Pasta, and Rice **31**

    Whole Grains and Ancient Grains 31

    Pasta Dishes................................34

    Nutritious Rice and Pilaf Dishes 37

Chapter 5: Fish and Seafood **41**

    Light and Refreshing Seafood Dishes................................41

    Omega-3 Rich Fish Recipes 44

    Quick and Easy Fish Recipes 47

Chapter 6: Poultry Recipes **50**

    Baked Poultry Dishes................................50

    Poultry Stews 53

    Quick and Easy Poultry Recipes 56

Chapter 7: Meat Recipes **60**

    Lean Red Meat Dishes 60

    Ground Meat Recipes................................63

    Slow-Cooked and Braised Meat Dishes 66

Chapter 8: Vegetable Recipes **70**

Vegetable Main Dishes 70

Nourishing Vegan Entrees 73

Vegetarian and Vegan Sides and Salads 77

Chapter 9: Soups **80**

Vegetable-Based Soups...80

Protein-Rich Soups 83

Grain and Legume Soups..86

Chapter 10: Desserts **89**

Guilt-Free Desserts for Heart Health...89

Nutrient-Dense Desserts..92

Healthy Alternatives to Traditional Sweets..................................95

BONUS Chapter: Heart Healthy Beverages **98**

Energizing Protein Shakes..98

Refreshing Juices and Mocktails...101

Cozy Warm Drinks..103

Conclusion **106**

60-Day Heart Healthy Meal Plan.. **107**

Nutritionist's Explanation for the 60-Day Meal Plan **110**

Index of Recipes **111**

Introduction

Welcome to your journey toward a healthier heart with our Heart Healthy Cookbook for Beginners. This book is designed to empower you with delicious, easy-to-make recipes that support cardiovascular health. Whether you're looking to prevent heart disease or manage existing conditions, this cookbook provides the essential tools to nourish your body and delight your taste buds.

How Diet Shapes Heart Health

Your diet plays a crucial role in heart health, influencing everything from blood pressure and cholesterol levels to inflammation and arterial health. Certain nutrients are essential for maintaining cardiovascular health. Fiber, which is abundant in whole grains, fruits, vegetables, and legumes, helps reduce cholesterol and regulate blood sugar. Healthy fats, especially unsaturated fats and omega-3s, found in foods like fish, nuts, and seeds, reduce inflammation and the risk of heart disease. Antioxidants, such as vitamins C and E and polyphenols found in berries, dark chocolate, and green tea, combat oxidative stress. Potassium, present in bananas, potatoes, and spinach, helps regulate blood pressure.

Foods to Embrace

Incorporating the right foods into your diet is essential for heart health. Fruits and vegetables are packed with essential vitamins, minerals, and antioxidants that support cardiovascular health. Aim for a colorful variety to ensure a broad spectrum of nutrients. Whole grains like oats, brown rice, and whole wheat not only provide fiber but also help lower cholesterol and improve blood vessel function. Lean proteins, including fish, poultry, beans, and legumes, offer the necessary protein without the drawbacks of excessive saturated fat. Healthy fats from avocados, nuts, seeds, and olive oil are excellent for managing cholesterol and reducing inflammation. Legumes such as beans, lentils, and chickpeas contribute significantly to lowering cholesterol and regulating blood sugar.

Foods to Limit

Conversely, certain foods should be limited to maintain optimal heart health. Saturated and trans fats, commonly found in red meat, full-fat dairy, and many processed foods, can raise LDL cholesterol levels, leading to plaque buildup in the arteries. High sodium intake, often from processed foods, can lead to hypertension, a major risk factor for heart disease. Additionally, excessive consumption of added sugars increases the risk of heart disease by contributing to weight gain and metabolic issues.

Building Heart-Healthy Eating Habits

Adopting heart-healthy eating habits is crucial. Plan balanced meals that incorporate a variety of food groups, ensuring each meal includes fruits, vegetables, whole grains, lean proteins, and healthy fats. Be diligent about reading labels to avoid hidden sugars, unhealthy fats, and high sodium. Cooking at home gives you control over ingredients and cooking methods, allowing for healthier meals tailored to your nutritional needs. Staying hydrated is also vital for maintaining healthy blood pressure and overall body functions.

The Impact of a Heart-Healthy Diet

The impact of a heart-healthy diet is profound. By making thoughtful food choices, you can significantly reduce cholesterol levels, control blood pressure, manage weight, and decrease inflammation, all of which contribute to overall well-being. Lowering LDL cholesterol and increasing HDL cholesterol helps prevent plaque buildup in the arteries, reducing the risk of heart disease and stroke. A diet rich in potassium and low in sodium supports healthy blood pressure levels, while maintaining a healthy weight reduces the strain on your heart. Additionally, antioxidant-rich foods reduce inflammation, further protecting your cardiovascular system. By understanding how your diet shapes heart health, you can make daily choices that nourish your body and protect your cardiovascular system, empowering you to take control of your health, one delicious meal at a time.

Balancing Cholesterol and Blood Pressure

Cholesterol and blood pressure are crucial for heart health. Cholesterol is needed for cell building, but too much can cause plaque buildup in arteries, increasing the risk of heart disease and stroke. Blood pressure, the force of blood against artery walls, must be at a healthy level to prevent heart overwork and vessel damage. High blood pressure, or hypertension, can lead to severe heart issues.

LDL, known as "bad" cholesterol, can cause plaque buildup in arteries, narrowing them and restricting blood flow. HDL, or "good" cholesterol, helps remove LDL from the bloodstream, transporting it to the liver for excretion. Balancing these cholesterol types is essential for heart health.

To balance cholesterol, increase fiber intake from oats, beans, lentils, fruits, and vegetables, which helps reduce LDL levels. Choose healthy fats like those in olive oil, avocados, nuts, and seeds, and consume omega-3 fatty acids from fish such as salmon and mackerel. Incorporate plant sterols and stanols found in fruits, vegetables, nuts, and seeds to block cholesterol absorption. Limit dietary cholesterol by moderating consumption of animal products.

High blood pressure often goes unnoticed until it causes major issues, damaging arteries, heart, brain, kidneys, and eyes. Reducing sodium intake by limiting processed foods and using herbs and spices instead of salt helps manage blood pressure. Eating potassium-rich foods like bananas, oranges, potatoes, spinach, and beans balances sodium levels and relaxes blood vessels. Limiting alcohol and caffeine is also important.

For heart health, embrace fruits and vegetables for their fiber, vitamins, and minerals. Whole grains like oats, brown rice, quinoa, and whole wheat provide essential nutrients and soluble fiber. Lean proteins such as fish, poultry, beans, and legumes offer protein without saturated fat. Healthy fats from avocados, nuts, seeds, and olive oil support heart health.

Limit saturated and trans fats found in red meat, full-fat dairy, and processed foods, as they raise LDL cholesterol. Reduce sodium intake from processed foods, canned soups, and certain condiments to avoid raising blood pressure. Avoid added sugars to prevent weight gain and reduce heart disease risk.

To maintain heart health, stay active to lower LDL cholesterol and raise HDL cholesterol, while also reducing blood pressure. Achieve and maintain a healthy weight to reduce heart strain and manage cholesterol and blood pressure. Quit smoking to prevent blood vessel damage and lower cholesterol and blood pressure.

Balancing cholesterol and blood pressure is vital for heart health. Thoughtful food choices and heart-healthy eating patterns can help manage these critical factors. This approach provides the knowledge and tools to support a healthy heart, enabling you to enjoy delicious meals while protecting your cardiovascular system.

Best Cooking Methods for Heart Health

Cooking methods play a crucial role in maintaining and enhancing the nutritional value of the foods we eat. When it comes to heart health, choosing the right cooking techniques can make a significant difference. By using methods that preserve nutrients and minimize unhealthy fats, you can create delicious meals that support cardiovascular wellness. This subchapter will explore the best cooking methods to keep your heart healthy and your taste buds satisfied.

Grilling

Grilling is a fantastic way to cook meats, fish, and vegetables without the need for added fats. This method allows excess fat to drip away from the food, reducing overall fat intake. When grilling, opt for lean cuts of meat and marinate them in heart-healthy ingredients like olive oil, lemon juice, and herbs to enhance flavor and nutritional value.

Baking

Baking is another excellent method for preparing heart-healthy meals. It requires little to no added fat and helps retain the natural flavors and nutrients of the food. When baking, use whole grains and incorporate plenty of vegetables to boost fiber intake. Baking fish with herbs and a drizzle of olive oil is a particularly heart-friendly option.

Steaming

Steaming is one of the healthiest ways to cook vegetables, fish, and even poultry. This method preserves vitamins and minerals that can be lost through other cooking techniques. Steaming also avoids the need for added fats, keeping the calorie content low. Enhance the flavor of steamed dishes with fresh herbs, spices, and a squeeze of lemon juice.

Sautéing

Sautéing allows for quick cooking with minimal fat, making it a great option for heart-healthy meals. Use a small number of heart-healthy oils like olive oil or avocado oil and cook over medium-high heat to retain the nutrients in your ingredients. Add plenty of vegetables and lean proteins for a balanced, nutritious dish.

Poaching

Poaching involves gently simmering food in water or broth, making it a low-fat cooking method that helps retain moisture and nutrients. This technique is perfect for cooking delicate proteins like fish, chicken, and eggs. Enhance the flavor of poached dishes with aromatic herbs, spices, and a splash of citrus.

Slow Cooking

Slow cooking is a convenient and healthy way to prepare meals, allowing flavors to meld together beautifully. It's especially good for cooking lean meats, beans, and vegetables without the need for added fats. Slow cooking helps break down fibers, making it easier to digest and absorb the nutrients.

Stir-Frying

Stir-frying is a quick and efficient way to cook a variety of ingredients with minimal oil. Use a heart-healthy oil, such as olive or canola oil, and cook over high heat while continuously stirring. This method is excellent for preserving the texture and nutrients of vegetables, lean meats, and tofu.

Tips for Heart-Healthy Cooking

Elevate your cooking game with heart-healthy practices that are as delicious as they are nutritious. Instead of reaching for butter or margarine, try oils rich in unsaturated fats such as olive, canola, or avocado oil. These oils not only enhance the flavor of your meals but also contribute to better heart health.

Cutting back on sodium is another great step. Rather than salt, use herbs, spices, citrus, and vinegar to give your dishes a burst of flavor. This not only keeps your meals tasty but also helps maintain healthy blood pressure levels.

Whole grains are your friends when it comes to heart health. Swap out refined grains for options like brown rice, quinoa, and whole wheat pasta. These alternatives are higher in fiber, which supports healthy cholesterol levels and keeps you feeling full longer.

Vegetables should be the highlight of your meals. Incorporate a variety of colorful, nutrient-dense options to ensure you're getting a broad spectrum of vitamins and minerals. Making veggies the star of your plate can also help in reducing overall calorie intake.

When it comes to sweetening your dishes, avoid added sugars. Opt for natural sweeteners like fruit, and use honey or maple syrup sparingly. This way, you can satisfy your sweet tooth without compromising your heart health.

Portion control is crucial, even with heart-healthy foods. Be mindful of serving sizes to avoid overeating and to help maintain a healthy weight.

By adopting these cooking methods, you can create meals that are not only nutritious but also packed with flavor. Grilling, baking, steaming, sautéing, poaching, slow cooking, and stir-frying are excellent techniques that preserve the nutritional value of your food. Combining these methods with smart ingredient choices ensures you stay on track with a heart-healthy diet, making your journey to better health enjoyable and sustainable.

Chapter 1: Breakfast

Starting your day with a nutritious breakfast is a key habit for better cardiovascular health. Breakfast kickstarts your metabolism and provides energy for the day ahead, playing a crucial role in maintaining a healthy heart. Choosing well-balanced nutrients in your morning meal helps regulate blood sugar levels, reduce cholesterol, and keep your heart functioning optimally. Studies show that people who eat a healthy breakfast have better heart health metrics than those who skip it.

In this chapter, you'll find a variety of delicious, heart-healthy breakfast recipes designed to provide essential nutrients for cardiovascular wellness. Each recipe is crafted to be low in sodium and saturated fats while being rich in fiber and other heart-beneficial ingredients. Transform the most important meal of the day into a powerful ally for your heart with these recipes. Enjoy knowing you are taking a vital step towards a healthier, more energetic life!

Tip for the chapter: Substitute almond milk in recipes with any plant-based milk of your choice.

Easy and Nutritious Breakfast Recipes

As breakfast is the foundation of a healthy day, setting the tone for your energy levels and overall well-being. This section is designed to highlight the importance of starting your day with meals that are not only quick and simple to prepare but also packed with nutrients that support cardiovascular health. Embrace these easy and nutritious breakfast ideas to boost your heart health and overall vitality every morning.

Avocado and Egg Toast

Yield: 2 servings / **Preparation Time:** 10 minutes / **Cooking Time:** 5 minutes

Ingredients:

- 2 slices whole grain or whole wheat bread
- 1 ripe avocado
- 2 large eggs
- 1 tablespoon extra-virgin olive oil
- 1/2 teaspoon lemon juice
- 1/4 teaspoon garlic powder (optional)
- 1/4 teaspoon red pepper flakes (optional)
- 1/4 teaspoon black pepper; a pinch of sea salt
- Fresh herbs for garnish (such as cilantro or parsley, optional)

Instructions:

1. Toast the slices of whole grain or whole wheat bread until they are golden and crispy. Using whole grain or whole wheat bread increases the fiber content, which is beneficial for heart health.
2. While the bread is toasting, cut the avocado in half, remove the pit, and scoop the flesh into a small bowl. Add the lemon juice, garlic powder (if using), and black pepper to the avocado. Mash the mixture with a fork until it reaches a creamy consistency. The lemon juice not only adds flavor but also prevents the avocado from browning.
3. Heat the extra virgin olive oil in a non-stick skillet over medium heat. Extra virgin olive oil is a heart-healthy fat that can help reduce bad cholesterol levels.
4. Crack the eggs into the skillet. Cook them sunny side up, over-easy, or scramble them, depending on your preference. Cooking the eggs over medium heat preserves their nutrients without adding unnecessary fats.
5. Spread the mashed avocado evenly over the toasted bread slices. Place the cooked eggs on top of the avocado spread. Sprinkle a pinch of sea salt and red pepper flakes (if using) over the top. Garnish with fresh herbs like cilantro or parsley for added flavor and a boost of nutrients.

Nutritional Information (per serving): Calories: 300 / Protein: 9g / Carbohydrates: 26g / Fats: 20g / Fiber: 7g / Cholesterol: 186mg / Sodium: 180mg / Potassium: 550mg

Spinach and Feta Omelet

Yield: 2 servings / **Preparation Time:** 10 minutes / **Cooking Time:** 10 minutes

Ingredients:

- 4 large eggs (or 2 whole eggs and 4 egg whites for a lower cholesterol option)
- 1 cup fresh spinach, chopped
- 1/4 cup crumbled feta cheese; 1/4 cup diced tomatoes
- 1 small onion, finely chopped
- 1 tablespoon olive oil
- 1/4 teaspoon black pepper; a pinch of sea salt
- fresh herbs for garnish (such as parsley or chives, optional)

Instructions:

1. Chop the spinach, onion, and tomatoes (if using). Crack the eggs into a bowl and beat them well. If using egg whites, separate the yolks from two eggs and combine with the whole eggs.
2. Heat the olive oil in a non-stick skillet over medium heat. Add the chopped onion and cook until it becomes translucent, about 2-3 minutes. Add the chopped spinach and tomatoes to the skillet. Cook for another 2-3 minutes until the spinach wilts. Pour the beaten eggs into the skillet with the vegetables. Tilt the pan to ensure the eggs cover the entire surface evenly. Cook the eggs without stirring for about 2-3 minutes, or until the edges start to set.
3. Sprinkle the crumbled feta cheese evenly over one half of the omelet. Add a pinch of sea salt and black pepper to taste. Using a spatula, gently fold the omelet in half over the filling. Cook for an additional 1-2 minutes until the eggs are fully set and the cheese is melted. Slide the omelet onto a plate. Garnish with fresh herbs if desired. Serve immediately with a side of whole-grain toast or a fresh fruit salad for a complete, heart-healthy meal.

Nutritional Information (per serving): Calories: 200 / Protein: 14g / Carbohydrates: 4g / Fats: 14g / Fiber: 1g / Cholesterol: 290mg (or 150mg if using egg whites) / Sodium: 300mg / Potassium: 400mg

Chia Seed Pudding with Fresh Fruit

Yield: 4 servings / **Preparation Time:** 10 minutes / **Setting Time:** 4 hours (or overnight)

Ingredients:

- 1/2 cup chia seeds
- 2 cups unsweetened almond milk
- 1/2 cup plain non-fat Greek yogurt
- 1 teaspoon vanilla extract
- 2 tablespoons honey or maple
- 1 cup mixed fresh fruit (such as berries, mango, kiwi, or banana)
- 1/4 cup chopped nuts (such as almonds or walnuts, optional)
- fresh mint leaves for garnish (optional)

Instructions:

1. In a medium-sized mixing bowl, whisk together the chia seeds, unsweetened almond milk, plain non-fat Greek yogurt, vanilla extract, and honey or maple syrup. Ensure that the chia seeds are evenly distributed throughout the liquid to prevent clumping. Let the mixture sit for about 10 minutes and whisk again to break up any clumps.
2. Cover the bowl with plastic wrap or divide the mixture into individual serving jars or containers. Refrigerate for at least 4 hours or overnight, allowing the chia seeds to absorb the liquid and form a pudding-like consistency.
3. While the pudding is setting, wash and cut the fresh fruit into bite-sized pieces. Once the chia pudding has set, give it a good stir. Divide the pudding evenly among four serving bowls or jars. Top each serving with a generous amount of fresh fruit and chopped nuts (if using). Garnish with fresh mint leaves if desired. Serve immediately or keep refrigerated until ready to eat.

Nutritional Information (per serving): Calories: 200 / Protein: 6g / Carbohydrates: 26g / Fats: 9g / Fiber: 10g / Cholesterol: 0mg / Sodium: 60mg / Potassium: 300mg

Tomato and Basil Breakfast Sandwich

Yield: 2 servings / **Preparation Time:** 10 minutes / **Cooking Time:** 5 minutes

Ingredients:
- 4 slices whole-grain bread
- 2 medium tomatoes, sliced
- 1/4 cup fresh basil leaves
- 1/2 cup low-fat ricotta cheese
- 1 tablespoon extra-virgin olive oil
- 1/2 teaspoon black pepper
- 1/4 teaspoon garlic powder (optional)
- 1 tablespoon balsamic glaze (optional)

Instructions:
1. Slice tomatoes, wash basil leaves, and toast whole-grain bread until golden and crispy. Spread 2 tablespoons of low-fat ricotta on each slice.
2. Top two slices with tomatoes, sprinkle with black pepper, sea salt, and garlic powder. Add basil leaves.
3. Drizzle with extra virgin olive oil and balsamic glaze (if desired). Top with remaining bread slices and serve immediately.

Nutritional Information (per serving): Calories: 250 / Protein: 10g / Carbohydrates: 28g / Fats: 12g / Fiber: 6g / Cholesterol: 15mg / Sodium: 350mg / Potassium: 500mg

High-Fiber Breakfast Options

Starting your day with high-fiber ingredients is a powerful way to support cardiovascular health. Fiber helps lower cholesterol levels, maintain healthy blood sugar levels, and keep you feeling full longer, which can aid in weight management. Choosing breakfasts rich in fiber not only supports heart health but also promotes digestive health and overall wellness. The following recipes ensure you're not just starting your day right but also making long-term strides toward better heart health. Enjoy these nourishing options and feel the difference they make in your daily energy and health.

Apple Cinnamon Quinoa Bowl

Yield: 4 servings / **Preparation Time:** 10 minutes / **Cooking Time:** 20 minutes

Ingredients:
- 1 cup quinoa, rinsed / 2 cups unsweetened almond milk
- 2 medium apples, peeled, cored, and diced
- 2 tablespoons honey or maple syrup
- 1 teaspoon vanilla extract
- 1 teaspoon ground cinnamon
- 1/4 teaspoon ground nutmeg (optional)
- 1/4 teaspoon salt (optional)
- 1/4 cup raisins or dried cranberries (optional for added sweetness)

Instructions:
1. Bring almond milk to a boil in a medium saucepan. Add rinsed quinoa, reduce heat, cover, and simmer for 15 minutes until tender.
2. In a separate saucepan, cook diced apples with honey or maple syrup, ground cinnamon, and salt over medium heat for 5 minutes until tender. Remove quinoa from heat, stir in vanilla extract, and mix in cooked apples. Fold in raisins or dried cranberries, if desired. Divide into four bowls and serve warm.

Nutritional Information (per serving): Calories: 250 / Protein: 6g / Carbohydrates: 42g / Fats: 8g / Fiber: 5g / Cholesterol: 0mg / Sodium: 150mg / Potassium: 300mg

Pumpkin Flaxseed Pancakes

Yield: 4 servings (12 pancakes) / **Preparation Time:** 15 minutes / **Cooking Time:** 15 minutes

Ingredients:

- 1 cup whole wheat flour
- 1/2 cup ground flaxseed
- 1/2 cup canned pumpkin puree
- 1 cup unsweetened almond
- 2 large eggs
- 1 tablespoon baking powder
- 1 teaspoon ground cinnamon

- 1/2 teaspoon ground nutmeg
- 1/2 teaspoon ground ginger
- 1/4 teaspoon salt
- 2 tablespoons honey or maple syrup
- 1 teaspoon vanilla extract
- 1 tablespoon olive oil (for cooking)

Instructions:

1. In a large bowl, whisk whole wheat flour, ground flaxseed, baking powder, cinnamon, nutmeg, ginger, and salt.
2. In another bowl, combine almond milk, pumpkin puree, eggs, honey or maple syrup, and vanilla extract. Whisk until smooth. Pour wet ingredients into dry ingredients and stir until just combined. Fold in optional ingredients if desired.
3. Heat a greased non-stick skillet over medium heat. Pour 1/4 cup batter per pancake. Cook until bubbles form and edges set, about 2-3 minutes. Flip and cook another 2-3 minutes until golden brown.
4. Serve warm with toppings like fresh fruit, Greek yogurt, maple syrup, or cinnamon.

Nutritional Information (per serving): Calories: 250 / Protein: 8g / Carbohydrates: 40g / Fats: 10g / Fiber: 8g / Cholesterol: 70mg / Sodium: 250mg / Potassium: 350mg

High-Fiber Breakfast Muffins

Yield: 12 muffins / **Preparation Time:** 15 minutes / **Cooking Time:** 20 minutes

Ingredients:

- 1 cup whole wheat flour
- 1/2 cup old-fashioned rolled oats
- 1/4 cup chia seeds
- 1/2 cup plain non-fat Greek yogurt
- 1/4 cup unsweetened almond milk
- 2 large eggs
- 1 cup grated carrots
- 1/2 cup blueberries (fresh or frozen)

- 1/4 cup chopped nuts (optional for added crunch)
- 1/2 cup brown sugar or coconut sugar
- 2 teaspoons baking powder
- 1 teaspoon baking soda
- 1 teaspoon ground cinnamon
- 1/4 teaspoon salt
- 1 teaspoon vanilla extract
- 1/2 cup unsweetened applesauce

Instructions:

1. Preheat oven to 375°F (190°C). Line a 12-cup muffin tin with paper liners or grease with non-stick spray.
2. In a large bowl, mix whole wheat flour, rolled oats, ground flaxseed, chia seeds, brown or coconut sugar, baking powder, baking soda, cinnamon, and salt.
3. In another bowl, whisk applesauce, Greek yogurt, almond milk, eggs, and vanilla extract. Combine with dry ingredients until just mixed. Fold in grated carrots, blueberries, and nuts if using.
4. Divide batter among muffin cups, filling each 3/4 full. Bake for 20-22 minutes, until a toothpick comes out clean. Cool in tin for 5 minutes, then transfer to a wire rack to cool completely.

Nutritional Information (per muffin): Calories: 160 / Protein: 5g / Carbohydrates: 26g / Fats: 5g / Fiber: 5g / Cholesterol: 35mg / Sodium: 150mg / Potassium: 150mg

Avocado and Black Bean Breakfast Wrap

Yield: 4 servings / **Preparation Time:** 10 minutes / **Cooking Time:** 10 minutes

Ingredients:

- 4 whole grain tortillas (8-inch)
- 1 ripe avocado, peeled, pitted, and mashed
- 1 cup canned black beans, drained and rinsed
- 4 large eggs (or 1 cup egg whites for lower cholesterol option)
- 1/2 cup diced tomatoes
- 1/2 cup chopped spinach
- 1/4 cup diced red onion
- 1/4 cup chopped fresh cilantro
- 1/2 teaspoon ground cumin
- 1/2 teaspoon paprika
- 1/4 teaspoon black pepper
- 1 tablespoon olive oil

Instructions:

1. Combine black beans, diced tomatoes, chopped spinach, red onion, cilantro, cumin, paprika, and black pepper in a bowl. Heat olive oil in a skillet over medium heat. Scramble eggs until fully cooked, then remove from heat.
2. Lay tortillas flat. Spread mashed avocado, then spoon black bean mixture and scrambled eggs on top. Fold and roll tightly to form wraps.

Nutritional Information (per serving): Calories: 350 / Protein: 14g / Carbohydrates: 40g / Fats: 16g / Fiber: 12g / Cholesterol: 185mg (or 0mg if using egg whites) / Sodium: 350mg / Potassium: 700mg

Berry Oatmeal Bake

Yield: 6 servings / **Preparation Time:** 15 minutes / **Cooking Time:** 35 minutes

Ingredients:

- 2 cups old-fashioned rolled oats
- 2 cups unsweetened almond milk
- 2 large eggs (or 1/2 cup unsweetened applesauce for a vegan option)
- 1 cup mixed fresh berries
- 1 teaspoon baking powder
- 1 teaspoon ground cinnamon
- 1/4 teaspoon salt
- 2 teaspoons vanilla extract
- 1/4 cup honey or maple syrup
- 1/4 cup chopped nuts
- 2 tablespoons chia seeds

Instructions:

1. Preheat your oven to 375°F (190°C). Lightly grease a 9x9-inch baking dish with a small amount of olive oil or non-stick cooking spray. In a large mixing bowl, combine the rolled oats, baking powder, ground cinnamon, and salt. Stir well to mix.
2. In a separate bowl, whisk together the almond milk, eggs (or applesauce), honey or maple syrup, and vanilla extract until well combined. Pour the wet ingredients into the dry ingredients and stir until well combined. Add the chia seeds. Gently fold in the mixed berries and chopped nuts, ensuring they are evenly distributed throughout the mixture.
3. Pour the mixture into the prepared baking dish. Spread it out evenly with a spatula. Bake in the preheated oven for 35 minutes or until the top is golden brown and the oats are set. Allow the oatmeal bake to cool for a few minutes before slicing. Serve warm.

Nutritional Information (per serving): Calories: 250 / Protein: 7g / Carbohydrates: 38g / Fats: 8g / Fiber: 6g / Cholesterol: 35mg (0mg if using applesauce)/ Sodium: 150mg/ Potassium: 200mg

Heart-Healthy Smoothies

Smoothies are an excellent way to start your day with a nutrient-packed breakfast that supports cardiovascular health. Quick to prepare and versatile, they can be loaded with fruits, vegetables, and other heart-healthy ingredients. Incorporating smoothies into your breakfast routine offers numerous benefits. They are rich in essential vitamins, minerals, and antioxidants that promote heart health. Additionally, they can be high in fiber, helping to lower cholesterol and maintain healthy blood pressure levels.

Oat and Flaxseed Smoothie

Yield: 2 servings / **Preparation Time:** 5 minutes / **Cooking Time:** None

Ingredients:

- 1/2 cup rolled oats
- 1 tablespoon ground flaxseed
- 1 tablespoon chia seeds
- 1 medium banana, sliced
- 1 cup unsweetened almond milk
- 1/2 cup plain non-fat Greek yogurt
- 1/2 teaspoon vanilla extract
- 1/2 teaspoon ground cinnamon
- 1 tablespoon honey or maple syrup (optional)

Instructions:

1. In a high-speed blender, combine the rolled oats, ground flaxseed, chia seeds, sliced banana, almond milk, Greek yogurt, vanilla extract, cinnamon, and honey or maple syrup (if using).
2. Blend on high speed until smooth and creamy. If the smoothie is too thick, add a little more almond milk until the desired consistency is reached. Pour the smoothie into two glasses and serve immediately.

Nutritional Information (per serving): Calories: 210 / Protein: 7g / Carbohydrates: 35g / Fats: 6g / Fiber: 8g / Cholesterol: 0mg / Sodium: 70mg / Potassium: 450mg

---

Green Detox Smoothie

Yield: 2 servings / **Preparation Time:** 5 minutes / **Cooking Time:** None

Ingredients:

- 1 cup fresh spinach leaves
- 1 cup kale leaves, stems removed
- 1 tablespoon chia seeds
- 1 tablespoon ground flaxseed
- 1 green apple, cored and chopped
- 1/2 cucumber, peeled and chopped
- 1/2 avocado
- 1 cup unsweetened almond milk
- 1/2 cup water (optional for thinner consistency)
- 1/2 lemon, juiced
- 1 teaspoon honey or maple syrup (optional for sweetness)

Instructions:

1. Wash the spinach and kale leaves thoroughly. Core and chop the green apple. Peel and chop the cucumber. Scoop out the flesh of the avocado. In a high-speed blender, combine the spinach, kale, green apple, cucumber, avocado, chia seeds, ground flaxseed, lemon juice, almond milk, and honey or maple syrup (if using).
2. Blend on high speed until smooth and creamy. If the smoothie is too thick, add water a little at a time until the desired consistency is reached. Pour the smoothie into two glasses and serve immediately.

Nutritional Information (per serving): Calories: 180 / Protein: 5g / Carbohydrates: 24g / Fats: 8g / Fiber: 8g / Cholesterol: 0mg / Sodium: 80mg / Potassium: 600mg

Berry Antioxidant Smoothie

Yield: 2 servings / **Preparation Time:** 5 minutes / **Cooking Time:** None

Ingredients:

- 1 cup fresh or frozen mixed berries
- 1 banana
- 1/2 cup plain non-fat Greek yogurt
- 1 cup unsweetened almond milk
- 1 tablespoon chia seeds
- 1 tablespoon ground flaxseed
- 1 teaspoon honey or maple syrup (optional)
- 1/2 teaspoon vanilla extract

Instructions:

1. Wash the fresh berries if using. Peel and slice the banana. In a high-speed blender, combine the mixed berries, banana, Greek yogurt, almond milk, chia seeds, ground flaxseed, honey or maple syrup (if using), and vanilla extract.
2. Blend on high speed until smooth and creamy. If the smoothie is too thick, add a little more almond milk until the desired consistency is reached. Pour the smoothie into two glasses and serve immediately.

Nutritional Information (per serving): Calories: 200 / Protein: 6g / Carbohydrates: 34g / Fats: 5g / Fiber: 8g / Cholesterol: 0mg / Sodium: 60mg / Potassium: 400mg

Banana Nut Smoothie Bowl

Yield: 2 servings / **Preparation Time:** 10 minutes / **Cooking Time:** None

Ingredients:

- 2 large ripe bananas, sliced and frozen
- 1/4 cup chopped nuts
- 1/2 cup unsweetened almond milk
- 1/4 cup granola (low-sugar, high-fiber variety)
- 1/2 cup plain non-fat Greek yogurt
- 1 tablespoon ground flaxseed
- 1 tablespoon chia seeds
- 1/4 teaspoon vanilla extract
- 1/4 teaspoon ground cinnamon
- Fresh berries for topping

Instructions:

1. In a high-speed blender, combine the frozen banana slices, almond milk, Greek yogurt, ground flaxseed, chia seeds, vanilla extract, and ground cinnamon. Blend until smooth and creamy. If the mixture is too thick, add a little more almond milk until the desired consistency is reached.
2. Divide the smoothie mixture evenly between two bowls. Top each bowl with granola, chopped nuts, fresh berries, and sliced banana. Seve immediately.

Nutritional Information (per serving): Calories: 320 / Protein: 10g / Carbohydrates: 45g / Fats: 12g / Fiber: 8g / Cholesterol: 0mg / Sodium: 75mg / Potassium: 600mg

Chapter 2: Snacks and Appetizers

Snacking throughout the day is a chance to nourish your body with essential nutrients that support cardiovascular health. Choosing well-balanced snacks helps maintain energy levels, curb unhealthy cravings, and provide vitamins and minerals that promote heart health. This chapter offers a selection of easy-to-prepare, heart-healthy snacks and appetizers. Each recipe provides a perfect balance of nutrients, allowing you to enjoy tasty treats while supporting your cardiovascular health. Embrace these snacks and make mindful eating a joyful part of your daily routine.

Heart-Boosting Snacks

Choosing snacks rich in fiber, healthy fats, and antioxidants can significantly improve cardiovascular health by helping to manage weight, stabilize blood sugar levels, and reduce cholesterol. Well-planned snacks provide sustained energy and prevent overeating at mealtimes, contributing to a healthier overall diet. These heart-boosting snacks are designed to be delicious, easy to prepare, and packed with nutrients that support your heart's wellbeing.

Veggie Sticks with Greek Yogurt Dip

Yield: 4 servings / **Preparation Time:** 15 minutes / **Cooking Time:** None

Ingredients:
- 1 cup carrot sticks
- 1 cup celery sticks
- 1 cup cucumber sticks
- 1 cup bell pepper strips (use a variety of colors for added nutrition and visual appeal)
- 1 cup plain non-fat Greek yogurt
- 1 tablespoon fresh lemon juice
- 1 tablespoon extra-virgin olive oil
- 1 teaspoon dried dill (or 1 tablespoon fresh dill, finely chopped)
- 1 teaspoon garlic powder
- 1/2 teaspoon onion powder
- 1/4 teaspoon salt; 1/4 teaspoon black pepper
- Optional: 1 tablespoon fresh parsley, finely chopped

Instructions:
1. Wash and cut the vegetables into sticks or strips. Arrange them on a serving platter.
2. In a medium bowl, combine the Greek yogurt, lemon juice, olive oil, dill, garlic powder, onion powder, salt, and black pepper. Mix well until all ingredients are thoroughly combined. If using fresh parsley, fold it in for added flavor and nutrients.
3. Serve the veggie sticks with the Greek yogurt dip immediately. You can also refrigerate the dip for up to 2 hours before serving to let the flavors meld.

Nutritional Information (per serving): Calories: 110 / Protein: 6g / Carbohydrates: 12g / Fats: 5g / Fiber: 4g / Cholesterol: 0mg / Sodium: 170mg / Potassium: 350mg

Carrot Sticks with Hummus

Yield: 4 servings / **Preparation Time:** 10 minutes / **Cooking Time:** None

Ingredients:
- 4 large carrots, peeled and cut into sticks
- 1 can (15 ounces) chickpeas, drained and rinsed
- 1/4 cup tahini
- 1 clove garlic, minced
- 2 tablespoons extra virgin olive oil
- 2 tablespoons fresh lemon juice
- 1/2 teaspoon ground cumin
- 1/2 teaspoon salt
- 1/4 teaspoon ground paprika (optional for garnish)
- Fresh parsley for garnish (optional)
- 2-3 tablespoons water (to desired consistency)

Instructions:
1. Wash, peel, and cut the carrots into sticks. Arrange them on a serving plate. In a food processor, combine the chickpeas, tahini, olive oil, lemon juice, garlic, cumin, and salt.
2. Process until smooth, scraping down the sides as needed. If the hummus is too thick, add water, one tablespoon at a time, until you reach the desired consistency.
3. Transfer the hummus to a serving bowl. Drizzle with a little extra virgin olive oil and sprinkle with paprika and chopped fresh parsley if desired. Serve the carrot sticks alongside the hummus for dipping.

Nutritional Information (per serving): Calories: 180 / Protein: 5g / Carbohydrates: 17g / Fats: 11g / Fiber: 6g / Cholesterol: 0mg / Sodium: 270mg / Potassium: 300mg

---

Apple Slices with Almond Butter

Yield: 2 servings / **Preparation Time:** 5 minutes / **Cooking Time:** None

Ingredients:
- 2 medium apples (any variety), cored and sliced
- 4 tablespoons almond butter (unsweetened and natural)
- 1 tablespoon chia seeds (optional for added fiber and Omega-3)
- 1 tablespoon ground flaxseed (optional for added fiber and Omega-3)
- 1/2 teaspoon ground cinnamon (optional for added flavor)
- 1 tablespoon unsweetened coconut flakes (optional for added texture and flavor)

Instructions:
1. Wash, core, and slice the apples into thin wedges. In a small bowl, stir the almond butter to ensure it is well-mixed. If desired, you can mix in the chia seeds, ground flaxseed, and ground cinnamon for added flavor and nutritional benefits.
2. Arrange the apple slices on a serving plate. Drizzle or spread the almond butter mixture over the apple slices. Sprinkle with unsweetened coconut flakes if using.

Nutritional Information (per serving): Calories: 220 / Protein: 5g / Carbohydrates: 26g / Fats: 12g / Fiber: 6g / Cholesterol: 0mg / Sodium: 0mg / Potassium: 300mg

Greek Yogurt with Honey and Walnuts

Yield: 2 servings / **Preparation Time:** 5 minutes / **Cooking Time:** None

Ingredients:
- 1 cup plain non-fat Greek yogurt
- 1/4 cup walnuts, chopped
- 2 tablespoons honey
- Optional: 1/2 teaspoon ground cinnamon
- Optional: fresh fruit for topping (such as berries, banana slices, or apple slices)

Instructions:
1. Divide the Greek yogurt evenly between two serving bowls. Drizzle 1 tablespoon of honey over each serving of yogurt.
2. Sprinkle 2 tablespoons of chopped walnuts over each bowl. Optional: Sprinkle a pinch of ground cinnamon over the top for added flavor. Serve immediately and enjoy!

Nutritional Information (per serving): Calories: 220 / Protein: 14g / Carbohydrates: 22g / Fats: 9g / Fiber: 2g / Cholesterol: 5mg / Sodium: 60mg / Potassium: 300mg

Whole-Grain Crackers with Avocado Spread

Yield: 4 servings / **Preparation Time:** 10 minutes / **Cooking Time:** None

Ingredients:
- 2 ripe avocados, peeled and pitted
- 1 tablespoon fresh lime juice
- 1 small garlic clove, minced
- 1/4 teaspoon ground cumin
- 1/4 teaspoon salt; 1/4 teaspoon black pepper
- 1/4 cup finely chopped red onion
- 1/4 cup finely chopped fresh cilantro (optional)
- 1 small jalapeño, seeded and minced (optional for added spice)
- 24 whole-grain crackers (about 6 crackers per serving)

Instructions:
1. In a medium bowl, mash the avocados with a fork until smooth. Add the lime juice, minced garlic, ground cumin, salt, and black pepper. Mix well to combine. Stir in the chopped red onion, cilantro, and jalapeño (if using) until evenly distributed.
2. Spread a generous amount of the avocado mixture onto each whole-grain cracker.
3. Arrange the crackers on a serving platter and serve immediately.

Nutritional Information (per serving): Calories: 220 / Protein: 4g / Carbohydrates: 24g / Fats: 13g / Fiber: 7g / Cholesterol: 0mg / Sodium: 250mg / Potassium: 450mg

Simple and Tasty Appetizers

Appetizers are a great way to enjoy delicious, heart-healthy options before a meal. Well-balanced appetizers help control hunger, prevent overeating, and provide steady energy. They are flavorful, easy to prepare, and packed with nutrients that support cardiovascular health, such as fiber, healthy fats, and antioxidants.

Hosting guests? These heart-healthy, crowd-pleasing appetizers ensure you stay on track with your diet while impressing your guests. Dive into these recipes and see how simple, tasty choices can make a big difference in your heart health.

Smoked Salmon and Cream Cheese Cucumber Bites

Yield: 4 servings / **Preparation Time:** 15 minutes / **Cooking Time:** None

Ingredients:
- 1 large cucumber
- 4 ounces smoked salmon, thinly sliced
- 4 ounces light cream cheese
- 1 tablespoon fresh dill, finely chopped
- Fresh dill sprigs for garnish
- 1 tablespoon fresh lemon juice
- Optional: 1/4 teaspoon garlic powder; 1/4 teaspoon black pepper

Instructions:
1. Wash and peel the cucumber. Slice it into 1/4-inch-thick rounds. Arrange the slices on a serving platter.
2. In a small bowl, combine the light cream cheese, chopped fresh dill, lemon juice, black pepper, and garlic powder (if using). Mix until smooth and well combined.
3. Spread a small amount of the cream cheese mixture on each cucumber slice. Top each with a piece of smoked salmon. Garnish each cucumber bite with a small sprig of fresh dill. Serve immediately.

Nutritional Information (per serving): Calories: 120 / Protein: 7g / Carbohydrates: 5g / Fats: 8g / Fiber: 1g / Cholesterol: 25mg / Sodium: 230mg / Potassium: 200mg

---

Bruschetta with Tomato and Basil

Yield: 4 servings / **Preparation Time:** 10 minutes / **Cooking Time:** 5 minutes

Ingredients:
- 8 slices whole-grain baguette or whole-wheat bread
- 4 medium tomatoes, diced
- 1/4 cup fresh basil leaves, chopped
- 2 cloves garlic, minced
- 2 tablespoons extra virgin olive oil
- 1 tablespoon balsamic vinegar
- 1/4 teaspoon sea salt; 1/4 teaspoon black pepper

Instructions:
1. Preheat the oven to 375°F (190°C). Arrange the baguette slices on a baking sheet. Lightly brush each slice with a little bit of olive oil. Toast in the preheated oven for about 5 minutes, or until the bread is golden and crispy.
2. In a medium bowl, combine the diced tomatoes, chopped basil, minced garlic, remaining olive oil, balsamic vinegar, sea salt, and black pepper. Mix well to combine all the flavors.
3. Spoon the tomato mixture evenly onto the toasted bread slices. Serve immediately while the bread is still warm and crispy.

Nutritional Information (per serving): Calories: 180 / Protein: 4g / Carbohydrates: 22g / Fats: 8g / Fiber: 3g / Cholesterol: 0mg / Sodium: 200mg / Potassium: 350mg

Caprese Skewers with Balsamic Glaze

Yield: 4 servings / **Preparation Time:** 15 minutes / **Cooking Time:** 10 minutes

Ingredients:

- 1 cup cherry tomatoes
- 1 cup fresh mozzarella balls (bocconcini)
- 1/2 cup fresh basil leaves
- 1/4 cup balsamic vinegar
- 1 tablespoon honey (optional for sweetness)
- 1 tablespoon olive oil
- 1/4 teaspoon salt
- 1/4 teaspoon black pepper
- Skewers (wooden or metal)

Instructions:

1. Wash the cherry tomatoes and basil leaves. Drain the fresh mozzarella balls.
2. In a small saucepan, combine the balsamic vinegar and honey (if using). Bring to a simmer over medium heat and let cook for about 8-10 minutes, or until the mixture has reduced by half and has a syrupy consistency. Remove from heat and let cool.
3. Thread a cherry tomato, a basil leaf, and a mozzarella ball onto each skewer. Repeat until all ingredients are used.
4. Arrange the skewers on a serving platter. Drizzle with olive oil and sprinkle with salt and black pepper. Drizzle the cooled balsamic glaze over the skewers just before serving.

Nutritional Information (per serving): Calories: 150 / Protein: 7g / Carbohydrates: 10g / Fats: 9g / Fiber: 1g / Cholesterol: 20mg / Sodium: 220mg / Potassium: 250mg

Cucumber Avocado Rolls

Yield: 4 servings / **Preparation Time:** 15 minutes / **Cooking Time:** None

Ingredients:

- 2 large cucumbers
- 1 ripe avocado, peeled and pitted
- 1 tablespoon fresh lemon juice
- 1 tablespoon extra-virgin olive oil
- 1 clove garlic, minced
- 1/4 teaspoon salt
- 1/4 teaspoon black pepper
- 1/4 cup finely chopped fresh herbs (such as dill, cilantro, or parsley)
- Toothpicks for securing the rolls

Instructions:

1. Wash the cucumbers and trim the ends. Using a mandoline slicer or a vegetable peeler, slice the cucumbers lengthwise into thin strips.
2. In a medium bowl, mash the avocado with a fork until smooth. Add the fresh lemon juice, olive oil, minced garlic, salt, and black pepper. Mix well to combine. Stir in the finely chopped herbs.
3. Lay out a cucumber strip on a flat surface. Spoon a small amount of the avocado mixture onto one end of the strip. Carefully roll up the cucumber strip, starting from the end with the filling. Secure the roll with a toothpick. Repeat with the remaining cucumber strips and avocado filling.
4. Arrange the cucumber avocado rolls on a serving platter. Serve immediately as a refreshing and nutritious appetizer.

Nutritional Information (per serving): Nutritional Information (per serving): Calories: 120 / Protein: 2g / Carbohydrates: 8g / Fats: 10g / Fiber: 4g / Cholesterol: 0mg / Sodium: 150mg / Potassium: 300mg

Stuffed Mini Bell Peppers with Quinoa

Yield: 4 servings / **Preparation Time:** 15 minutes / **Cooking Time:** 25 minutes

Ingredients:
- 12 mini bell peppers
- 1 cup cooked quinoa
- 1/2 cup black beans, rinsed and drained
- 1/2 cup corn kernels (fresh or frozen)
- 1/2 cup diced tomatoes
- 1/4 cup finely chopped red onion
- 1/4 cup finely chopped fresh cilantro
- 1 tablespoon olive oil
- 1 teaspoon ground cumin
- 1/2 teaspoon smoked paprika
- 1/2 teaspoon garlic powder
- 1/2 teaspoon salt
- 1/4 teaspoon black pepper

Instructions:
1. Preheat oven to 375°F (190°C). Slice tops off mini bell peppers, remove seeds, and place on a parchment-lined baking sheet.
2. Mix cooked quinoa, black beans, corn, tomatoes, red onion, cilantro, olive oil, cumin, smoked paprika, garlic powder, salt, and pepper in a bowl. Fill peppers with the mixture.
3. Bake for 20-25 minutes until peppers are tender and slightly browned. Serve warm.

Nutritional Information (per serving): Calories: 120 / Protein: 2g / Carbohydrates: 8g / Fats: 10g / Fiber: 4g / Cholesterol: 0mg / Sodium: 150mg / Potassium: 300mg

Low-Sodium Snack Options

Low-sodium snacks are beneficial for managing blood pressure and reducing the strain on your cardiovascular system. Incorporating these snacks into your daily routine can help you stay energized, satisfied, and on track with your heart-healthy goals. Whether you're at home, at work, or on the go, these snacks will keep you feeling great and your heart health in check.

Baked Kale Chips

Yield: 4 servings / **Preparation Time:** 10 minutes / **Cooking Time:** 20 minutes

Ingredients:
- 1 bunch kale, washed and thoroughly dried
- 1 tablespoon olive oil
- 1/4 teaspoon garlic powder
- 1/4 teaspoon onion powder
- 1/8 teaspoon salt
- 1/8 teaspoon black pepper
- 1/4 teaspoon smoked paprika (optional)

Instructions:
1. Preheat oven to 300°F (150°C). Remove kale stems and tear leaves into bite-sized pieces. Ensure kale is dry.
2. Toss kale with olive oil in a large bowl. Sprinkle with garlic powder, onion powder, smoked paprika (if using), salt, and pepper. Toss to coat evenly.
3. Spread kale in a single layer on a parchment-lined baking sheet. Bake for 15-20 minutes until edges are crisp. Cool slightly before serving warm or at room temperature.

Nutritional Information (per serving): Calories: 60 / Protein: 2g / Carbohydrates: 5g / Fats: 4g / Fiber: 2g / Cholesterol: 0mg / Sodium: 75mg / Potassium: 300mg

Rice Cakes with Avocado and Cherry Tomatoes

Yield: 4 servings / **Preparation Time:** 10 minutes / **Cooking Time:** None

Ingredients:
- 4 whole-grain rice cakes
- 2 ripe avocados, peeled and pitted
- 1 cup cherry tomatoes, halved
- 1 tablespoon fresh lemon juice
- 1 tablespoon extra-virgin olive oil
- 1/4 teaspoon garlic powder
- 1/4 teaspoon black pepper
- 1/8 teaspoon salt
- Optional: Fresh basil or cilantro leaves for garnish

Instructions:
1. In a medium bowl, mash the avocados with a fork until smooth but slightly chunky. Add the fresh lemon juice, olive oil, garlic powder, black pepper, and salt. Mix well to combine. Wash and halve the cherry tomatoes.
2. Spread a generous amount of the avocado mixture on each whole-grain rice cake. Top with halved cherry tomatoes, arranging them evenly.
3. If desired, garnish with fresh basil or cilantro leaves for added flavor and color. Serve immediately as a nutritious snack or light meal.

Nutritional Information (per serving): Calories: 210 / Protein: 3g / Carbohydrates: 22g / Fats: 14g / Fiber: 6g / Cholesterol: 0mg / Sodium: 120mg / Potassium: 500mg

Air-Popped Popcorn with Nutritional Yeast

Yield: 4 servings / **Preparation Time:** 5 minutes / **Cooking Time:** 5 minutes

Ingredients:
- 1/2 cup popcorn kernels
- 2 tablespoons nutritional yeast
- 1 tablespoon olive oil
- 1/4 teaspoon garlic powder (optional)
- 1/4 teaspoon onion powder (optional)
- 1/8 teaspoon salt (optional)

Instructions:
1. Using an air popper, pop the 1/2 cup of popcorn kernels according to the manufacturer's instructions. This should yield about 8 cups of popped popcorn.
2. In a large mixing bowl, drizzle the olive oil over the freshly popped popcorn. Toss to coat evenly.
3. Sprinkle the nutritional yeast, garlic powder, onion powder, and salt over the popcorn. Toss again to ensure the seasonings are evenly distributed. Serve immediately as a nutritious snack.

Nutritional Information (per serving): Calories: 110 / Protein: 4g / Carbohydrates: 18g / Fats: 2g / Fiber: 4g / Cholesterol: 0mg / Sodium: 30mg / Potassium: 100mg

Plain Greek Yogurt with Fresh Berries

Yield: 4 servings / **Preparation Time:** 5 minutes / **Cooking Time:** None

Ingredients:
- 2 cups plain non-fat Greek yogurt
- 1 cup fresh strawberries, hulled and sliced
- 1 cup fresh blueberries
- 1 cup fresh raspberries
- 1 tablespoon honey (optional for added sweetness)
- 1/2 teaspoon vanilla extract (optional for flavor)
- 1/4 cup chopped nuts (such as almonds or walnuts, optional for added crunch)
- 1 tablespoon chia seeds (optional for added fiber and Omega-3)

Instructions:
1. Wash the strawberries, blueberries, and raspberries thoroughly. Hull and slice the strawberries.
2. In a large bowl, combine the Greek yogurt, honey (if using), and vanilla extract (if using). Stir until well mixed.
3. Divide the yogurt mixture evenly among four bowls or parfait glasses.
4. Top each serving with a mix of the fresh strawberries, blueberries, and raspberries.
5. Sprinkle each serving with chopped nuts and chia seeds if desired for added texture and nutritional benefits.

Nutritional Information (per serving): Calories: 140 / Protein: 12g / Carbohydrates: 18g / Fats: 2g / Fiber: 4g / Cholesterol: 0mg / Sodium: 60mg / Potassium: 300mg

Apple Chips with Cinnamon

Yield: 4 servings / **Preparation Time:** 10 minutes / **Cooking Time:** 2-3 hours

Ingredients:
- 4 medium apples (any variety)
- 1 teaspoon ground cinnamon
- Optional: 1 teaspoon sugar or sugar substitute (if additional sweetness is desired)

Instructions:
1. Preheat your oven to 200°F (95°C). Line two baking sheets with parchment paper.
2. Wash and core the apples. Using a mandoline slicer or a sharp knife, slice the apples into thin rings, about 1/8-inch thick. Arrange the apple slices in a single layer on the prepared baking sheets. Sprinkle the ground cinnamon evenly over the apple slices. If using sugar, sprinkle it over the slices as well.
3. Place the baking sheets in the preheated oven. Bake for 1 hour, then flip the apple slices over and continue baking for another 1-2 hours, or until the apple slices are dry and crisp. Check periodically to ensure they do not burn.
4. Remove the apple chips from the oven and let them cool completely on the baking sheets. They will continue to crisp up as they cool. Store in an airtight container for up to one week.

Nutritional Information (per serving): Calories: 60 / Protein: 0g / Carbohydrates: 16g / Fats: 0g / Fiber: 3g / Cholesterol: 0mg / Sodium: 0mg / Potassium: 120mg

Chapter 3: Salads

Salads are a nutrient powerhouse that can significantly boost cardiovascular health. Incorporating fresh vegetables, fruits, and heart-healthy toppings provides essential vitamins, minerals, and antioxidants that support heart function and reduce heart disease risk. Eating salads daily can help maintain a healthy weight, control blood pressure, and improve cholesterol levels—key factors for heart health. This chapter offers vibrant and delicious salads that are nutritious and satisfying. Each recipe focuses on low saturated fats and sodium while being rich in fiber, healthy fats, and essential nutrients. These salads are easy to prepare and versatile enough to be enjoyed as a main course or side dish.

Leafy Greens and Vegetable Salads

Leafy greens like spinach, dill, and arugula are packed with vitamins, minerals, and antioxidants that promote cardiovascular health. High in dietary fiber, they help lower cholesterol and maintain healthy blood pressure. Incorporating these salads into your daily routine enhances heart health, aids in weight management, and reduces heart disease risk. Explore this subchapter for delicious, easy-to-prepare recipes that make eating healthy delightful.

Strawberry Spinach Salad with Poppy Seed Dressing

Yield: 4 servings / **Preparation Time:** 15 minutes / **Cooking Time:** None

Ingredients:
- 6 cups fresh spinach leaves, washed and dried
- 2 cups fresh strawberries, hulled and sliced
- 1/4 cup red onion, thinly sliced
- 1/4 cup almonds, sliced or slivered (toasted if desired)
- 1/4 cup feta cheese, crumbled
- 1/4 cup extra virgin olive oil
- 2 tablespoons apple cider vinegar
- 1 tablespoon honey
- 1 teaspoon Dijon mustard
- 1 teaspoon poppy seeds
- 1/4 teaspoon salt
- 1/4 teaspoon black pepper

Instructions:
1. In a large salad bowl, combine the fresh spinach leaves, sliced strawberries, and thinly sliced red onion. Sprinkle the almonds and feta cheese over the top.
2. In a small bowl or a jar with a tight-fitting lid, combine the extra virgin olive oil, apple cider vinegar, honey, Dijon mustard, poppy seeds, salt, and black pepper. Whisk or shake well until all ingredients are well combined.
3. Drizzle the poppy seed dressing over the salad just before serving. Toss gently to coat the salad ingredients evenly with the dressing. Serve immediately and enjoy.

Nutritional Information (per serving): Calories: 220 / Protein: 5g / Carbohydrates: 18g / Fats: 15g / Fiber: 5g / Cholesterol: 10mg / Sodium: 180mg / Potassium: 500mg

Roasted Beet and Arugula Salad

Yield: 4 servings / **Preparation Time:** 15 minutes / **Cooking Time:** 45 minutes

Ingredients:

- 4 medium beets, washed and trimmed
- 4 cups fresh arugula
- 1/4 cup walnuts, toasted and chopped
- 1/4 cup crumbled goat cheese
- 1/4 cup red onion, thinly sliced
- 1/4 cup extra virgin olive oil
- 2 tablespoons balsamic vinegar
- 1 tablespoon honey or maple syrup
- 1 teaspoon Dijon mustard
- 1/4 teaspoon salt
- 1/4 teaspoon black pepper

Instructions:

1. Preheat the oven to 400°F (200°C). Wrap each beet individually in aluminum foil and place them on a baking sheet. Roast in the preheated oven for 40-45 minutes, or until tender when pierced with a fork. Allow the beets to cool, then peel and cut them into wedges or slices.
2. In a small bowl, whisk together the olive oil, balsamic vinegar, honey or maple syrup, Dijon mustard, salt, and black pepper until well combined.
3. In a large salad bowl, combine the arugula, roasted beets, toasted walnuts, and red onion. Drizzle the dressing over the salad and toss gently to combine. Sprinkle with crumbled goat cheese if desired. Serve immediately and enjoy as a nutritious and flavorful salad.

Nutritional Information (per serving): Calories: 220 / Protein: 4g / Carbohydrates: 18g / Fats: 15g / Fiber: 5g / Cholesterol: 5mg / Sodium: 180mg / Potassium: 500mg

Cucumber and Dill Salad

Yield: 4 servings / **Preparation Time:** 10 minutes / **Cooking Time:** None

Ingredients:

- 2 large cucumbers, thinly sliced
- 1/4 cup red onion, thinly sliced
- 1/4 cup fresh dill, chopped
- 1/4 cup plain non-fat Greek yogurt
- 1 tablespoon apple cider vinegar
- 1 tablespoon olive oil
- 1/4 teaspoon salt; 1/4 teaspoon black pepper

Instructions:

1. Wash and thinly slice the cucumbers and red onion. Place them in a large salad bowl.
2. In a small bowl, whisk together the Greek yogurt, apple cider vinegar, olive oil, salt, and black pepper until well combined.
3. Add the chopped fresh dill to the bowl with the cucumbers and onions. Pour the dressing over the salad, toss gently to combine all ingredients evenly. Serve immediately or refrigerate for up to an hour to allow the flavors to meld.

Nutritional Information (per serving): Calories: 80 / Protein: 3g / Carbohydrates: 7g / Fats: 5g / Fiber: 1g / Cholesterol: 0mg / Sodium: 150mg / Potassium: 250mg.

Citrus and Fennel Salad

Yield: 4 servings / **Preparation Time:** 15 minutes / **Cooking Time:** None

Ingredients:

- 2 large oranges, peeled and segmented
- 1 large grapefruit, peeled and segmented
- 1 large fennel bulb, thinly sliced
- 1/4 cup red onion, thinly sliced
- 1/4 cup pomegranate seeds
- 1/4 cup fresh mint leaves, chopped
- 1/4 cup fresh parsley, chopped
- 2 tablespoons extra virgin olive oil
- 1 tablespoon fresh lemon juice
- 1 tablespoon fresh orange juice
- 1 teaspoon honey (optional)
- 1/4 teaspoon salt
- 1/4 teaspoon black pepper

Instructions:

1. Peel the oranges and grapefruit, removing as much of the white pith as possible. Segment the fruit and set aside in a large salad bowl.
2. Thinly slice the fennel bulb and red onion. Add them to the salad bowl with the citrus segments. If using, add the pomegranate seeds, chopped mint leaves, and chopped parsley to the bowl.
3. In a small bowl, whisk together the olive oil, lemon juice, orange juice, honey (if using), salt, and black pepper until well combined. Pour the dressing over the salad ingredients and toss gently to combine. Serve immediately.

Nutritional Information (per serving): Calories: 140 / Protein: 2g / Carbohydrates: 20g / Fats: 7g / Fiber: 5g / Cholesterol: 0mg / Sodium: 150mg / Potassium: 450mg.

Kale and Radish Salad with Lemon-Tahini Dressing

Yield: 4 servings / **Preparation Time:** 15 minutes / **Cooking Time:** none

Ingredients

- 4 cups kale, washed and chopped (remove stems)
- 1 cup radishes, thinly sliced
- 1 ripe avocado, sliced
- 1/4 cup chopped almonds, toasted
- 1/4 cup thinly sliced red onion
- 1/4 cup crumbled feta cheese (optional)
- 3 tablespoons tahini
- 2 tablespoons fresh lemon juice
- 1 tablespoon extra-virgin olive oil
- 1 teaspoon honey or maple syrup
- 1 clove garlic, minced
- 2-3 tablespoons water (to desired consistency)
- salt and pepper to taste

Instructions

1. In a large salad bowl, combine the chopped kale, sliced radishes, avocado, toasted almonds, and red onion. If using, sprinkle the crumbled feta cheese on top.
2. In a small bowl, whisk together the tahini, lemon juice, olive oil, honey or maple syrup, garlic, salt, and pepper. Add water gradually to reach desired consistency.
3. Drizzle the lemon-tahini dressing over the salad and toss gently to combine.
4. Serve immediately and enjoy this fresh, heart-healthy salad.

Nutritional Information (per serving): Calories: 250 / Protein: 5g / Carbohydrates: 12g / Fats: 21g / Fiber: 6g / Cholesterol: 0mg (if feta cheese is excluded) / Sodium: 60mg (if feta cheese is excluded) / Potassium: 580mg

Protein-Packed Salads

Including protein in your salads is essential for maintaining muscle mass, supporting metabolic functions, and keeping you full and energized throughout the day. Protein-packed salads provide the necessary amino acids your body needs to repair tissues and produce enzymes and hormones. Lean proteins can help lower blood pressure, reduce cholesterol levels, and promote overall cardiovascular health. Explore our recipes to discover how easy and enjoyable it is to include high-quality proteins in your diet, all while supporting your heart health.

Mediterranean Chickpea Salad

Yield: 4 servings / **Preparation Time:** 15 minutes / **Cooking Time:** None

Ingredients:

- 1 can (15 ounces) chickpeas, drained and rinsed
- 1 cup cherry tomatoes, halved
- 1 cucumber, diced
- 1/2 red bell pepper, diced
- 1/4 cup red onion, finely chopped
- 1/4 cup Kalamata olives, pitted and halved
- 1/4 cup feta cheese, crumbled (optional)
- 1/4 cup fresh parsley, chopped
- 2 tablespoons fresh lemon juice
- 2 tablespoons extra virgin olive oil
- 1 teaspoon dried oregano
- 1/4 teaspoon salt
- 1/4 teaspoon black pepper

Instructions:

1. Wash and prepare the cherry tomatoes, cucumber, red bell pepper, and red onion. Halve the cherry tomatoes, dice the cucumber and red bell pepper, and finely chop the red onion.
2. In a large mixing bowl, combine the chickpeas, cherry tomatoes, cucumber, red bell pepper, red onion, Kalamata olives, feta cheese (if using), and fresh parsley.
3. In a small bowl, whisk together the fresh lemon juice, extra virgin olive oil, dried oregano, salt, and black pepper until well combined. Pour the dressing over the salad and toss gently to coat all the ingredients evenly.
4. Serve immediately or refrigerate for up to an hour to allow the flavors to meld.

Nutritional Information (per serving): Calories: 220 / Protein: 6g / Carbohydrates: 22g / Fats: 12g / Fiber: 6g / Cholesterol: 0mg / Sodium: 300mg / Potassium: 400mg

Salmon and Mixed Greens Salad

Yield: 4 servings / **Preparation Time:** 15 minutes / **Cooking Time:** 10 minutes

Ingredients:

- 6 cups mixed greens (such as spinach, arugula, and baby kale)
- 4 salmon fillets (4-6 ounces each)
- 1 cup cherry tomatoes, halved
- 1 cucumber, sliced
- 1 avocado, sliced
- 1/2 red onion, thinly sliced
- 2 tablespoons olive oil
- 1 tablespoon fresh lemon juice
- 1/2 teaspoon salt; 1/2 teaspoon black pepper
- 2 tablespoons fresh lemon juice
- 1 tablespoon Dijon mustard
- 1 tablespoon honey or maple syrup
- 1 clove garlic, minced

Instructions:

1. Preheat the oven to 400°F (200°C). Season the salmon fillets with olive oil, fresh lemon juice, salt, and black pepper. Place the salmon fillets on a baking sheet lined with parchment paper.
2. Bake in the preheated oven for about 10 minutes, or until the salmon is cooked through and flakes easily with a fork. Allow to cool slightly.
3. While the salmon is baking, wash and prepare the mixed greens, cherry tomatoes, cucumber, red onion, and avocado. In a small bowl, whisk together the extra virgin olive oil, fresh lemon juice, Dijon mustard, honey or maple syrup, minced garlic, salt, and black pepper until well combined.
4. In a large salad bowl, combine the mixed greens, cherry tomatoes, cucumber, red onion, and avocado.
5. Place the cooked salmon fillets on top of the salad. Drizzle the dressing over the salad and toss gently to combine all the ingredients. Serve immediately and enjoy this nutritious and delicious salad.

Nutritional Information (per serving): Calories: 450 / Protein: 32g / Carbohydrates: 15g / Fats: 30g / Fiber: 6g / Cholesterol: 75mg / Sodium: 400mg / Potassium: 1000mg

---

Turkey and Cranberry Salad

Yield: 4 servings / **Preparation Time:** 15 minutes / **Cooking Time:** 10 minutes

Ingredients:

- 2 cups turkey breast, diced or shredded
- 4 cups mixed greens (such as spinach, arugula, and romaine)
- 1/2 cup dried cranberries (unsweetened, if possible)
- 1/2 cup chopped celery
- 1/4 cup chopped red onion
- 1/4 cup crumbled feta or goat cheese (optional)
- 3 tablespoons extra virgin olive oil
- 2 tablespoons apple cider vinegar
- 1 tablespoon Dijon mustard
- 1 tablespoon honey or maple syrup
- 1/4 teaspoon salt
- 1/4 teaspoon black pepper

Instructions:

1. Season the turkey breast with salt and pepper, cook it in a skillet over medium heat until cooked through (about 5-7 minutes per side), and let it cool before dicing.
2. Wash and prepare the mixed greens, chop the celery and red onion. In a small bowl, whisk together the extra virgin olive oil, apple cider vinegar, Dijon mustard, honey or maple syrup, salt, and black pepper until well combined.
3. In a large salad bowl, combine the mixed greens, diced turkey, dried cranberries, chopped celery, and red onion. Add the toasted nuts and crumbled cheese if using.
4. Pour the dressing over the salad and toss gently to combine all the ingredients. Serve immediately and enjoy this nutritious and delicious salad.

Nutritional Information (per serving): Calories: 300 / Protein: 20g / Carbohydrates: 20g / Fats: 15g / Fiber: 5g / Cholesterol: 45mg / Sodium: 350mg / Potassium: 500mg

Egg and Spinach Salad

Yield: 4 servings / **Preparation Time:** 10 minutes / **Cooking Time:** 10 minutes

Ingredients:

- 6 large eggs
- 6 cups fresh baby spinach
- 1 cup cherry tomatoes, halved
- 1 cucumber, sliced
- 1/4 red onion, thinly sliced
- 1 avocado, diced
- 1/4 cup toasted sunflower seeds (optional)
- 3 tablespoons extra virgin olive oil
- 2 tablespoons fresh lemon juice
- 1 tablespoon Dijon mustard
- 1 tablespoon honey or maple syrup
- 1 clove garlic, minced
- 1/4 teaspoon salt
- 1/4 teaspoon black pepper

Instructions:

1. Place the eggs in a saucepan and cover with cold water. Bring to a boil over medium-high heat. Once boiling, remove from heat and let the eggs sit in the hot water for 9-12 minutes, depending on desired doneness. Drain and cool the eggs under cold running water. Peel and slice the eggs.
2. While the eggs are cooking, wash and prepare the baby spinach, cherry tomatoes, cucumber, red onion, and avocado. In a small bowl, whisk together the extra virgin olive oil, fresh lemon juice, Dijon mustard, honey or maple syrup, minced garlic, salt, and black pepper until well combined.
3. In a large salad bowl, combine the baby spinach, cherry tomatoes, cucumber, and red onion. Add the diced avocado and toasted sunflower seeds (if using).
4. Place the sliced eggs on top of the salad. Drizzle the dressing over the salad and toss gently to combine all the ingredients. Serve immediately and enjoy this nutritious and delicious salad.

Nutritional Information (per serving): Calories: 300 / Protein: 12g / Carbohydrates: 14g / Fats: 24g / Fiber: 6g / Cholesterol: 210mg / Sodium: 250mg / Potassium: 750mg

Avocado and Black Bean Salad

Yield: 4 servings / **Preparation Time:** 15 minutes / **Cooking Time:** None

Ingredients:

- 1 can (15 ounces) black beans, drained and rinsed
- 1 cup cherry tomatoes, halved
- 1 cup corn kernels (fresh or frozen, thawed)
- 1 red bell pepper, diced
- 1 avocado, diced
- 1/4 red onion, finely chopped
- 1/4 cup fresh cilantro, chopped
- 2 tablespoons extra virgin olive oil
- 2 tablespoons fresh lime juice
- 1 teaspoon ground cumin
- 1/4 teaspoon salt
- 1/4 teaspoon black pepper

Instructions:

1. Prepare cherry tomatoes, corn, red bell pepper, avocado, red onion, and cilantro. Combine with black beans in a large bowl.
2. Whisk olive oil, lime juice, cumin, salt, and pepper in a small bowl.
3. Pour dressing over salad, toss to coat, and serve immediately or refrigerate for up to an hour.

Nutritional Information (per serving): Calories: 220 / Protein: 6g / Carbohydrates: 26g / Fats: 12g / Fiber: 10g / Cholesterol: 0mg / Sodium: 240mg / Potassium: 650mg

Fruit Salads

Fruit salads are rich in dietary fiber, helping to lower cholesterol and regulate blood pressure. Their natural sweetness makes them a nutritious snack or refreshing side dish, satisfying sweet cravings without added sugars or unhealthy fats. Fruits like berries, citrus, and apples have heart-protective properties, reducing inflammation and improving arterial function. Including fruit salads in your diet ensures you receive diverse nutrients while enjoying bursts of flavor and color. Explore our fruit salad recipes to add delightful and impactful dishes to your meals.

Mixed Berry and Almond Salad

Yield: 4 servings / **Preparation Time:** 10 minutes / **Cooking Time:** None

Ingredients:

- 2 cups mixed greens (spinach, arugula, baby kale)
- 1 cup fresh strawberries, hulled and sliced
- 1 cup fresh blueberries
- 1 cup fresh raspberries
- 1/4 cup sliced almonds, toasted
- 1/4 cup crumbled goat cheese (optional)
- 3 tablespoons extra virgin olive oil
- 2 tablespoons balsamic vinegar
- 1 tablespoon honey or maple syrup
- 1 teaspoon Dijon mustard
- 1/4 teaspoon salt
- 1/4 teaspoon black pepper

Instructions:

1. Combine mixed greens, sliced strawberries, blueberries, and raspberries in a large bowl. Toast sliced almonds in a dry skillet over medium heat for 3-5 minutes until golden.
2. Cool. Whisk olive oil, balsamic vinegar, honey/maple syrup, Dijon mustard, salt, and pepper in a small bowl.
3. Add toasted almonds and goat cheese (if using) to the salad. Drizzle with dressing and toss gently. Serve immediately.

Nutritional Information (per serving): Calories: 220 / Protein: 4g / Carbohydrates: 20g / Fats: 14g / Fiber: 6g / Cholesterol: 5mg (if goat cheese is used) / Sodium: 200mg / Potassium: 350mg

---

Tropical Fruit and Spinach Salad

Yield: 4 servings / **Preparation Time:** 15 minutes / **Cooking Time:** None

Ingredients:

- 6 cups fresh baby spinach
- 1/2 cup sliced strawberries
- 1 cup fresh pineapple, diced
- 1 cup fresh mango, diced
- 1 cup fresh papaya, diced
- 1/4 red onion, thinly sliced
- 1/4 cup sliced almonds or macadamia nuts
- 3 tablespoons extra virgin olive oil
- 2 tablespoons fresh lime juice
- 1 tablespoon honey or maple syrup
- 1 teaspoon Dijon mustard
- 1/4 teaspoon salt; 1/4 teaspoon black pepper

Instructions:

1. Prepare baby spinach, pineapple, mango, papaya, and strawberries in a large bowl.
2. Whisk olive oil, lime juice, honey/maple syrup, Dijon mustard, salt, and pepper.
3. Add nuts to the salad. Drizzle with dressing, toss gently, and serve immediately.

Nutritional Information (per serving): Calories: 200 / Protein: 3g / Carbohydrates: 28g / Fats: 10g / Fiber: 5g / Cholesterol: 0mg / Sodium: 150mg / Potassium: 500m

Pear and Pecan Salad

Yield: 4 servings / **Preparation Time:** 15 minutes / **Cooking Time:** None

Ingredients:

- 6 cups mixed greens (such as spinach, arugula, and romaine)
- 2 ripe pears, cored and thinly sliced
- 1/2 cup pecans, toasted and chopped
- 1/4 cup red onion, thinly sliced
- 1/4 cup dried cranberries
- 3 tablespoons extra virgin olive oil
- 2 tablespoons apple cider vinegar
- 1 tablespoon Dijon mustard
- 1 tablespoon honey or maple syrup
- 1 clove garlic, minced
- 1/4 teaspoon salt
- 1/4 teaspoon black pepper

Instructions:

1. In a large salad bowl, combine the mixed greens, sliced pears, toasted pecans, red onion, and dried cranberries.
2. In a dry skillet over medium heat, toast the pecans until they are golden brown and fragrant, about 3-5 minutes. Stir frequently to prevent burning. Allow to cool.
3. In a small bowl, whisk together the extra virgin olive oil, apple cider vinegar, Dijon mustard, honey or maple syrup, minced garlic, salt, and black pepper until well combined.
4. Drizzle the dressing over the salad and toss gently to combine all the ingredients.
5. Serve immediately and enjoy this nutritious and delicious salad.

Nutritional Information (per serving): Calories: 240 / Protein: 3g / Carbohydrates: 20g / Fats: 18g / Fiber: 5g / Cholesterol: 0mg / Sodium: 200mg / Potassium: 400mg

Orange and Pomegranate Salad

Yield: 4 servings / **Preparation Time:** 15 minutes / **Cooking Time:** None

Ingredients:

- 4 oranges, peeled and segmented
- 1 cup pomegranate seeds
- 4 cups mixed greens (such as spinach, arugula, and romaine)
- 1/4 cup red onion, thinly sliced
- 1/4 cup chopped fresh mint
- 1/4 cup toasted almonds or walnuts
- 3 tablespoons extra virgin olive oil
- 2 tablespoons fresh lemon juice
- 1 tablespoon honey or maple syrup
- 1 teaspoon Dijon mustard
- 1/4 teaspoon salt; 1/4 teaspoon black pepper

Instructions:

1. Peel and segment oranges, remove seeds, and place in a large bowl. Add pomegranate seeds.
2. Add washed mixed greens and red onion to the bowl.
3. Toast almonds/walnuts in a dry skillet over medium heat for 3-5 minutes until golden. Cool and add to the salad.
4. Whisk olive oil, lemon juice, honey/maple syrup, Dijon mustard, salt, and pepper in a small bowl.
5. Drizzle dressing over the salad, toss gently, garnish with mint, and serve immediately.

Nutritional Information (per serving): Calories: 220 / Protein: 3g / Carbohydrates: 25g / Fats: 14g / Fiber: 6g Cholesterol: 0mg / Sodium: 150mg / Potassium: 450mg

Chapter 4: Grains, Pasta, and Rice

Grains, pasta, and rice are an important source of complex carbohydrates, providing sustained energy and numerous health benefits. These slow carb options are essential for maintaining cardiovascular health, as they are packed with fiber, vitamins, and minerals that support heart function, lower cholesterol levels, and help regulate blood pressure.

This chapter offers a variety of nutritious recipes that incorporate grains, pasta, and rice in heart-healthy ways, ensuring that every meal contributes positively to your well-being. Dive in and discover how these essential foods can be both satisfying and beneficial for your heart.

Whole Grains and Ancient Grains

Whole grains and ancient grains are powerhouses of nutrition that play a crucial role in a heart-healthy diet. Whole grains, such as brown rice, oats, and whole wheat, retain all parts of the grain kernel, providing fiber, vitamins, and minerals that support cardiovascular health. Ancient grains like quinoa, farro, and spelt are nutrient-dense, minimally processed grains that have been cultivated for centuries. Both whole grains and ancient grains help reduce cholesterol, regulate blood pressure, and provide sustained energy. In this subchapter, explore delicious recipes that harness the benefits of these grains to enhance your heart health.

Barley and Mushroom Stew

Yield: 4 servings / **Preparation Time:** 15 minutes / **Cooking Time:** 45 minutes

Ingredients:

- 1 cup pearl barley
- 2 tablespoons olive oil
- 1 large onion, chopped
- 3 cloves garlic, minced
- 3 carrots, diced
- 2 celery stalks, diced
- 1-pound mixed mushrooms (such as cremini, shiitake, and button), sliced
- 1 can (14.5 ounces) diced tomatoes, with juice

- 4 cups low-sodium vegetable broth
- 1 teaspoon dried thyme
- 1 teaspoon dried rosemary
- 1 bay leaf
- 1/2 teaspoon salt
- 1/4 teaspoon black pepper
- 2 cups fresh spinach, roughly chopped
- 1/4 cup fresh parsley, chopped (optional)

Instructions:

1. Rinse the barley under cold water and set aside.
2. In a large pot, heat the olive oil over medium heat. Add the chopped onion and garlic, and sauté for about 5 minutes until the onion becomes translucent. Add the diced carrots and celery. Cook for another 5 minutes, stirring occasionally.
3. Add the sliced mushrooms to the pot. Cook for 5-7 minutes, or until the mushrooms have released their moisture and started to brown.
4. Add the rinsed barley, diced tomatoes (with juice), vegetable broth, dried thyme, dried rosemary, bay leaf, salt, and black pepper. Stir to combine.
5. Bring the mixture to a boil, then reduce the heat to low. Cover the pot and let the stew simmer for about 30 minutes, or until the barley is tender and the flavors have melded together.
6. Stir in the chopped spinach and cook for an additional 5 minutes until the spinach is wilted. Remove the bay leaf and stir in the fresh parsley (if using). Ladle the stew into bowls and serve hot.

Nutritional Information (per serving): Calories: 320 / Protein: 9g / Carbohydrates: 55g / Fats: 8g / Fiber: 10g / Cholesterol: 0mg / Sodium: 350mg / Potassium: 750mg

Mediterranean Quinoa Salad

Yield: 4 servings / **Preparation Time:** 15 minutes / **Cooking Time:** 15 minutes

Ingredients:

- 1 cup quinoa, rinsed
- 2 cups water or low-sodium vegetable broth
- 1 cup cherry tomatoes, halved
- 1 cucumber, diced
- 1/2 red onion, thinly sliced
- 1/2 cup Kalamata olives, pitted and halved
- 1/4 cup crumbled feta cheese (optional)
- 2 tablespoons fresh parsley, chopped
- 2 tablespoons fresh mint, chopped
- 2 tablespoons virgin olive oil
- 2 tablespoons fresh lemon juice
- 1 clove garlic, minced
- 1/2 teaspoon dried oregano
- Salt and pepper to taste

Instructions:

1. Combine quinoa and water (or vegetable broth) in a saucepan. Bring to a boil, then reduce heat to low, cover, and simmer for 15 minutes or until the quinoa is tender and the liquid is absorbed. Fluff with a fork and let cool.
2. In a large bowl, combine cooked quinoa, cherry tomatoes, cucumber, red onion, kalamata olives, feta cheese (if using), parsley, and mint.
3. Whisk together olive oil, lemon juice, garlic, oregano, salt, and pepper in a small bowl. Pour the dressing over the salad and toss gently to combine. Serve immediately or refrigerate for up to an hour to allow flavors to meld.

Nutritional Information (per serving): Calories: 250 / Protein: 7g / Carbohydrates: 28g / Fats: 12g / Fiber: 5g / Cholesterol: 10mg (if using feta) / Sodium: 200mg / Potassium: 400mg

Farro and Vegetable Medley

Yield: 4 servings / **Preparation Time:** 15 minutes / **Cooking Time:** 30 minutes

Ingredients:

- 1 cup farro, rinsed
- 2 cups low-sodium vegetable broth
- 1 tablespoon olive oil
- 1 red bell pepper, diced
- 1 yellow bell pepper, diced
- 1 zucchini, diced
- 1 yellow squash, diced
- 1 red onion, chopped
- 2 cloves garlic, minced
- 1 cup cherry tomatoes, halved
- 1/2 teaspoon salt
- 1/4 teaspoon black pepper
- 1 teaspoon dried thyme
- 1 teaspoon dried oregano
- 1/4 cup fresh basil, chopped
- 1/4 cup grated Parmesan cheese (optional)

Instructions:

1. Cook farro in vegetable broth: boil, reduce heat, cover, and simmer for 20 minutes until tender. Set aside.
2. Heat olive oil in a large skillet over medium heat. Sauté onion and garlic for 3 minutes. Add bell peppers, zucchini, and squash; cook for 5-7 minutes until tender but crisp.
3. Add cooked farro, cherry tomatoes, salt, pepper, thyme, and oregano; stir and cook for 5 minutes.
4. Remove from heat. Stir in basil and sprinkle with Parmesan cheese, if desired.
5. Serve the Farro and Vegetable Medley warm in bowls.

Nutritional Information (per serving): Calories: 280 / Protein: 7g / Carbohydrates: 45g / Fats: 8g / Fiber: 7g / Cholesterol: 0mg (with no Parmesan cheese) or 7mg (with Parmesan cheese) / Sodium: 200mg / Potassium: 550mg

Spelt and Roasted Butternut Squash Salad

Yield: 4 servings / **Preparation Time:** 15 minutes / **Cooking Time:** 40 minutes

Ingredients:

- 1 cup spelt, rinsed
- 2 cups low-sodium vegetable broth or water
- 2 cups butternut squash, peeled and cubed
- 1 tablespoon olive oil
- 1/2 teaspoon salt
- 1/4 teaspoon black pepper
- 1 teaspoon Dijon mustard
- 1/4 cup dried cranberries
- 1/4 cup chopped pecans, toasted
- 2 cups baby spinach, roughly chopped
- 3 tablespoons olive oil
- 2 tablespoons apple cider vinegar
- 1 tablespoon honey or maple syrup
- 1 clove garlic, minced

Instructions:

1. In a medium saucepan, combine the rinsed spelt and vegetable broth (or water). Bring to a boil, then reduce heat to low. Cover and simmer for about 30 minutes, or until the spelt is tender. Drain any excess liquid and set aside.
2. Preheat the oven to 400°F (200°C). Place the cubed butternut squash on a baking sheet. Drizzle with olive oil and season with salt and black pepper. Toss to coat evenly. Roast the squash in the preheated oven for 25-30 minutes, or until tender and slightly caramelized.
3. In a small bowl, whisk together the olive oil, apple cider vinegar, honey or maple syrup, Dijon mustard, minced garlic, salt, and pepper until well combined.
4. In a large bowl, combine the cooked spelt, roasted butternut squash, dried cranberries, toasted pecans, and baby spinach. Pour the dressing over the salad and toss gently to combine. Serve the salad warm or at room temperature.

Nutritional Information (per serving): Calories: 320 / Protein: 7g / Carbohydrates: 45g / Fats: 12g / Fiber: 8g / Cholesterol: 0mg (with no feta) or 25mg (with feta) / Sodium: 200mg / Potassium: 500mg

Lentil and Vegetable Stew

Yield: 6 servings / **Preparation Time:** 15 minutes / **Cooking Time:** 45 minutes

Ingredients:

- 1 cup dried green or brown lentils, rinsed
- 4 cups low-sodium vegetable broth
- 2 tablespoons olive oil
- 1 large onion, chopped
- 2 cloves garlic, minced
- 3 carrots, diced
- 2 celery stalks, diced
- 1 red bell pepper, chopped
- 1 zucchini, chopped
- 1 can (14.5 ounces) diced tomatoes, with juice
- 2 teaspoons ground cumin
- 1 teaspoon dried thyme
- 1 teaspoon smoked paprika
- 1/2 teaspoon turmeric
- 1/4 teaspoon black pepper
- 1 bay leaf
- 2 cups fresh spinach, roughly chopped
- 1/4 cup fresh parsley, chopped
- juice of 1 lemon

Instructions:

1. Rinse the lentils under cold water and set aside. In a large pot, heat the olive oil over medium heat. Add the chopped onion and garlic, and sauté for about 5 minutes until the onion becomes translucent. Add the diced carrots, celery, red bell pepper, and zucchini. Cook for another 5-7 minutes, stirring occasionally.
2. Add the rinsed lentils to the pot, along with the diced tomatoes (including juice), vegetable broth, ground cumin, dried thyme, smoked paprika, turmeric, black pepper, and bay leaf. Stir well to combine.

3. Bring the mixture to a boil, then reduce the heat to low. Cover the pot and let the stew simmer for about 30 minutes, or until the lentils and vegetables are tender.
4. Once the lentils and vegetables are cooked, stir in the chopped spinach and fresh parsley (if using). Cook for an additional 5 minutes until the spinach is wilted.
5. Remove the bay leaf and stir in the lemon juice. Ladle the stew into bowls and serve hot.

Nutritional Information (per serving): Calories: 250 / Protein: 12g / Carbohydrates: 40g / Fats: 6g / Fiber: 12g / Cholesterol: 0mg / Sodium: 300mg / Potassium: 700mg

Pasta Dishes

Pasta dishes can be a delightful and nutritious part of a heart-healthy diet. When made with whole grain or legume-based pasta, these dishes provide a good source of slow-digesting carbohydrates, fiber, and essential nutrients. They help maintain steady blood sugar levels and keep you feeling full and satisfied. Incorporating pasta dishes into your meal can be beneficial for your heart health, especially when paired with heart-friendly ingredients like vegetables, lean proteins, and healthy fats. Enjoy the variety and flavors that pasta dishes bring to your diet while supporting your cardiovascular health.

Spaghetti Squash with Marinara

Yield: 4 servings / **Preparation Time:** 10 minutes / **Cooking Time:** 45 minutes

Ingredients:
- 1 large spaghetti squash
- 1 can (28 ounces) crushed tomatoes
- 2 tablespoons olive oil
- Salt and pepper to taste
- 1 small onion, finely chopped
- 2 cloves garlic, minced
- 1 teaspoon dried oregano
- 1 teaspoon dried basil
- 1/4 teaspoon red pepper flakes (optional)
- 1/2 teaspoon salt
- 1/4 teaspoon black pepper
- 1/4 cup fresh basil, chopped
- fresh basil leaves (optional topping)

Instructions:
1. Preheat the oven to 400°F (200°C).
2. Line a baking sheet with parchment paper. Cut the spaghetti squash in half lengthwise and scoop out the seeds. Drizzle the inside of each half with olive oil and season with salt and pepper. Place the squash halves cut-side down on the prepared baking sheet. Roast in the preheated oven for 40-45 minutes, or until the squash is tender and easily pierced with a fork.
3. While the squash is roasting, heat 1 tablespoon of olive oil in a large skillet over medium heat. Add the chopped onion and cook for about 5 minutes, or until softened. Add the minced garlic and cook for an additional 1-2 minutes, until fragrant.
4. Stir in the crushed tomatoes, dried oregano, dried basil, red pepper flakes (if using), salt, and black pepper. Simmer the sauce for about 20 minutes, stirring occasionally. Stir it into the sauce just before serving.
5. Once the squash is roasted and cool enough to handle, use a fork to scrape the flesh into spaghetti-like strands.
6. Divide the spaghetti squash strands among four plates. Top each serving with a generous portion of marinara sauce. Serve the dish warm, with fresh basil leaves if desired.

Nutritional Information (per serving): Calories: 180 / Protein: 4g / Carbohydrates: 28g / Fats: 7g / Fiber: 6g / Cholesterol: 0mg / Sodium: 380mg / Potassium: 750mg

One-Pot Pesto Pasta with Peas

Yield: 4 servings / **Preparation Time:** 10 minutes / **Cooking Time:** 20 minutes

Ingredients:
- 12 ounces whole wheat pasta (penne, fusilli, or spaghetti)
- 4 cups low-sodium vegetable broth
- 1 cup frozen peas
- 2 cups fresh basil leaves
- 1/4 cup pine nuts (or walnuts)
- 2 cloves garlic, minced
- 1/2 teaspoon salt
- 1/4 teaspoon black pepper
- 1 tablespoon olive oil
- 1 tablespoon lemon juice
- Cherry tomatoes, halved (optional)
- Fresh basil leaves (optional)

Instructions:
1. Blend basil, garlic, olive oil, lemon juice, salt, and pepper in a food processor until smooth. Set aside.
2. In a large pot, cook pasta, broth, minced garlic, salt, and pepper. Bring to a boil, then simmer for 10 minutes.
3. Add peas and cook for 5 minutes until pasta is al dente and peas are tender. Adjust liquid if needed.
4. Remove from heat and stir in pesto. Serve pasta in bowls topped with cherry tomatoes and fresh basil.

Nutritional Information (per serving): Calories: 350 / Protein: 10g / Carbohydrates: 55g / Fats: 14g / Fiber: 10g / Cholesterol: 0mg / Sodium: 350mg / Potassium: 400mg

Chickpea Pasta with Spinach and Garlic

Yield: 4 servings / **Preparation Time:** 10 minutes / **Cooking Time:** 15 minutes

Ingredients:
- 12 ounces chickpea pasta (such as Banza)
- 5 cups fresh spinach, roughly chopped
- 4 cloves garlic, minced; fresh parsley, chopped
- 1 can (15 ounces) chickpeas, drained and rinsed
- 1/4 cup low-sodium vegetable broth
- 1/4 teaspoon salt
- 1/4 teaspoon black pepper
- 2 tablespoons olive oil
- 1 tablespoon lemon juice]
- Zest of 1 lemon
- 1/4 teaspoon red pepper flakes (optional)

Instructions:
1. Bring a large pot of water to a boil. Add the chickpea pasta and cook according to the package instructions until al dente. Drain and set aside.
2. In a large skillet, heat the olive oil over medium heat. Add the minced garlic and red pepper flakes (if using) and sauté for about 1 minute, until fragrant.
3. Add the chopped spinach to the skillet and cook, stirring occasionally, until wilted, about 2-3 minutes. Add the drained chickpeas and vegetable broth to the skillet. Cook for another 2-3 minutes, allowing the flavors to meld together. Season with salt and black pepper.
4. Add the cooked chickpea pasta to the skillet and toss to combine. Cook for an additional 2 minutes to heat through.
5. Remove from heat, add lemon juice, and lemon zest. Garnish with fresh parsley.

Nutritional Information (per serving): Calories: 350 / Protein: 18g / Carbohydrates: 45g / Fats: 12g / Fiber: 10g / Cholesterol: 0mg / Sodium: 300mg / Potassium: 600mg

Whole Grain Penne with Broccoli and Olive Oil

Yield: 4 servings/ **Preparation Time:** 10 minutes / **Cooking Time:** 20 minutes

Ingredients:
- 12 ounces whole grain penne pasta
- 4 cups broccoli florets
- 3 tablespoons extra virgin olive oil
- 2 tablespoons lemon juice
- zest of 1 lemon
- 1/2 teaspoon salt
- 1/4 teaspoon black pepper
- 1/4 teaspoon red pepper flakes (optional)
- 4 cloves garlic, minced
- fresh parsley, chopped (optional for garnish)

Instructions:
1. Boil water, add salt and whole grain penne, cook until al dente (10-12 minutes). Reserve 1/2 cup pasta water, drain, and set aside.
2. Steam or boil broccoli florets until tender (5-7 minutes). Boil with pasta in the last 3-4 minutes to save time.
3. Heat olive oil in a skillet over medium heat. Sauté minced garlic and red pepper flakes for 1-2 minutes. Add pasta and broccoli, toss to coat.
4. Add reserved pasta water, salt, black pepper, lemon zest, and juice. Toss until combined and heated through. Serve with fresh parsley if desired.

Nutritional Information (per serving): Calories: 350 / Protein: 10g / Carbohydrates: 55g / Fats: 12g / Fiber: 10g / Cholesterol: 0mg / Sodium: 250mg / Potassium: 600mg.

Lentil Pasta with Roasted Red Pepper Sauce

Yield: 4 servings / **Preparation Time:** 10 minutes / **Cooking Time:** 30 minutes

Ingredients:
- 12 ounces lentil pasta (such as red lentil or green lentil pasta)
- 1 can (14.5 ounces) diced tomatoes, with juice
- 1/4 cup unsweetened almond milk or low-fat milk
- 2 tablespoons olive oil
- 2 large red bell peppers
- 1 small onion, finely chopped
- 3 cloves garlic, minced
- 1/4 teaspoon red pepper flakes (optional)
- 1/2 teaspoon dried basil
- 1/2 teaspoon dried oregano
- 1/4 teaspoon salt
- 1/4 teaspoon black pepper
- 1/4 cup fresh basil leaves, chopped (optional)

Instructions:
1. Preheat oven to 450°F (230°C). Roast whole red bell peppers on a foil-lined baking sheet for 20-25 minutes, turning occasionally. Place in a bowl, cover with plastic wrap, steam for 10 minutes, peel, seed, and chop. Set aside.
2. Boil water in a large pot, cook lentil pasta until al dente, drain, and set aside.
3. Heat 1 tablespoon olive oil in a large skillet over medium heat. Cook chopped onion for 5 minutes until softened. Add minced garlic and red pepper flakes, cook for 1-2 minutes. Stir in chopped roasted red peppers, diced tomatoes, dried basil, dried oregano, salt, and pepper. Simmer for 10 minutes.
4. Cool sauce slightly, blend until smooth, return to skillet, and stir in almond or low-fat milk. Simmer for 2-3 minutes.
5. Add cooked pasta to skillet, toss with sauce, heat through. Serve in bowls topped with fresh basil leaves.

Nutritional Information (per serving): Calories: 350 / Protein: 18g / Carbohydrates: 55g / Fats: 10g / Fiber: 12g / Cholesterol: 0mg / Sodium: 350mg / Potassium: 750mg

Nutritious Rice and Pilaf Dishes

Rice and pilaf dishes can be a cornerstone of a heart-healthy diet. Using whole grains like brown or wild rice, they provide essential fiber, vitamins, and minerals that support cardiovascular health.

Benefits of Whole Grains

Whole grains retain the bran, germ, and endosperm, making them more nutritious than refined grains. They help lower cholesterol, regulate blood sugar, and improve digestion. Nutrients like magnesium, selenium, and B vitamins reduce blood pressure and inflammation, promoting heart health.

Incorporating Heart-Friendly Ingredients

- **Vegetables**: Enhance with bell peppers, spinach, carrots, and tomatoes for vitamins and antioxidants.
- **Lean Proteins**: Add chicken, turkey, tofu, or legumes for protein without unhealthy fats.
- **Healthy Fats**: Use olive oil, avocado, and nuts to reduce bad cholesterol and provide essential fatty acids.

Enjoying the Health Benefits

These versatile dishes allow for the inclusion of various heart-friendly ingredients, creating nutritious and flavorful meals. Regularly incorporating them into your diet supports a strong, healthy heart and overall wellness. Enjoy the benefits and flavors of these nutritious rice and pilaf dishes as part of your heart-healthy diet.

Balsamic Glazed Portobello Mushrooms with Wild Rice

Yield: 4 servings / **Preparation Time:** 15 minutes / **Cooking Time:** 45 minutes

Ingredients:

- 1 cup wild rice, rinsed
- 2 ½ cups low-sodium vegetable broth or water
- 4 large portobello mushroom caps, stems removed
- 1 small onion, finely chopped
- 2 cloves garlic, minced
- 1/2 teaspoon dried thyme
- 1/2 teaspoon dried oregano
- 1/4 teaspoon salt; 1/4 teaspoon black pepper
- 2 tablespoons balsamic vinegar
- 2 tablespoons olive oil
- 1 tablespoon low-sodium soy sauce
- 1 tablespoon maple syrup or honey
- 1/4 teaspoon dried rosemary

Instructions:

1. In a medium pot, boil low-sodium vegetable broth or water. Add rinsed wild rice, reduce heat, cover, and simmer for 40-45 minutes until tender. In a large skillet, heat 1 tbsp olive oil over medium heat.
2. Sauté chopped onion and garlic until translucent (5 minutes). Stir in cooked wild rice, dried thyme, dried oregano, salt, and black pepper. Keep warm.
3. Preheat oven to 400°F (200°C). In a small bowl, whisk balsamic vinegar, olive oil, low-sodium soy sauce, maple syrup or honey, minced garlic, dried rosemary, and black pepper.
4. Place portobello mushroom caps on a parchment-lined baking sheet. Brush with balsamic glaze. Bake for 20-25 minutes, flipping halfway, until tender and caramelized.
5. Serve wild rice on plates, topped with a balsamic-glazed portobello mushroom cap. Garnish with fresh herbs if desired.

Nutritional Information (per serving): Calories: 250 / Protein: 6g / Carbohydrates: 40g / Fats: 9g / Fiber: 5g / Cholesterol: 0mg / Sodium: 280mg / Potassium: 750mg

Brown Rice and Vegetable Stir-Fry

Yield: 4 servings **Preparation Time:** 15 minutes   **Cooking Time:** 30 minutes

Ingredients:
- 1 cup brown rice, rinsed
- 2 ½ cups low-sodium vegetable broth or water
- 1 red bell pepper, sliced
- 1 yellow bell pepper, sliced
- 1 medium carrot, julienned
- 1 cup broccoli florets
- 1 cup snap peas
- 1 small red onion, sliced
- 2 cloves garlic, minced
- 1 teaspoon fresh ginger, minced
- 2 tablespoons low-sodium soy sauce
- 1 tablespoon rice vinegar
- 1 tablespoon olive oil
- 1 tablespoon hoisin sauce
- 1/4 cup chopped fresh cilantro (optional)
- 1/4 cup chopped green onions (optional)

Instructions:
1. In a medium pot, bring the low-sodium vegetable broth or water to a boil. Add the rinsed brown rice, reduce the heat to low, cover, and simmer for 30-35 minutes or until the rice is tender and the liquid is absorbed. Remove from heat and let it sit covered for 5 minutes, then fluff with a fork.
2. In a large skillet or wok, heat the olive oil over medium-high heat. Add the sliced red and yellow bell peppers, broccoli florets, snap peas, julienned carrot, and sliced red onion.
3. Stir-fry for about 5-7 minutes until the vegetables are tender-crisp. Add the minced garlic and fresh ginger to the skillet, and stir-fry for an additional 1-2 minutes until fragrant.
4. In a small bowl, mix the low-sodium soy sauce, rice vinegar, hoisin sauce. Pour the sauce over the vegetables in the skillet and toss to coat evenly. Cook for another 2-3 minutes until everything is well combined and heated through.
5. Add the cooked brown rice to the skillet and stir to mix with the vegetables and sauce. Optionally, garnish with chopped fresh cilantro, green onions before serving.

Nutritional Information (per serving): Calories: 250 / Protein: 5g / Carbohydrates: 45g / Fats: 5g / Fiber: 6g / Cholesterol: 0mg / Sodium: 320mg / Potassium: 550mg

Wild Rice and Cranberry Pilaf

Yield: 4 servings / **Preparation Time:** 15 minutes / **Cooking Time:** 45 minutes

Ingredients:
- 1 cup wild rice, rinsed
- 2 ½ cups low-sodium vegetable broth or water
- 1 tablespoon olive oil
- 1 small onion, finely chopped
- 2 cloves garlic, minced
- 1/2 cup dried cranberries
- 1/4 cup chopped pecans, toasted
- 1/4 teaspoon salt
- 1/4 teaspoon black pepper
- 1/2 teaspoon dried thyme
- 1/2 teaspoon dried rosemary
- Optional: 2 cups fresh spinach, roughly chopped (for added fiber, vitamins, and minerals)
- Optional: 1 tablespoon chia seeds (for added omega-3 fatty acids, fiber, and protein)

Instructions:

1. In a medium saucepan, bring the low-sodium vegetable broth or water to a boil. Add the rinsed wild rice, reduce the heat to low, cover, and simmer for about 45 minutes, or until the rice is tender and most of the liquid is absorbed. Remove from heat and let it sit covered for 5 minutes, then fluff with a fork.
2. While the rice is cooking, heat the olive oil in a large skillet over medium heat. Add the chopped onion and cook, stirring occasionally, until the onion is soft and translucent, about 5 minutes. Add the minced garlic and cook for another 1-2 minutes, until fragrant.
3. Add the cooked wild rice to the skillet with the onions and garlic. Stir to combine. Stir in the dried cranberries, toasted pecans, salt, black pepper, thyme, and rosemary.
4. Cook for another 2-3 minutes, stirring frequently, until everything is well mixed and heated through.

Nutritional Information (per serving): Calories: 280 / Protein: 6g / Carbohydrates: 45g / Fats: 9g / Fiber: 5g / Cholesterol: 0mg / Sodium: 140mg / Potassium: 300mg

---

Lemon Herb Rice with Grilled Vegetables

Yield: 4 servings / **Preparation Time:** 15 minutes / **Cooking Time:** 35 minutes

Ingredients:

- 1 cup brown rice, rinsed
- 2 cups low-sodium vegetable broth or water
- 1 red bell pepper, sliced into strips
- 1 yellow bell pepper, sliced into strips
- 1 zucchini, sliced into rounds
- 1 yellow squash, sliced into rounds
- 1 red onion, sliced into rings
- 2 cloves garlic, minced
- 2 tablespoons olive oil
- 1 tablespoon fresh parsley, chopped
- 1 tablespoon fresh dill, chopped
- Zest of 1 lemon
- juice of 1 lemon
- 1 teaspoon dried oregano
- 1 teaspoon dried thyme
- 1/4 teaspoon salt
- 1/4 teaspoon black pepper

Instructions:

1. In a medium saucepan, bring the low-sodium vegetable broth or water to a boil. Add the rinsed brown rice, reduce the heat to low, cover, and simmer for about 30-35 minutes, or until the rice is tender and the liquid is absorbed. Remove from heat and let it sit covered for 5 minutes.
2. In a small pan, heat 1 tablespoon of olive oil over medium heat. Add the minced garlic and cook for 1-2 minutes until fragrant. Fluff the rice with a fork and stir in the garlic, lemon zest, lemon juice, parsley, dill, salt, and black pepper.
3. Preheat the grill to medium-high heat. In a large bowl, toss the bell peppers, zucchini, squash, and red onion with 1 tablespoon of olive oil, dried oregano, dried thyme, salt, and black pepper. Grill the vegetables for about 5-7 minutes per side, until they are tender and have nice grill marks. Remove from the grill and set aside.
4. Arrange the grilled vegetables on a serving platter. Serve the lemon herb rice alongside the vegetables or mix the grilled vegetables into the rice. Optionally, garnish with additional fresh herbs and a drizzle of lemon juice for extra flavor.

Nutritional Information (per serving): Calories: 250 / Protein: 5g / Carbohydrates: 40g / Fats: 8g / Fiber: 5g / Cholesterol: 0mg / Sodium: 180mg / Potassium: 500mg

Spinach and Feta Stuffed Peppers

Yield: 4 servings / **Preparation Time:** 20 minutes / **Cooking Time:** 40 minutes

Ingredients:
- 4 large bell peppers, tops cut off and seeds removed
- 1 cup cooked brown rice
- 1/4 cup low-sodium vegetable broth or water
- 1 tablespoon olive oil
- 1 small onion, finely chopped
- 2 cloves garlic, minced
- 4 cups fresh spinach, roughly chopped
- 1/2 cup crumbled feta cheese
- 1/4 cup chopped fresh parsley
- 1/2 teaspoon dried oregano
- 1/2 teaspoon dried thyme
- 1/2 teaspoon salt
- 1/4 teaspoon black pepper

Instructions:
1. Preheat your oven to 375°F (190°C). Cut the tops off the bell peppers and remove the seeds. Arrange them in a baking dish.
2. Heat the olive oil in a large skillet over medium heat. Add the chopped onion and garlic, and sauté until the onion is translucent, about 5 minutes. Add the chopped spinach to the skillet and cook until wilted, about 3 minutes.
3. In a large bowl, combine the cooked brown rice, sautéed onions, garlic, spinach, crumbled feta cheese, chopped parsley, dried oregano, dried thyme, salt, and black pepper. Mix well.
4. Spoon the rice mixture into each bell pepper, packing it down slightly. Pour the low-sodium vegetable broth or water into the bottom of the baking dish to keep the peppers moist during baking.
5. Cover the baking dish with aluminum foil and bake for 30 minutes. If using, remove the foil and sprinkle the tops of the peppers with grated Parmesan cheese, then bake for an additional 10 minutes until the cheese is melted and the peppers are tender.
6. Remove the stuffed peppers from the oven and let them cool slightly before serving. Garnish with additional chopped parsley if desired.

Nutritional Information (per serving): Calories: 230 / Protein: 7g / Carbohydrates: 30g / Fats: 10g / Fiber: 5g / Cholesterol: 20mg (if feta cheese is used) / Sodium: 320mg / Potassium: 500mg

Chapter 5: Fish and Seafood

Fish and seafood are essential components of a heart-healthy diet, offering a wealth of nutrients that can significantly enhance cardiovascular health. Rich in omega-3 fatty acids, vitamins, and minerals, these ingredients help reduce inflammation, lower blood pressure, and decrease the risk of heart disease. Incorporating fish and seafood into your meals can be a delicious and effective way to support your heart and overall well-being. Dive into this chapter to discover a variety of nutritious and delectable recipes that make it easy to enjoy the heart-boosting benefits of fish and seafood.

Light and Refreshing Seafood Dishes

Light and refreshing seafood dishes are a fantastic way to support cardiovascular health while enjoying flavorful meals. These dishes are typically low in saturated fats and calories, yet rich in essential nutrients like omega-3 fatty acids, which help reduce inflammation and support heart function. Incorporating light seafood dishes into your diet can help maintain healthy cholesterol levels, lower blood pressure, and improve overall heart health. Enjoy the variety of delicious, heart-friendly seafood recipes that are perfect for any occasion.

Ceviche with Fresh Lime and Cilantro

Yield: 4 servings / **Preparation Time:** 20 minutes / **Setting Time:** 30 minutes

Ingredients:
- 1 lb. fresh white fish (such as tilapia, sea bass, or halibut), diced into small pieces
- 1 avocado, diced
- 1 jalapeño pepper, finely chopped (seeds removed for less heat)
- 1 cup cherry tomatoes, quartered
- 1/2 cup fresh cilantro, chopped
- 1 cup fresh lime juice (about 8-10 limes)
- 1/2 cup fresh lemon juice (about 4-5 lemons)
- 1/4 teaspoon salt
- 1/4 teaspoon black pepper
- Lettuce leaves or whole-grain tortilla chips for serving

Instructions:
1. Place the diced fish in a glass or ceramic bowl. Pour the fresh lime and lemon juice over the fish, ensuring that all the pieces are fully submerged. Cover the bowl and refrigerate for 30 minutes, or until the fish is opaque and firm, indicating it is "cooked" by the acidity of the citrus juices.
2. While the fish is marinating, finely chop the red onion, jalapeño pepper, cherry tomatoes, cilantro, and cucumber. Dice the avocado just before serving to keep it fresh.
3. Once the fish is "cooked," drain off most of the citrus juice, leaving a little to keep the ceviche moist. Add the chopped red onion, jalapeño, cherry tomatoes, cilantro, cucumber, and avocado to the fish. Gently toss to combine.
4. Season the ceviche with salt and black pepper to taste. Serve the ceviche chilled, on a bed of lettuce leaves or with whole-grain tortilla chips for a heart-healthy, crunchy accompaniment.

Nutritional Information (per serving): Calories: 200 / Protein: 25g / Carbohydrates: 15g / Fats: 7g / Fiber: 5g / Cholesterol: 35mg / Sodium: 220mg / Potassium: 700mg

Tuna and White Bean Salad

Yield: 4 servings / **Preparation Time:** 15 minutes / **Cooking Time:** None

Ingredients:
- 2 cans (5 ounces each) tuna packed in water, drained
- 1 can (15 ounces) white beans (such as cannellini or navy beans), drained and rinsed
- 1/2 red onion, finely chopped
- 1 clove garlic, minced
- 1 cup cherry tomatoes, halved
- 1/4 cup fresh parsley, chopped
- 1/2 cucumber, diced
- 2 tablespoons fresh lemon juice (about 1 lemon)
- 2 tablespoons olive oil
- 1/4 teaspoon salt; 1/4 teaspoon black pepper
- Optional: 1/4 cup Kalamata olives, pitted and sliced

Instructions:
1. In a small bowl, whisk together the fresh lemon juice, olive oil, minced garlic, salt, and black pepper until well combined.
2. In a large bowl, combine the drained tuna, white beans, red onion, cherry tomatoes, cucumber, and parsley. If using, add the sliced Kalamata olives. Pour the dressing over the salad ingredients. Toss gently to combine, ensuring all ingredients are well-coated with the dressing.
3. Divide the salad into four servings and serve immediately or cover and refrigerate for up to 2 days.

Nutritional Information (per serving): Calories: 280 / Protein: 24g / Carbohydrates: 20g / Fats: 12g / Fiber: 6g / Cholesterol: 20mg / Sodium: 360mg / Potassium: 600mg

Shrimp and Mango Salad

Yield: 4 servings / **Preparation Time:** 15 minutes / **Cooking Time:** 10 minutes

Ingredients:
- 1 lb. large shrimp, peeled and deveined
- 1 large mango, peeled, pitted, and diced
- 1 red bell pepper, diced
- 1/2 red onion, finely chopped
- 1 avocado, diced
- 1/4 cup fresh cilantro, chopped
- 4 cups mixed salad greens
- 2 tablespoons olive oil
- 2 tablespoons fresh lime juice
- 1 teaspoon ground cumin
- 1/4 teaspoon salt; 1/4 teaspoon black pepper
- 2 tablespoons olive oil
- 2 tablespoons fresh lime juice
- 1 teaspoon honey or agave nectar

Instructions:
1. Toss shrimp with olive oil, lime juice, cumin, salt, and pepper. Cook in a hot skillet for 2-3 minutes per side until pink and opaque. Set aside.
2. Combine diced mango, red bell pepper, red onion, avocado, and cilantro in a large bowl.
3. Whisk olive oil, lime juice, honey/agave, salt, and pepper. Add shrimp to the salad bowl, pour dressing over, and toss gently.
4. Divide mixed salad greens among four plates. Top with shrimp and mango mixture. Serve immediately.

Nutritional Information (per serving): Calories: 320 / Protein: 25g / Carbohydrates: 20g / Fats: 18g / Fiber: 7g / Cholesterol: 170mg / Sodium: 320mg / Potassium: 750mg

Scallop and Citrus Salad

Yield: 4 servings / **Preparation Time:** 15 minutes / **Cooking Time:** 5 minutes

Ingredients:

- 1 lb. sea scallops, rinsed and patted dry
- 1 orange, peeled and segmented
- 1 grapefruit, peeled and segmented
- 1 avocado, diced
- 1/2 red onion, thinly sliced
- 4 cups mixed salad greens (such as arugula, spinach, and romaine)
- 1/4 cup fresh mint leaves, chopped
- 3 tablespoons olive oil
- 2 tablespoons fresh lemon juice
- 1 tablespoon fresh orange juice
- 1/4 teaspoon salt
- 1/4 teaspoon black pepper
- 1 teaspoon honey or agave nectar

Instructions:

1. Whisk olive oil, lemon juice, orange juice, honey/agave, salt, and pepper in a small bowl.
2. Heat 1 tbsp olive oil in a skillet over medium-high heat. Season scallops with salt and pepper, then cook for 2-3 minutes per side until golden and opaque. Set aside.
3. In a large bowl, combine mixed greens, orange segments, grapefruit segments, avocado, red onion, and mint. Add scallops and drizzle with dressing. Toss gently, then divide among four plates. Serve immediately.

Nutritional Information (per serving): Calories: 320 / Protein: 20g / Carbohydrates: 20g / Fats: 20g / Fiber: 8g / Cholesterol: 35mg / Sodium: 300mg / Potassium: 750mg

Citrus-Marinated Shrimp Salad

Yield: 4 servings / **Preparation Time:** 20 minutes / **Marinating Time:** 30 minutes / **Cooking Time:** 10 minutes

Ingredients:

- 1 lb. large shrimp, peeled and deveined
- 1/4 cup fresh orange juice
- 1/4 cup fresh lime juice
- 1/4 cup fresh lemon juice
- 4 cups mixed salad greens (e.g., arugula, spinach, and lettuce)
- 1/2 cup cherry tomatoes, halved
- 1/4 cup red onion, thinly sliced
- 1/4 cup fresh cilantro, chopped
- 1 avocado, sliced
- 2 cloves garlic, minced
- 2 tablespoons olive oil
- 1/4 teaspoon salt; 1/4 teaspoon black pepper
- 1 teaspoon honey

Instructions:

1. Combine orange juice, lemon juice, lime juice, olive oil, garlic, cumin, salt, and pepper in a large bowl. Toss shrimp in the mixture, cover, and refrigerate for 30 minutes.
2. In a large bowl, combine mixed greens, cherry tomatoes, cucumber, red onion, avocado, and cilantro.
3. Heat a skillet over medium-high heat. Remove shrimp from marinade and cook for 2-3 minutes per side until pink and opaque. Let cool slightly.
4. Whisk olive oil, lemon juice, lime juice, honey/agave, salt, and pepper in a small bowl.
5. Add cooked shrimp to the salad, drizzle with dressing, and toss gently. Divide among four plates and serve immediately.

Nutritional Information (per serving): Calories: 280 / Protein: 25g / Carbohydrates: 12g / Fats: 15g / Fiber: 6g / Cholesterol: 170mg / Sodium: 450mg / Potassium: 700mg.

Omega-3 Rich Fish Recipes

Incorporating Omega-3 rich fish recipes into your heart-healthy diet is essential for maintaining optimal cardiovascular health. Omega-3 fatty acids, found abundantly in fish, like salmon, mackerel, and sardines, play a crucial role in reducing inflammation, lowering triglyceride levels, and preventing heart disease. These healthy fats also support brain function and overall well-being. By including Omega-3 rich fish in your meals, you can enjoy delicious dishes while reaping significant heart health benefits.

Baked Cod with Mediterranean Vegetables

Yield: 4 servings / **Preparation Time:** 15 minutes / **Cooking Time:** 25 minutes

Ingredients:

- 4 (6-ounce) cod fillets
- 2 tablespoons olive oil
- 1 lemon, sliced
- 1 zucchini, sliced
- 1 red bell pepper, sliced
- 1 yellow bell pepper, sliced
- 1 red onion, sliced
- 3 cloves garlic, minced
- 1 cup cherry tomatoes, halved
- 1/4 cup Kalamata olives, pitted and halved
- 1 teaspoon dried oregano
- 1 teaspoon dried thyme
- 1/2 teaspoon salt; 1/4 teaspoon black pepper
- Fresh parsley, chopped for garnish

Instructions:

1. Preheat your oven to 400°F (200°C). In a large mixing bowl, combine the zucchini, red bell pepper, yellow bell pepper, red onion, cherry tomatoes, Kalamata olives, and minced garlic. Drizzle with 1 tablespoon of olive oil and sprinkle with dried oregano, dried thyme, salt, and black pepper. Toss to combine.
2. Place the cod fillets in a large baking dish. Arrange the mixed vegetables around the cod fillets. Place lemon slices over the cod fillets. Drizzle the remaining 1 tablespoon of olive oil over the cod and vegetables.
3. Bake in the preheated oven for 20-25 minutes, or until the cod is opaque and flakes easily with a fork and the vegetables are tender. Garnish with chopped fresh parsley before serving. Serve immediately.

Nutritional Information (per serving): Calories: 310 / Protein: 30g / Carbohydrates: 12g / Fats: 16g / Fiber: 4g / Cholesterol: 65mg / Sodium: 450mg / Potassium: 850mg

---

Herb-Crusted Salmon with Quinoa

Yield: 4 servings / **Preparation Time:** 15 minutes / **Cooking Time:** 20 minutes

Ingredients:

- 4 (6-ounce) salmon fillets
- 1 cup quinoa, rinsed
- 2 cups low-sodium vegetable broth or water
- 1 cup baby spinach, chopped
- 1/2 cup cherry tomatoes, halved
- 1/4 cup red onion, finely chopped
- 2 tablespoons olive oil
- 2 tablespoons Dijon mustard
- 1 tablespoon fresh lemon juice
- 1 teaspoon lemon zest
- 1/2 cup whole wheat breadcrumbs
- 1/4 cup grated Parmesan cheese
- 2 tablespoons fresh parsley, chopped
- 1 tablespoon fresh dill, chopped
- 1 tablespoon fresh chives, chopped
- 1/4 teaspoon salt
- 1/4 teaspoon black pepper
- 1 clove garlic, minced

Instructions:

1. Preheat your oven to 400°F (200°C). Line a baking sheet with parchment paper.
2. In a small bowl, mix the Dijon mustard, lemon juice, and lemon zest. Brush this mixture over the top of the salmon fillets. In another bowl, combine the whole wheat breadcrumbs, Parmesan cheese, parsley, dill, chives, salt, and black pepper. Press this mixture onto the top of the salmon fillets to create a crust.
3. Place the salmon fillets on the prepared baking sheet and drizzle with olive oil. Bake in the preheated oven for 15-20 minutes, or until the salmon is opaque and flakes easily with a fork.
4. While the salmon is baking, heat the olive oil in a medium saucepan over medium heat. Add the minced garlic and cook for about 1 minute until fragrant.
5. Add the quinoa and vegetable broth (or water) to the saucepan. Bring to a boil, then reduce the heat to low, cover, and simmer for about 15 minutes, or until the quinoa is cooked and the liquid is absorbed. Stir in the chopped spinach, cherry tomatoes, and red onion. Season with salt and pepper to taste. Cook for an additional 2-3 minutes, until the spinach is wilted, and the vegetables are heated through.
6. Divide the quinoa mixture among four plates. Place a salmon fillet on top of each serving of quinoa. Garnish with additional fresh herbs if desired.

Nutritional Information (per serving): Calories: 450 / Protein: 38g / Carbohydrates: 30g / Fats: 22g / Fiber: 5g / Cholesterol: 75mg / Sodium: 400mg / Potassium: 900mg

---

Sardine and Tomato Pasta

Yield: 4 servings / **Preparation Time:** 10 minutes / **Cooking Time:** 20 minutes

Ingredients:

- 8 ounces whole-grain pasta (spaghetti or linguine)
- 1 (4-ounce) can sardines in olive oil, drained and flaked
- 1 (14.5-ounce) can diced tomatoes, no salt added
- 2 tablespoons olive oil
- 3 cloves garlic, minced; 1 small onion, finely chopped
- 1/2 teaspoon dried oregano
- 1/4 teaspoon salt; 1/4 teaspoon black pepper
- 1/4 teaspoon red pepper flakes (optional)
- 1/4 cup fresh parsley, chopped
- Zest of 1 lemon
- fresh lemon wedges for serving

Instructions:

1. In a large pot of boiling, salted water, cook the whole-grain pasta according to the package instructions until al dente. Drain and set aside.
2. In a large skillet, heat the olive oil over medium heat. Add the minced garlic and chopped onion, and sauté until fragrant and the onion is translucent, about 3-5 minutes.
3. Stir in the diced tomatoes (with their juice), red pepper flakes (if using), dried oregano, salt, and black pepper. Bring to a simmer and cook for about 10 minutes, stirring occasionally. Add the flaked sardines to the skillet and gently stir to combine. Cook for an additional 2-3 minutes to heat through.
4. Add the cooked pasta to the skillet and toss to coat with the sauce. If the sauce is too thick, add a bit of the pasta cooking water to achieve the desired consistency. Stir in the chopped fresh parsley, and lemon zest. Toss to combine. Divide the pasta among four plates. Serve with fresh lemon wedges on the side for squeezing over the top.

Nutritional Information (per serving): Calories: 350 / Protein: 18g / Carbohydrates: 45g / Fats: 12g / Fiber: 7g / Cholesterol: 40mg / Sodium: 380mg / Potassium: 700mg

Flaxseed-Crusted Mackerel

Yield: 4 servings / **Preparation Time:** 10 minutes / **Cooking Time:** 15 minutes

Ingredients:
- 4 (6-ounce) mackerel fillets
- 1/2 cup ground flaxseeds
- 1 tablespoon olive oil
- 1 tablespoon Dijon mustard
- 1/2 teaspoon dried thyme
- 1/4 teaspoon salt
- 1/4 teaspoon black pepper
- 1 teaspoon lemon zest
- Fresh lemon wedges (for serving)
- Fresh parsley, chopped (for garnish)

Instructions:
1. Preheat your oven to 375°F (190°C). Line a baking sheet with parchment paper. In a small bowl, combine the ground flaxseeds, lemon zest, dried thyme, salt, and black pepper.
2. Pat the mackerel fillets dry with paper towels. Brush each fillet with a thin layer of Dijon mustard. Press the mustard-coated side of each fillet into the flaxseed mixture, ensuring an even coating. Place the fillets on the prepared baking sheet, crust side up.
3. Drizzle the fillets with olive oil. Bake in the preheated oven for 12-15 minutes, or until the mackerel is opaque and flakes easily with a fork. Transfer the baked mackerel to serving plates. Garnish with fresh parsley and serve with lemon wedges on the side.

Nutritional Information (per serving): Calories: 350 / Protein: 28g / Carbohydrates: 3g / Fats: 25g / Fiber: 6g / Cholesterol: 60mg / Sodium: 280mg / Potassium: 700mg

Miso-Glazed Sea Bass

Yield: 4 servings / **Preparation Time:** 10 minutes / **Marinating Time:** 30 minutes / **Cooking Time:** 15 minutes

Ingredients:
- 4 (6-ounce) sea bass fillets
- 3 tablespoons white miso paste
- 3 tablespoons sake
- 3 tablespoons mirin
- 2 tablespoons low-sodium soy sauce
- 1 tablespoon honey or agave nectar
- 1 teaspoon fresh ginger, grated
- 1 teaspoon sesame oil
- 2 green onions, thinly sliced (optional for garnish)
- 1 tablespoon sesame seeds (optional for garnish)

Instructions:
1. In a small bowl, whisk together the miso paste, sake, mirin, low-sodium soy sauce, honey (or agave nectar), grated ginger, and sesame oil until smooth.
2. Place the sea bass fillets in a shallow dish. Pour the marinade over the fish, ensuring they are well-coated. Cover and refrigerate for at least 30 minutes.
3. Preheat your oven to 400°F (200°C). Line a baking sheet with parchment paper. Place the marinated sea bass fillets on the prepared baking sheet. Bake in the preheated oven for 12-15 minutes, or until the fish is opaque and flakes easily with a fork.
4. Transfer the baked sea bass to a serving platter. Garnish with thinly sliced green onions and sesame seeds, if desired.

Nutritional Information (per serving): Calories: 250 / Protein: 30g / Carbohydrates: 12g / Fats: 9g / Fiber: 0g / Cholesterol: 60mg / Sodium: 500mg / Potassium: 750mg

Quick and Easy Fish Recipes

In today's fast-paced world, finding time to prepare heart-healthy meals can be challenging. That's why this subchapter is a lifesaver for those committed to maintaining cardiovascular health without spending hours in the kitchen. Fish is a fantastic source of lean protein and essential nutrients, including Omega-3 fatty acids, which are crucial for heart health. These recipes are designed to be both time-efficient and nutritious, making it simple to incorporate heart-healthy fish into your diet.

Quick Lemon Pepper Baked Fish

Yield: 4 servings / **Preparation Time:** 10 minutes / **Cooking Time:** 15 minutes

Ingredients:

- 4 (6-ounce) white fish fillets (such as cod, tilapia, or haddock)
- 2 tablespoons olive oil
- 2 tablespoons fresh lemon juice
- 1 teaspoon black pepper; 1/2 teaspoon salt
- 1 teaspoon garlic powder
- 1 teaspoon dried oregano
- 1 teaspoon lemon zest
- Lemon wedges (for serving)
- Fresh parsley, chopped (for garnish)

Instructions:

1. Preheat your oven to 400°F (200°C). Line a baking sheet with parchment paper or lightly grease it with olive oil.
2. In a small bowl, whisk together the olive oil, lemon juice, lemon zest, black pepper, salt, garlic powder, and dried oregano. Place the fish fillets on the prepared baking sheet. Brush the marinade evenly over each fillet, ensuring they are well-coated.
3. Bake in the preheated oven for 12-15 minutes, or until the fish is opaque and flakes easily with a fork. Garnish with chopped fresh parsley and serve with lemon wedges on the side.

Nutritional Information (per serving): Calories: 220 / Protein: 30g / Carbohydrates: 1g / Fats: 11g / Fiber: 0g / Cholesterol: 75mg / Sodium: 300mg / Potassium: 450mg

---

Pan-Seared Scallops with Garlic Butter

Yield: 4 servings / **Preparation Time:** 10 minutes / **Cooking Time:** 10 minutes

Ingredients:

- 1 pound sea scallops, patted dry
- 2 tablespoons olive oil
- 2 tablespoons unsalted butter
- 3 cloves garlic, minced
- 2 tablespoons fresh parsley, chopped
- 1/4 teaspoon salt; 1/4 teaspoon black pepper
- Juice of 1 lemon
- Lemon wedges (for serving)

Instructions:

1. Pat scallops dry and season with salt and pepper.
2. Heat olive oil in a skillet over medium-high heat. Cook scallops for 2-3 minutes per side until golden and opaque. Set aside.
3. Reduce heat to medium, melt butter in the skillet, and sauté garlic for 1 minute. Add lemon juice and stir. Return scallops to the skillet and spoon garlic butter over them. Sprinkle with parsley.
4. Serve scallops with additional lemon wedges.

Nutritional Information (per serving): Calories: 210 / Protein: 22g / Carbohydrates: 3g / Fats: 12g / Fiber: 0g / Cholesterol: 60mg / Sodium: 290mg / Potassium: 450mg

Simple Tuna Steak with Soy Sauce and Ginger

Yield: 4 servings / **Preparation Time:** 10 minutes / **Cooking Time:** 8 minutes

Ingredients:

- 4 (6-ounce) tuna steaks
- 1/4 cup low-sodium soy sauce
- 1 tablespoon olive oil
- 1 tablespoon rice vinegar
- 1 tablespoon honey
- 1 tablespoon fresh ginger, grated
- 1 teaspoon sesame oil
- 1/4 teaspoon black pepper
- 2 cloves garlic, minced
- 2 green onions, sliced (for garnish)
- sesame seeds (for garnish, optional)

Instructions:

1. In a small bowl, whisk together the soy sauce, grated ginger, minced garlic, rice vinegar, honey, sesame oil, and black pepper. Place the tuna steaks in a shallow dish and pour the marinade over them. Let them marinate for at least 15 minutes, or up to 30 minutes in the refrigerator, turning the steaks occasionally.
2. Heat the olive oil in a large skillet over medium-high heat until hot. Remove the tuna steaks from the marinade (reserve the marinade) and place them in the hot skillet.
3. Sear the steaks for about 3-4 minutes on each side for medium-rare, or longer if you prefer them more well-done.
4. While the tuna is cooking, pour the reserved marinade into a small saucepan. Bring it to a boil, then reduce the heat and simmer for about 3 minutes until slightly thickened.
5. Place the seared tuna steaks on serving plates. Drizzle the reduced marinade over the top and garnish with sliced green onions and sesame seeds, if using.

Nutritional Information (per serving): Calories: 220 / Protein: 30g / Carbohydrates: 4g / Fats: 8g / Fiber: 0g / Cholesterol: 55mg / Sodium: 380mg / Potassium: 600mg

Fish Fillet Sandwiches with Tartar Sauce

Yield: 4 servings / **Preparation Time:** 15 minutes / **Cooking Time:** 15 minutes

Ingredients:

- 4 (4-ounce) white fish fillets (such as cod or tilapia)
- 1/2 cup whole wheat flour
- 1/2 teaspoon salt
- 1/2 teaspoon black pepper
- 1 teaspoon paprika
- 2 tablespoons olive oil
- 2 tablespoons lemon juice
- 2 tablespoons pickle relish
- 1/2 cup plain Greek yogurt
- 1 teaspoon Dijon mustard
- 2 tablespoons fresh dill, chopped
- 1 tablespoon capers, drained and chopped
- 4 whole wheat sandwich buns
- 1 cup lettuce, shredded
- 1 large tomato, sliced

Instructions:

1. In a shallow dish, combine the whole wheat flour, salt, black pepper, and paprika. Dredge each fish fillet in the flour mixture, coating evenly. Heat the olive oil in a large skillet over medium-high heat.
2. Add the fish fillets and cook for about 3-4 minutes on each side until golden brown and cooked through. Drizzle with lemon juice and set aside.
3. In a small bowl, mix the Greek yogurt, pickle relish, chopped capers, lemon juice, Dijon mustard, and fresh dill.
4. Toast the whole wheat buns if desired. Spread a generous amount of tartar sauce on the bottom half of each bun. Place a fish fillet on top, followed by shredded lettuce and tomato slices. Cover with the top half of the bun.

Nutritional Information (per serving): Calories: 350 / Protein: 28g / Carbohydrates: 40g / Fats: 12g / Fiber: 6g / Cholesterol: 60mg / Sodium: 580mg / Potassium: 500mg

---

Easy Fish Curry with Coconut Milk

Yield: 4 servings / **Preparation Time:** 15 minutes / **Cooking Time:** 25 minutes

Ingredients:
- 1 lb. (450g) white fish fillets (such as cod or tilapia), cut into chunks
- 1 can (14 oz) light coconut milk
- 1 can (14 oz) diced tomatoes; no salt added
- 1 cup low-sodium vegetable or fish broth
- 1 red bell pepper, sliced
- 1 green bell pepper, sliced
- 1 medium zucchini, sliced
- 1 tablespoon olive oil
- 1 tablespoon fresh lime juice
- 1 medium onion, finely chopped
- 2 cloves garlic, minced
- 1 tablespoon fresh ginger, grated
- 1-2 tablespoons curry powder
- 1 teaspoon ground cumin
- 1 teaspoon ground coriander
- 1/2 teaspoon turmeric powder

Instructions:
1. Heat the olive oil in a large skillet over medium heat. Add the chopped onion and sauté until softened, about 5 minutes. Add the minced garlic and grated ginger, cooking for an additional 1-2 minutes until fragrant.
2. Stir in the curry powder, ground cumin, ground coriander, and turmeric powder. Cook for 1 minute to toast the spices. Pour in the light coconut milk, diced tomatoes, and vegetable or fish broth. Stir well to combine.
3. Add the sliced red and green bell peppers and zucchini to the skillet. Bring the mixture to a simmer and cook for about 10 minutes until the vegetables are tender.
4. Gently place the fish chunks into the skillet, submerging them in the sauce. Simmer for about 5-7 minutes until the fish is cooked through and flakes easily with a fork. Stir in the fresh lime juice and season with salt and pepper to taste. Serve the curry over brown rice or quinoa for a complete meal.

Nutritional Information (per serving): Calories: 300 / Protein: 25g / Carbohydrates: 18g / Fats: 14g / Fiber: 4g / Cholesterol: 55mg / Sodium: 350mg / Potassium: 900m

Chapter 6: Poultry Recipes

Poultry is a cornerstone of heart-healthy eating, offering lean protein that supports cardiovascular health without the high saturated fats found in red meat. In this chapter, we present a variety of delicious and nutritious poultry recipes that are perfect for beginners. These dishes are designed to be easy to prepare while providing essential nutrients that promote heart health. Enjoy the benefits of incorporating poultry into your diet, including improved cholesterol levels, better heart function, and a tasty way to maintain a balanced, heart-healthy lifestyle.

Baked Poultry Dishes

Baking poultry is an excellent method for creating heart-healthy meals that are both delicious and nutritious. This cooking technique helps retain the lean protein and essential nutrients in poultry without adding unhealthy fats. In this subchapter, you'll discover a variety of baked poultry recipes that are easy to prepare and perfect for maintaining cardiovascular health. Choosing baked poultry dishes allows you to enjoy flavorful meals that support your heart, keep cholesterol levels in check, and promote overall well-being.

Baked Chicken Parmesan

Yield: 4 servings / **Preparation Time:** 15 minutes / **Cooking Time:** 25-30 minutes

Ingredients:
- 4 boneless, skinless chicken breasts
- 1 cup whole wheat breadcrumbs
- 1 large egg, beaten
- 1/2 cup grated Parmesan cheese
- 1 teaspoon dried oregano
- 1 teaspoon dried basil
- 1/2 teaspoon garlic powder
- 1/2 teaspoon onion powder
- 1/2 teaspoon black pepper
- 1/4 teaspoon salt
- 1 cup marinara sauce (low sodium, no sugar added)
- 1 cup part-skim mozzarella cheese, shredded
- Fresh basil or parsley for garnish (optional)

Instructions:
1. Preheat your oven to 400°F (200°C). Line a baking sheet with parchment paper or lightly grease it with olive oil.
2. In a shallow dish, combine the whole wheat breadcrumbs, grated Parmesan cheese, dried oregano, dried basil, garlic powder, onion powder, black pepper, and salt.
3. Dip each chicken breast into the beaten egg, ensuring it is fully coated, then press it into the breadcrumb mixture, coating both sides evenly.
4. Place the breaded chicken breasts on the prepared baking sheet. Bake in the preheated oven for 20-25 minutes, or until the chicken is cooked through and reaches an internal temperature of 165°F (75°C).
5. Remove the baking sheet from the oven. Spoon marinara sauce over each chicken breast, then sprinkle with shredded mozzarella cheese. Return to the oven and bake for an additional 5-7 minutes, or until the cheese is melted and bubbly.
6. Garnish with fresh basil or parsley, if desired. Serve with a side of whole grain pasta, steamed vegetables, or a fresh green salad for a complete, heart-healthy meal.

Nutritional Information (per serving): Calories: 350 / Protein: 40g / Carbohydrates: 15g / Fats: 15g / Fiber: 3g / Cholesterol: 110mg / Sodium: 480mg / Potassium: 600mg

Herb-Roasted Turkey Breast

Yield: 4 servings / **Preparation Time:** 10 minutes / **Cooking Time:** 1 hour 15 minutes to 1 hour 30 minutes

Ingredients:

- 1 boneless turkey breast (about 2-3 pounds)
- 1 cup low-sodium chicken broth
- 4 cloves garlic, minced
- 1 teaspoon salt
- 1/2 teaspoon black pepper
- 2 tablespoons olive oil
- 1 lemon, zested and juiced
- Chopped fresh herbs: 2 tablespoons rosemary, 2 tablespoons thyme, 2 tablespoons parsley, 1 tablespoon fresh sage

Instructions:

1. Preheat your oven to 375°F (190°C). In a small bowl, combine the olive oil, rosemary, thyme, parsley, sage, minced garlic, salt, pepper, lemon zest, and lemon juice. Mix well to form a paste.
2. Pat the turkey breast, dry with paper towels. Rub the herb mixture all over the turkey breast, making sure it is evenly coated.
3. Place the seasoned turkey breast on a rack in a roasting pan. Pour the low-sodium chicken broth into the bottom of the pan. Roast in the preheated oven for about 1 hour 15 minutes to 1 hour 30 minutes, or until the internal temperature reaches 165°F (75°C) when measured with a meat thermometer.
4. Remove the turkey breast from the oven and let it rest for 10-15 minutes before slicing. This helps retain the juices and keep the meat tender. Slice the turkey breast and serve with a side of steamed vegetables, whole grains, or a fresh salad for a complete, heart-healthy meal.

Nutritional Information (per serving): Calories: 280 / Protein: 40g / Carbohydrates: 2g / Fats: 12g / Fiber: 1g / Cholesterol: 100mg / Sodium: 350mg / Potassium: 500mg

Baked Honey Mustard Chicken

Yield: 4 servings / **Preparation Time:** 10 minutes / **Cooking Time:** 30-35 minutes

Ingredients:

- 4 boneless, skinless chicken breasts
- 3 tablespoons Dijon mustard
- 2 tablespoons honey
- 1 tablespoon olive oil
- 2 cloves garlic, minced
- 1 teaspoon dried rosemary
- 1/2 teaspoon salt
- 1/2 teaspoon black pepper
- 1 tablespoon chopped fresh parsley (optional, for garnish)

Instructions:

1. Preheat your oven to 375°F (190°C).
2. In a small bowl, whisk together the Dijon mustard, honey, olive oil, minced garlic, dried rosemary, salt, and black pepper until well combined. Place the chicken breasts in a baking dish. Pour the honey mustard sauce over the chicken, making sure each piece is well coated.
3. Cover the baking dish with aluminum foil and bake in the preheated oven for 20 minutes. Remove the foil and bake for an additional 10-15 minutes, or until the chicken is cooked through and reaches an internal temperature of 165°F (75°C).
4. Let the chicken rest for a few minutes before serving. Garnish with chopped fresh parsley if desired. Serve with a side of steamed vegetables or a fresh salad for a complete, heart-healthy meal.

Nutritional Information (per serving): Calories: 260 / Protein: 30g / Carbohydrates: 10g / Fats: 10g / Fiber: 0g / Cholesterol: 75mg / Sodium: 400mg / Potassium: 500mg

Lemon Pepper Baked Turkey

Yield: 4 servings / **Preparation Time:** 10 minutes / **Cooking Time:** 40-45 minutes

Ingredients:

- 4 turkey breast cutlets (about 4-6 ounces each)
- 2 tablespoons olive oil
- 5 tablespoons fresh lemon juice
- 1 tablespoon lemon zest
- 2 cloves garlic, minced
- 1 teaspoon dried thyme
- 1 teaspoon black pepper
- 1/2 teaspoon salt
- 1/4 teaspoon paprika
- Fresh parsley, chopped (optional, for garnish)

Instructions:

1. Preheat your oven to 375°F (190°C).
2. In a small bowl, combine the olive oil, fresh lemon juice, lemon zest, minced garlic, dried thyme, black pepper, salt, and paprika. Mix well to create a marinade. Place the turkey breast cutlets in a baking dish. Pour the marinade over the turkey, ensuring each piece is well coated. Let it marinate for at least 10 minutes to allow the flavors to infuse.
3. Cover the baking dish with aluminum foil and bake in the preheated oven for 25 minutes. Remove the foil and bake for an additional 15-20 minutes, or until the turkey is cooked through and reaches an internal temperature of 165°F (75°C).
4. Let the turkey rest for a few minutes before serving. Garnish with chopped fresh parsley if desired. Serve with a side of steamed vegetables or a fresh salad for a complete, heart-healthy meal.

Nutritional Information (per serving): Calories: 220 / Protein: 30g / Carbohydrates: 2g / Fats: 10g / Fiber: 0g / Cholesterol: 70mg / Sodium: 300mg / Potassium: 400mg

---

Baked Lemon Rosemary Chicken Thighs

Yield: 4 servings / **Preparation Time:** 15 minutes / **Cooking Time:** 40 minutes

Ingredients:

- 8 bone-in, skinless chicken thighs
- 2 tablespoons olive oil
- 3 cloves garlic, minced
- 2 tablespoons fresh lemon juice
- 1 tablespoon lemon zest
- 2 tablespoons fresh rosemary, chopped
- 1 teaspoon dried thyme
- 1/2 teaspoon salt
- 1/4 teaspoon black pepper
- Lemon slices, for garnish; fresh rosemary sprigs, for garnish (optional)

Instructions:

1. Preheat your oven to 375°F (190°C). In a small bowl, mix the olive oil, minced garlic, lemon juice, lemon zest, chopped rosemary, dried thyme, salt, and black pepper.
2. Place the chicken thighs in a large bowl or Ziplock bag. Pour the marinade over the chicken, ensuring each piece is well coated. Let it marinate for at least 15 minutes, or up to 2 hours in the refrigerator for more flavor.
3. Place the marinated chicken thighs in a single layer in a baking dish. Pour any remaining marinade over the top. Bake in the preheated oven for 35-40 minutes, or until the chicken reaches an internal temperature of 165°F (74°C) and is no longer pink in the center. Garnish with fresh lemon slices and rosemary sprigs if desired. Serve hot.

Nutritional Information (per serving): Calories: 250 / Protein: 25g / Carbohydrates: 2g / Fats: 16g / Fiber: 1g / Cholesterol: 120mg / Sodium: 300mg / Potassium: 380mg

Poultry Stews

Stewing is perfect for creating hearty, flavorful poultry dishes that fit a heart-healthy diet. By gently simmering chicken or turkey with vegetables, herbs, and spices, you can craft nutrient-rich meals low in saturated fats and high in essential vitamins and minerals. Stews enhance natural flavors without excessive salt or unhealthy fats. This subchapter offers delicious, nourishing poultry stews that are easy to prepare and incredibly satisfying, helping you maintain cardiovascular health with wholesome, comforting meals.

Moroccan Chicken Stew

Yield: 6 servings / **Preparation Time:** 20 minutes / **Cooking Time:** 40 minutes

Ingredients:
- 1 lb (450g) boneless, skinless chicken thighs, cut into bite-sized pieces
- 2 cups low-sodium chicken broth
- 1 large onion, finely chopped
- 3 cloves garlic, minced
- 1 bell pepper, diced
- 2 carrots, sliced
- 1 zucchini, sliced
- 1 can (15 oz) chickpeas, drained and rinsed
- 1 can (14.5 oz) diced tomatoes; no salt added
- 1 tablespoon tomato paste
- 1 tablespoon olive oil
- 1 teaspoon ground cumin
- 1 teaspoon ground coriander
- 1 teaspoon ground cinnamon
- 1 teaspoon ground turmeric
- 1/2 teaspoon ground ginger
- 1/2 teaspoon ground paprika
- 1/4 teaspoon cayenne pepper; salt, black pepper to taste
- 1/4 cup dried apricots, chopped
- Fresh cilantro, chopped (for garnish)
- Cooked quinoa or brown rice (for serving)

Instructions:
1. Cut chicken into bite-sized pieces. Chop the onion, mince the garlic, slice the carrots and zucchini, and dice the bell pepper. Chop the dried apricots.
2. Heat olive oil in a large pot over medium heat. Add chicken pieces and cook until browned on all sides, about 5-7 minutes. Remove chicken and set aside.
3. In the same pot, add the chopped onion and garlic. Sauté for 2-3 minutes until fragrant. Add carrots, bell pepper, and zucchini. Cook for an additional 5 minutes until vegetables start to soften.
4. Stir in the cumin, coriander, cinnamon, turmeric, ginger, paprika, and cayenne pepper (if using). Cook for 1-2 minutes until spices are fragrant. Add the browned chicken back to the pot. Stir in the diced tomatoes, chickpeas, tomato paste, and chicken broth. Add chopped dried apricots.
5. Bring the stew to a boil, then reduce heat to low. Cover and let simmer for 25-30 minutes until the chicken is cooked through and the vegetables are tender. Season with salt and black pepper to taste. Garnish with fresh cilantro. Serve hot over cooked quinoa or brown rice.

Nutritional Information (per serving): Calories: 310 / Protein: 25g / Carbohydrates: 34g / Fats: 9g / Fiber: 8g / Cholesterol: 55mg / Sodium: 310mg / Potassium: 900mg

Turkey Chili

Yield: 6 servings / **Preparation Time:** 15 minutes / **Cooking Time:** 45 minutes

Ingredients:

- 1 lb. (450g) ground turkey, lean
- 1 cup low-sodium chicken broth
- 1 large onion, diced
- 3 cloves garlic, minced
- 1 large red bell pepper, diced
- 1 large green bell pepper, diced
- 1 medium carrot, peeled and diced
- 1 can (14.5 oz) diced tomatoes; no salt added
- 1 can (15 oz) black beans, drained and rinsed
- 1 can (15 oz) kidney beans, drained and rinsed
- 1 can (15 oz) corn kernels, drained
- 1 tablespoon olive oil
- 2 tablespoons tomato paste
- 1 tablespoon chili powder
- 1 teaspoon ground cumin
- 1 teaspoon smoked paprika
- 1/2 teaspoon ground black pepper; salt to taste
- 1/4 teaspoon cayenne pepper (optional, for added heat)
- 1 teaspoon dried oregano
- 1 bay leaf
- Fresh cilantro, chopped (optional, for garnish)

Instructions:

1. Dice the onion, bell peppers, and carrot. Mince the garlic.
2. In a large pot or Dutch oven, heat the olive oil over medium heat. Add the ground turkey and cook until browned, about 5-7 minutes. Break it up into crumbles as it cooks. Add the diced onion, garlic, red bell pepper, green bell pepper, and carrot to the pot. Cook until the vegetables are softened, about 5 minutes.
3. Stir in the diced tomatoes, black beans, kidney beans, corn, and low-sodium chicken broth. Add the tomato paste, chili powder, ground cumin, smoked paprika, black pepper, cayenne pepper (if using), dried oregano, and bay leaf. Stir to combine all ingredients.
4. Bring the mixture to a boil, then reduce the heat to low. Let the chili simmer, uncovered, for about 30 minutes, stirring occasionally, until the flavors are well combined, and the chili has thickened. Remove the bay leaf before serving. Ladle the turkey chili into bowls. Garnish with fresh cilantro if desired.

Nutritional Information (per serving): Calories: 320 / Protein: 28g / Carbohydrates: 35g / Fats: 8g / Fiber: 12g / Cholesterol: 50mg / Sodium: 450mg / Potassium: 800mg

Creamy Chicken and Mushroom Casserole

Yield: 6 servings / **Preparation Time:** 20 minutes / **Cooking Time:** 40 minutes

Ingredients:

- 1 lb. (450g) boneless, skinless chicken breasts, cut into bite-sized pieces
- 8 oz (225g) mushrooms, sliced
- 1 cup low-sodium chicken broth
- 1 cup unsweetened almond milk (or low-fat milk)
- 1 tablespoon olive oil
- 1 large onion, finely chopped
- 3 cloves garlic, minced
- 1/4 cup whole wheat flour
- 1 teaspoon dried thyme
- 1 teaspoon dried parsley
- 1/2 teaspoon ground black pepper
- 1/2 teaspoon salt (optional)
- 1 cup cooked quinoa
- 1/2 cup low-fat Greek yogurt
- 1/2 cup grated Parmesan cheese (optional for extra flavor)
- Fresh parsley, chopped (optional for garnish)

Instructions:

1. Preheat your oven to 375°F (190°C).

2. In a large skillet, heat the olive oil over medium heat. Add the chicken pieces and cook until browned on all sides, about 5-7 minutes. Remove the chicken and set aside. In the same skillet, add the chopped onion and minced garlic. Sauté for 2-3 minutes until the onion becomes translucent. Add the sliced mushrooms and cook until they release their juices and become tender, about 5 minutes.
3. Sprinkle the whole wheat flour over the vegetables and stir well to combine. Gradually add the low-sodium chicken broth and unsweetened almond milk, stirring constantly to avoid lumps. Add the dried thyme, dried parsley, ground black pepper, and salt (if using). Continue to stir until the sauce thickens, about 5 minutes.
4. Return the cooked chicken to the skillet and add the cooked quinoa. Stir to combine everything evenly. Remove from heat and stir in the low-fat Greek yogurt until well combined. Transfer the mixture to a lightly greased casserole dish.
5. Sprinkle the top with grated Parmesan cheese if desired. Bake in the preheated oven for 25-30 minutes, until the top is golden, and the casserole is heated through. Garnish with fresh chopped parsley if desired. Serve warm and enjoy!

Nutritional Information (per serving): Calories: 280 / Protein: 28g / Carbohydrates: 20g / Fats: 10g / Fiber: 4g / Cholesterol: 55mg / Sodium: 310mg / Potassium: 600mg

---

Turkey and Quinoa Stew

Yield: 4 servings / **Preparation Time:** 20 minutes / **Cooking Time:** 45 minutes

Ingredients:

- 1 lb. ground turkey (preferably lean)
- 1 medium onion, chopped
- 2 cloves garlic, minced
- 2 medium carrots, diced
- 2 celery stalks, diced
- 1 red bell pepper, diced
- 1 zucchini, diced
- 1 cup quinoa, rinsed
- 4 cups low-sodium chicken broth
- 1 can (14.5 ounces) diced tomatoes; no salt added
- 1 teaspoon dried thyme
- 1 teaspoon dried oregano
- 1/2 teaspoon ground black pepper
- 1/2 teaspoon salt (optional)
- 1 tablespoon olive oil
- 2 cups baby spinach, roughly chopped
- 1/4 cup fresh parsley, chopped (optional)

Instructions:

1. In a large pot, heat the olive oil over medium heat.
2. Add the ground turkey and cook until browned, breaking it up with a spoon as it cooks. This should take about 5-7 minutes.
3. Add the chopped onion and garlic to the pot, cooking for another 3-4 minutes until the onion becomes translucent.
4. Stir in the carrots, celery, red bell pepper, and zucchini, cooking for an additional 5 minutes. Add the rinsed quinoa, chicken broth, diced tomatoes (with their juice), thyme, oregano, black pepper, and salt (if using). Stir well to combine.
5. Bring the mixture to a boil, then reduce the heat to low. Cover the pot and let it simmer for 25-30 minutes, or until the quinoa and vegetables are tender.
6. Stir in the chopped spinach and let it cook for an additional 2-3 minutes until wilted. Ladle the stew into bowls and garnish with fresh parsley, if desired.

Nutritional Information (per serving): Calories: 340 / Protein: 28g / Carbohydrates: 42g / Fats: 10g / Fiber: 8g / Cholesterol: 60mg / Sodium: 420mg / Potassium: 1000mg

Yield: 4 servings / **Preparation Time:** 15 minutes / **Cooking Time:** 45 minutes

Ingredients:
- 1 lb. (450g) boneless, skinless chicken breast, cut into bite-sized pieces
- 2 large carrots, peeled and sliced
- 2 celery stalks, sliced
- 1 large potato, peeled and diced
- 1 red bell pepper, diced
- 1 zucchini, sliced
- 1 cup green beans, trimmed and cut into 1-inch pieces
- 1 can (14.5 oz) diced tomatoes; no salt added
- 4 cups low-sodium chicken broth
- 2 tablespoons olive oil
- 1 large onion, diced
- 3 cloves garlic, minced
- 1 teaspoon dried thyme
- 1 teaspoon dried oregano
- 1 bay leaf
- Salt and pepper to taste
- Fresh parsley, chopped (optional, for garnish)

Instructions:
1. Cut the chicken into bite-sized pieces and season lightly with salt and pepper. Dice and slice all vegetables as specified.
2. In a large pot or Dutch oven, heat 1 tablespoon of olive oil over medium heat. Add the chicken pieces and cook until they are browned on all sides, about 5-7 minutes. Remove the chicken from the pot and set aside.
3. In the same pot, add the remaining tablespoon of olive oil. Add the diced onion and cook until translucent, about 5 minutes. Add the minced garlic and cook for another 1-2 minutes until fragrant.
4. Add the carrots, celery, and potato to the pot. Cook for 5 minutes, stirring occasionally. Stir in the diced red bell pepper, zucchini, and green beans. Return the cooked chicken to the pot.
5. Pour in the can of diced tomatoes (with juices) and the low-sodium chicken broth. Add the dried thyme, dried oregano, and bay leaf. Stir everything together and bring to a boil.
6. Reduce the heat to low and let the stew simmer for about 30 minutes, or until the vegetables are tender and the flavors are well combined. Season with additional salt and pepper to taste.
7. Remove the bay leaf before serving. Garnish with chopped fresh parsley if desired. Serve hot with a side of whole grain bread or a green salad for a complete, heart-healthy meal.

Nutritional Information (per serving): Calories: 320 / Protein: 25g / Carbohydrates: 30g / Fats: 10g / Fiber: 6g / Cholesterol: 60mg / Sodium: 350mg / Potassium: 900mg

Quick and Easy Poultry Recipes

Having a collection of quick and easy poultry recipes is essential for maintaining a heart-healthy diet without compromising on time or taste. These recipes are designed to be simple, efficient, and packed with nutrients, making it easier for you to incorporate heart-friendly meals into your busy schedule. By focusing on lean poultry and straightforward preparation methods, these dishes provide a healthy dose of protein, essential vitamins, and minerals, all while being low in saturated fats and sodium. Embrace the convenience of these quick and easy poultry recipes to support your cardiovascular health effortlessly and deliciously.

Quick Teriyaki Chicken Stir-Fry

Yield: 4 servings / **Preparation Time:** 10 minutes / **Cooking Time:** 15 minutes

Ingredients:

- 1 lb. (450g) boneless, skinless chicken breast, thinly sliced
- 1/2 cup low-sodium chicken broth
- 1 tablespoon cornstarch mixed with 2 tablespoons water
- 1 large bell pepper, sliced
- 1 medium broccoli head, cut into florets
- 1 medium carrot, julienned
- 1/2 cup snap peas
- 2 tablespoons low-sodium soy sauce
- 2 tablespoons honey
- 1 tablespoon rice vinegar
- 1 tablespoon olive oil
- 2 cloves garlic, minced
- 1 teaspoon grated ginger
- 1 green onion, sliced (for garnish)

Instructions:

1. In a small bowl, whisk together the low-sodium soy sauce, honey, rice vinegar, garlic, and ginger. Set aside.
2. Heat 1 tablespoon of olive oil in a large skillet or wok over medium-high heat. Add the thinly sliced chicken breast and cook until browned and cooked through, about 5-7 minutes. Remove the chicken from the skillet and set aside.
3. In the same skillet, add the bell pepper, broccoli, carrot, and snap peas. Stir-fry for about 5 minutes until the vegetables are tender-crisp. Return the cooked chicken to the skillet with the vegetables. Pour in the prepared sauce and add the low-sodium chicken broth. Bring to a simmer and cook for 2-3 minutes.
4. Stir in the cornstarch-water mixture and cook until the sauce has thickened, about 1-2 minutes. Garnish with sliced green onions if desired. Serve hot over brown rice or quinoa for an extra boost of fiber and nutrients.

Nutritional Information (per serving): Calories: 250 / Protein: 25g / Carbohydrates: 20g / Fats: 8g / Fiber: 4g / Cholesterol: 55mg / Sodium: 320mg / Potassium: 750mg

Lemon Garlic Chicken Tenders

Yield: 4 servings / **Preparation Time:** 10 minutes / **Cooking Time:** 15 minutes

Ingredients:

- 1 lb. (450g) chicken tenders
- 2 tablespoons olive oil
- 3 cloves garlic, minced
- Zest and juice of 1 lemon
- 1 teaspoon dried oregano
- 1 teaspoon dried thyme
- 1/2 teaspoon black pepper
- 1/4 teaspoon salt (optional)
- 1 tablespoon chopped fresh parsley (optional, for garnish)

Instructions:

1. Combine olive oil, minced garlic, lemon zest, lemon juice, dried oregano, dried thyme, black pepper, and salt in a medium bowl to create a marinade. Toss chicken tenders in the marinade and let sit for at least 10 minutes, up to 30 minutes in the fridge.
2. Preheat a non-stick skillet or grill pan over medium-high heat. Cook chicken tenders for 5-7 minutes on each side until golden brown and cooked through (165°F or 75°C).
3. Transfer chicken to a serving plate, garnish with fresh parsley if desired, and serve hot with steamed vegetables or a green salad.

Nutritional Information (per serving): Calories: 210 / Protein: 28g / Carbohydrates: 2g / Fats: 10g / Fiber: 0.5g / Cholesterol: 75mg / Sodium: 180mg / Potassium: 450mg

Spicy Chicken Wraps

Yield: 4 servings / **Preparation Time:** 15 minutes / **Cooking Time:** 15 minutes

Ingredients:

- 1 lb. (450g) boneless, skinless chicken breasts, thinly sliced
- 1/2 cup sliced red onion
- 1/2 cup shredded carrots
- 1/2 cup sliced bell peppers (any color)
- 4 whole grain tortillas (8-inch)
- 1 cup shredded lettuce
- 1/2 cup diced tomatoes
- 1/4 cup plain Greek yogurt (for a healthier sauce option)
- 2 tablespoons olive oil
- 1 tablespoon fresh lime juice
- 2 cloves garlic, minced
- 1 tablespoon chili powder
- 1 teaspoon cumin
- 1 teaspoon smoked paprika
- 1/2 teaspoon cayenne pepper (adjust to taste)
- 1/2 teaspoon salt (optional)
- 1/4 teaspoon black pepper

Instructions:

1. Combine olive oil, minced garlic, chili powder, cumin, smoked paprika, cayenne pepper, salt, and black pepper in a bowl. Toss thinly sliced chicken breasts in the mixture and marinate for at least 10 minutes.
2. Preheat a non-stick skillet over medium-high heat. Cook chicken for 5-7 minutes on each side until fully cooked. Let rest, then slice into strips.
3. Mix Greek yogurt with lime juice and chopped cilantro for the sauce. Lay out whole grain tortillas and add shredded lettuce, diced tomatoes, sliced red onions, shredded carrots, and sliced bell peppers.
4. Top with chicken strips and drizzle with the yogurt sauce. Roll up tortillas, fold in the sides, slice in half, and serve immediately.

Nutritional Information (per serving): Calories: 310 / Protein: 25g / Carbohydrates: 35g / Fats: 9g / Fiber: 7g / Cholesterol: 55mg / Sodium: 450mg / Potassium: 620mg

Turkey and Spinach Quesadillas

Yield: 4 servings / **Preparation Time:** 10 minutes / **Cooking Time:** 10 minutes

Ingredients:

- 1 lb. (450g) ground turkey
- 4 whole wheat tortillas (8-inch)
- 1 tablespoon olive oil
- 1 small onion, finely chopped
- 2 cloves garlic, minced
- 1 teaspoon cumin
- 1 teaspoon paprika
- 1/2 teaspoon chili powder
- 1/2 teaspoon black pepper
- 2 cups fresh spinach, chopped
- 1 cup reduced-fat shredded cheddar cheese
- Optional: 1/4 cup chopped fresh cilantro
- Optional: 1/4 cup Greek yogurt (for dipping)
- Optional: 1/4 cup salsa (for dipping)

Instructions:

1. In a large skillet, heat olive oil over medium heat. Add the finely chopped onion and minced garlic, and sauté for 2-3 minutes until the onion becomes translucent. Add the ground turkey to the skillet, breaking it apart with a spatula, and cook until browned and no longer pink, about 5-7 minutes. Stir in cumin, paprika, chili powder, and black pepper. Mix well to coat the turkey evenly with the spices.

2. Add the chopped spinach to the skillet with the cooked turkey. Stir until the spinach is wilted and well combined with the turkey mixture, about 2-3 minutes. Remove the skillet from heat.
3. Place a whole wheat tortilla on a clean surface. Spread 1/4 of the turkey and spinach mixture evenly over half of the tortilla. Sprinkle 1/4 cup of shredded cheddar cheese over the turkey mixture. Fold the tortilla in half to cover the filling. Repeat with the remaining tortillas and filling.
4. Preheat a large non-stick skillet or griddle over medium heat. Place one assembled quesadilla in the skillet and cook for 2-3 minutes on each side until the tortilla is golden brown and the cheese is melted. Remove the quesadilla from the skillet and keep warm. Repeat with the remaining quesadillas. Cut each quesadilla into wedges and serve immediately. Optionally, garnish with chopped fresh cilantro and serve with Greek yogurt and salsa for dipping.

Nutritional Information (per serving): Calories: 350 / Protein: 28g / Carbohydrates: 28g / Fats: 14g / Fiber: 4g / Cholesterol: 70mg / Sodium: 450mg / Potassium: 620mg

---

Easy Chicken Fajitas

Yield: 4 servings / **Preparation Time:** 15 minutes / **Cooking Time:** 15 minutes

Ingredients:

- 1 lb. (450g) boneless, skinless chicken breasts, thinly sliced
- 8 small whole wheat tortillas
- 1 red bell pepper, thinly sliced
- 1 yellow bell pepper, thinly sliced
- 1 green bell pepper, thinly sliced
- 1 large onion, thinly sliced
- 2 cloves garlic, minced
- 1 tablespoon olive oil
- Juice of 1 lime
- 1 teaspoon chili powder
- 1 teaspoon ground cumin
- 1 teaspoon paprika
- 1/2 teaspoon dried oregano
- 1/2 teaspoon black pepper
- 1/4 teaspoon salt (optional for a low-sodium diet)
- Optional topping: fresh cilantro
- Optional topping: Greek yogurt or low-fat sour cream
- Optional topping: Avocado slices
- Optional topping: Salsa

Instructions:

1. In a large bowl, combine the sliced chicken, chili powder, ground cumin, paprika, dried oregano, black pepper, and minced garlic. Mix well to coat the chicken evenly with the spices. In a separate bowl, combine the sliced bell peppers and onion.
2. Heat 1 tablespoon of olive oil in a large skillet over medium-high heat. Add the seasoned chicken to the skillet and cook for 5-7 minutes until the chicken is fully cooked and no longer pink, stirring occasionally. Remove the chicken from the skillet and set aside.
3. In the same skillet, add the sliced bell peppers and onion. Cook for 5-7 minutes until the vegetables are tender-crisp, stirring occasionally.
4. Return the cooked chicken to the skillet with the vegetables. Stir to combine and heat through, about 2-3 minutes. Squeeze the juice of 1 lime over the chicken and vegetable mixture and stir.
5. Warm the whole wheat tortillas in a dry skillet or microwave. Fill each tortilla with the chicken and vegetable mixture. Add optional toppings such as fresh cilantro, Greek yogurt, avocado slices, and salsa if desired.

Nutritional Information (per serving): Calories: 320 / Protein: 27g / Carbohydrates: 28g / Fats: 10g / Fiber: 6g / Cholesterol: 65mg / Sodium: 280mg / Potassium: 620mg

Chapter 7: Meat Recipes

In this chapter we explore the benefits of incorporating lean meat into a heart-healthy diet. While often overlooked, lean cuts of meat can be an excellent source of essential nutrients such as protein, iron, and B vitamins, all of which play a vital role in maintaining overall cardiovascular health. By choosing the right cuts and cooking methods, meat can be enjoyed as part of a balanced diet that supports heart health. In this chapter, we offer delicious and nutritious meat recipes that are low in saturated fats and sodium, helping you enjoy the flavors you love while keeping your heart strong and healthy.

Lean Red Meat Dishes

Incorporating lean red meat dishes into your meal plan can provide essential nutrients without compromising heart health. Lean cuts of red meat, such as tenderloin, sirloin, and round, are excellent sources of high-quality protein, iron, and vital vitamins like B12. These nutrients support muscle health, oxygen transport, and energy levels. By choosing lean red meat and preparing it with heart-healthy cooking methods, you can enjoy delicious and satisfying meals that contribute to a balanced, nutritious diet.

Grilled Sirloin with Chimichurri Sauce

Yield: 4 servings / **Preparation Time:** 15 minutes / **Cooking Time:** 10-15 minutes

Ingredients:

- 1 lb. (450g) lean sirloin steak
- 1 cup fresh parsley, finely chopped
- 1/2 cup fresh cilantro, finely chopped
- 3 cloves garlic, minced
- 1/4 cup red wine vinegar
- Juice of 1 lemon
- 2 tablespoons olive oil
- 1 teaspoon garlic powder
- 1 teaspoon paprika
- 1 teaspoon red pepper flakes
- 1 teaspoon black pepper
- Salt to taste
- Optional: 1 avocado, sliced or cubed
- Optional: 2 cups fresh spinach leaves
- Optional: 1 cup halved cherry tomatoes
- Optional: 1 cup cooked quinoa
- Optional: 1/4 cup chopped walnuts

Instructions:

1. Preheat the grill to medium-high heat. In a small bowl, mix the olive oil, black pepper, garlic powder, and paprika. Rub the seasoning mixture evenly over both sides of the sirloin steak. Let it marinate for about 10 minutes at room temperature. Place the steak on the preheated grill.
2. Cook for 5-7 minutes per side for medium-rare, or until it reaches your desired level of doneness. Remove the steak from the grill and let it rest for 5 minutes before slicing.
3. In a medium bowl, combine the chopped parsley, cilantro, red wine vinegar, olive oil, minced garlic, red pepper flakes, salt, black pepper, and lemon juice. Stir well to combine all the ingredients.
4. Slice the grilled sirloin steak thinly against the grain. Drizzle the chimichurri sauce generously over the sliced steak. Serve with a side of mixed greens or roasted vegetables for a complete meal.

Nutritional Information (per serving): Calories: 310 / Protein: 28g / Carbohydrates: 4g / Fats: 20g / Fiber: 1g / Cholesterol: 70mg / Sodium: 290mg / Potassium: 560mg

Lean Beef and Vegetable Stir-Fry

Yield: 4 servings / **Preparation Time:** 15 minutes / **Cooking Time:** 15 minutes

Ingredients:

- 1 lb. (450g) lean beef sirloin, thinly sliced
- 1/4 cup water
- 1 red bell pepper, sliced
- 1 yellow bell pepper, sliced
- 1 medium carrot, julienned
- 3 green onions, chopped
- 1 cup broccoli florets
- 1 cup snow peas
- 2 tablespoons low-sodium soy sauce

- 2 tablespoons hoisin sauce
- 1 tablespoon olive oil
- 1 tablespoon cornstarch
- 2 cloves garlic, minced
- 1 tablespoon ginger, minced
- 1 tablespoon sesame seeds (optional)
- 1 tablespoon rice vinegar
- 1 teaspoon honey
- 1 teaspoon sesame oil

Instructions:

1. In a bowl, combine the thinly sliced beef, 2 tablespoons of low-sodium soy sauce, and cornstarch. Mix well and set aside for 10 minutes.
2. In a small bowl, whisk together the remaining 2 tablespoons of low-sodium soy sauce, hoisin sauce, rice vinegar, honey, sesame oil, and water. Set aside.
3. Heat 1 tablespoon of olive oil in a large skillet or wok over medium-high heat. Add the marinated beef and stir-fry for 3-4 minutes until the beef is browned and cooked through. Remove the beef from the skillet and set aside.
4. In the same skillet, add the minced garlic and ginger, and stir-fry for 1 minute until fragrant. Add the bell peppers, carrot, broccoli, and snow peas. Stir-fry for 5-7 minutes until the vegetables are tender-crisp.
5. Return the cooked beef to the skillet and pour in the prepared sauce. Stir well to combine and cook for an additional 2-3 minutes until everything is heated through. Garnish with chopped green onions and sesame seeds, if desired.
6. Serve the stir-fry over brown rice or quinoa for a complete meal.

Nutritional Information (per serving): Calories: 300 / Protein: 28g / Carbohydrates: 20g / Fats: 12g / Fiber: 4g / Cholesterol: 60mg / Sodium: 400mg / Potassium: 700mg

Seared Venison with Berry Sauce

Yield: 4 servings / **Preparation Time:** 15 minutes / **Cooking Time:** 20 minutes

Ingredients:

- 4 venison steaks (4-6 oz each)
- 1 cup mixed berries (blueberries, raspberries, and blackberries)
- 1/2 cup low-sodium chicken broth
- 1/4 cup balsamic vinegar
- 2 tablespoons olive oil
- 2 tablespoons honey

- 1 teaspoon sea salt
- 1/2 teaspoon freshly ground black pepper
- 1 tablespoon fresh thyme leaves
- 2 cloves garlic, minced
- 1 teaspoon cornstarch mixed with 1 tablespoon water (optional for thickening)

Instructions:

1. Pat venison steaks dry, rub with olive oil, sea salt, black pepper, minced garlic, and thyme. Marinate for 10-15 minutes.
2. In a saucepan, simmer mixed berries, chicken broth, balsamic vinegar, and honey for 10 minutes until thickened. Stir in cornstarch mixture if needed. Set aside.

3. Heat a skillet over medium-high heat. Sear steaks for 3-4 minutes per side for medium-rare (135°F/57°C). Let rest for 5 minutes. Slice steaks, arrange on plates, and top with berry sauce. Garnish with thyme leaves if desired.

Nutritional Information (per serving): Calories: 300 / Protein: 30g / Carbohydrates: 15g / Fats: 12g / Fiber: 3g / Cholesterol: 70mg / Sodium: 300mg / Potassium: 600mg

---

Rosemary Garlic Lamb Chops

Yield: 4 servings / **Preparation Time:** 10 minutes / **Cooking Time:** 15 minutes

Ingredients:
- 8 lamb chops (approximately 2 lbs.)
- 1 lemon, zested and juiced
- lemon wedges
- 3 cloves garlic, minced
- 2 tablespoons fresh rosemary, chopped
- fresh rosemary sprigs
- 2 tablespoons olive oil
- 1 teaspoon freshly ground black pepper
- 1/2 teaspoon sea salt

Instructions:
1. In a small bowl, combine the chopped rosemary, minced garlic, olive oil, black pepper, sea salt, lemon zest, and lemon juice. Rub the mixture evenly over the lamb chops.
2. Let the lamb chops marinate for at least 30 minutes, or up to 2 hours in the refrigerator.
3. Preheat your grill to medium-high heat. Place the marinated lamb chops on the preheated grill. Grill for 3-4 minutes per side for medium-rare, or longer if you prefer them well done. Use a meat thermometer to check the internal temperature; it should read 145°F (63°C) for medium-rare.
4. Remove the lamb chops from the grill and let them rest for 5 minutes before serving.
5. Serve the lamb chops garnished with fresh rosemary sprigs and lemon wedges. Pair with a side of steamed vegetables, quinoa, or a fresh salad for a balanced, heart-healthy meal.

Nutritional Information (per serving): Calories: 300 / Protein: 25g / Carbohydrates: 2g / Fats: 21g / Fiber: 1g / Cholesterol: 75mg / Sodium: 200mg / Potassium: 350mg

---

Baked Herb-Crusted Pork Tenderloin

Yield: 4 servings / **Preparation Time:** 15 minutes / **Cooking Time:** 25-30 minutes

Ingredients:
- 1.5 lbs. (680g) pork tenderloin
- 1 tablespoon olive oil
- 1 teaspoon dried rosemary
- 1 teaspoon dried thyme
- 1 teaspoon dried oregano
- 1 teaspoon garlic powder
- 1/2 teaspoon black pepper
- Zest of 1 lemon

Instructions:
1. Preheat your oven to 400°F (200°C).
2. In a small bowl, mix the dried rosemary, thyme, oregano, garlic powder, black pepper, salt (if using), and lemon zest. Rub the pork tenderloin with olive oil, then coat it evenly with the herb mixture.
3. Place the seasoned pork tenderloin on a baking sheet lined with parchment paper or in a baking dish. Bake in the preheated oven for 25-30 minutes, or until the internal temperature reaches 145°F (63°C). Remove the pork from the oven and let it rest for 5-10 minutes before slicing.

4. Slice the pork tenderloin into medallions. Serve with a side of steamed vegetables or a mixed green salad for a complete meal.

Nutritional Information (per serving): Calories: 200 / Protein: 28g / Carbohydrates: 2g / Fats: 9g / Fiber: 0g / Cholesterol: 80mg / Sodium: 150mg / Potassium: 450mg

Ground Meat Recipes

Ground meat can be a versatile and nutritious addition to a heart-healthy diet. Lean ground meats, such as turkey, chicken, and lean beef, provide essential proteins and nutrients while keeping saturated fats to a minimum. They can be easily incorporated into a variety of dishes, offering both convenience and flavor. Additionally, ground meat dishes are considerably easier to cook, making them a perfect choice for quick, nutritious meals. This subchapter showcases recipes that utilize ground meat to create delicious, heart-friendly meals that support cardiovascular health, ensuring you can enjoy satisfying, wholesome dishes without compromising your dietary goals.

Lean Beef Tacos with Fresh Salsa

Yield: 4 servings / **Preparation Time:** 15 minutes / **Cooking Time:** 15 minutes

Ingredients:
- 1 lb. lean ground beef (93% lean)
- 8 small whole wheat tortillas
- 1 tablespoon olive oil
- juice of 1 lime
- 1 small onion, finely chopped
- 2 cloves garlic, minced
- 1 teaspoon ground cumin
- Optional toppings: shredded lettuce; avocado slices; low-fat Greek yogurt or sour cream; shredded low-fat cheese
- 1 teaspoon chili powder
- 1/2 teaspoon paprika
- 1/4 teaspoon black pepper
- 2 medium tomatoes, diced
- 1/2 small red onion, finely chopped
- 1 jalapeño, seeded and finely chopped (optional)
- 1/4 cup fresh cilantro, chopped

Instructions:
1. In a medium bowl, combine diced tomatoes, red onion, jalapeño (if using), cilantro, lime juice, salt, and pepper. Mix well and set aside to let the flavors meld.
2. In a large skillet, heat the olive oil over medium heat. Add the chopped onion and cook until soft, about 3-4 minutes. Add the minced garlic and cook for an additional 1 minute.
3. Add the ground beef to the skillet, breaking it apart with a spoon, and cook until browned, about 5-7 minutes. Drain any excess fat from the skillet. Add the ground cumin, chili powder, paprika, and black pepper. Stir to combine and cook for another 2 minutes to allow the spices to blend with the meat.
4. Warm the whole wheat tortillas in a dry skillet over medium heat, about 30 seconds per side, or in the microwave for 10-15 seconds. Divide the cooked beef evenly among the tortillas.
5. Top each taco with fresh salsa and any optional toppings such as shredded lettuce, avocado slices, low-fat Greek yogurt, or shredded low-fat cheese.
6. Serve the tacos immediately with any additional toppings on the side.

Nutritional Information (per serving): Calories: 360 / Protein: 25g / Carbohydrates: 30g / Fats: 15g / Fiber: 6g / Cholesterol: 70mg / Sodium: 290mg / Potassium: 650mg

Gound Beef and Vegetable Stuffed Peppers

Yield: 4 servings / **Preparation Time:** 20 minutes / **Cooking Time:** 35 minutes

Ingredients:

- 4 large bell peppers (any color), tops cut off and seeds removed
- 1 lb. ground beef (preferably lean)
- 1 cup cooked brown rice
- 1 small onion, finely chopped
- 2 cloves garlic, minced
- 1 zucchini, diced
- 1 carrot, grated

- 1 cup baby spinach, chopped
- 1/2 cup low-sodium chicken broth
- 1 can (14.5 oz) diced tomatoes (no salt added)
- 1 teaspoon dried oregano
- 1 teaspoon dried basil
- 1/2 teaspoon ground black pepper
- 1/4 teaspoon salt
- 2 tablespoons olive oil

Instructions:

1. Preheat your oven to 375°F (190°C). Cut the tops off the bell peppers and remove the seeds and membranes. Set aside.
2. In a large skillet, heat 1 tablespoon of olive oil over medium heat. Add the chopped onion and minced garlic, and cook until the onion is translucent, about 3-4 minutes. Add the ground chicken to the skillet, breaking it apart with a spoon, and cook until no longer pink, about 5-6 minutes.
3. Add the diced zucchini and grated carrot and cook for another 3-4 minutes until the vegetables are tender. Stir in the chopped spinach and cook until wilted, about 2 minutes. Add the cooked brown rice, diced tomatoes, chicken broth, oregano, basil, black pepper, and salt. Stir to combine and let it simmer for 5 minutes to allow the flavors to meld.
4. Place the prepared bell peppers in a baking dish. Drizzle the remaining olive oil over the peppers. Fill each bell pepper with the chicken and vegetable mixture, pressing down gently to pack the filling.
5. Cover the baking dish with foil and bake in the preheated oven for 25 minutes. Remove the foil and bake for an additional 10 minutes until the peppers are tender and the tops are slightly browned.
6. Let the stuffed peppers cool slightly before serving. Enjoy them as a main dish or a hearty side.

Nutritional Information (per serving): Calories: 300 / Protein: 28g / Carbohydrates: 25g / Fats: 10g / Fiber: 6g / Cholesterol: 70mg / Sodium: 320mg / Potassium: 900mg

Lean Beef and Spinach Lasagna

Yield: 8 servings / **Preparation Time:** 20 minutes / **Cooking Time:** 1 hour

Ingredients:

- 1 lb. lean ground beef
- 12 whole-wheat lasagna noodles
- 1 cup water
- 1 large egg
- 1 package (10 ounces) frozen spinach, thawed and drained
- 1 medium onion, finely chopped
- 3 cloves garlic, minced
- 1 can (28 ounces) low-sodium crushed tomatoes

- 1 can (15 ounces) low-sodium tomato sauce
- 1 can (6 ounces) low-sodium tomato paste
- 1 container (15 ounces) part-skim ricotta cheese
- 1 cup low-fat cottage cheese
- 1/4 cup grated Parmesan cheese
- 2 cups shredded part-skim mozzarella cheese
- 1 tablespoon dried basil
- 1 teaspoon dried oregano
- 1/2 teaspoon salt; 1/4 teaspoon black pepper

Instructions:

1. In a large skillet, cook the lean ground beef over medium heat until browned. Drain any excess fat. Add the chopped onion and minced garlic to the skillet. Cook until the onion is translucent. Stir in the crushed tomatoes, tomato sauce, tomato paste, water, dried basil, dried oregano, salt, and pepper. Bring to a boil, then reduce the heat and let it simmer for 30 minutes, stirring occasionally.
2. In a medium bowl, combine the ricotta cheese, low-fat cottage cheese, egg, salt, pepper, Parmesan cheese, and thawed spinach. Mix until well blended. Cook the lasagna noodles according to the package instructions. Drain and set aside.
3. Preheat your oven to 375°F (190°C). Spread a thin layer of the meat sauce at the bottom of a 9x13-inch baking dish. Place 3 cooked lasagna noodles over the sauce. Spread 1/3 of the cheese mixture over the noodles. Top with 1/3 of the meat sauce. Repeat the layers twice more, ending with the remaining meat sauce. Sprinkle the shredded mozzarella cheese evenly over the top.
4. Cover the baking dish with aluminum foil. Bake in the preheated oven for 25 minutes. Remove the foil and bake for an additional 15 minutes, or until the cheese is bubbly and lightly browned. Let the lasagna cool for about 10 minutes before serving.

Nutritional Information (per serving): Calories: 375 / Protein: 30g / Carbohydrates: 40g / Fats: 12g / Fiber: 7g / Cholesterol: 65mg / Sodium: 580mg / Potassium: 950mg

---

Turkey Meatballs with Marinara Sauce

Yield: 4 servings / **Preparation Time:** 20 minutes / **Cooking Time:** 40 minutes

Ingredients:

- 1 pound ground turkey (preferably lean)
- 1 large egg
- 1 (28-ounce) can crushed tomatoes (low sodium)
- 1/2 cup whole wheat breadcrumbs
- 1/4 cup grated Parmesan cheese
- 1/4 cup finely chopped fresh parsley
- 1 teaspoon dried oregano
- 1 teaspoon dried basil
- 1/2 teaspoon salt
- 1/4 teaspoon black pepper
- salt to taste
- 1 tablespoon olive oil
- 1 small onion, finely chopped
- 3 cloves garlic, minced

Instructions:

1. Preheat your oven to 375°F (190°C) and line a baking sheet with parchment paper. In a large mixing bowl, combine the ground turkey, whole wheat breadcrumbs, grated Parmesan cheese, chopped parsley, egg, minced garlic, dried oregano, dried basil, salt, and black pepper. Mix until all ingredients are well incorporated.
2. Shape the mixture into 1 1/2-inch meatballs and place them on the prepared baking sheet. Bake in the preheated oven for 20-25 minutes, or until the meatballs are cooked through and golden brown.
3. While the meatballs are baking, heat olive oil in a large saucepan over medium heat. Add the finely chopped onion and cook until it becomes translucent, about 5 minutes. Add the minced garlic and cook for another minute until fragrant.
4. Pour in the crushed tomatoes, dried oregano, dried basil, and red pepper flakes (if using). Stir to combine. Bring the sauce to a simmer and let it cook for about 15-20 minutes, stirring occasionally. Season with salt and pepper to taste.
5. Once the meatballs are cooked, transfer them to the saucepan with the marinara sauce. Gently stir to coat the meatballs with the sauce. Simmer for an additional 5 minutes to allow the flavors to meld together.
6. Serve the turkey meatballs and marinara sauce over whole wheat spaghetti or zucchini noodles or enjoy them on their own.

Nutritional Information (per serving): Calories: 350 / Protein: 28g / Carbohydrates: 22g / Fats: 16g / Fiber: 5g / Cholesterol: 95mg / Sodium: 480mg / Potassium: 900mg

Ground Turkey Lettuce Wraps

Yield: 4 servings / **Preparation Time:** 15 minutes / **Cooking Time:** 15 minutes

Ingredients:

- 1 pound ground turkey (93% lean)
- 1/2 cup water chestnuts, finely chopped
- 1 head of butter lettuce or iceberg lettuce, leaves separated
- 1/4 cup chopped green onions
- 1 small onion, finely chopped
- 2 cloves garlic, minced
- 1 red bell pepper, finely diced
- 1 carrot, shredded

- 1 tablespoon olive oil
- 3 tablespoons low-sodium soy sauce
- 2 tablespoons hoisin sauce
- 1 tablespoon rice vinegar
- 1 teaspoon fresh ginger, grated
- 1 teaspoon sesame oil
- Optional: 1 tablespoon chopped fresh cilantro
- Optional: 1 tablespoon sesame seeds

Instructions:

1. Heat olive oil in a large skillet over medium-high heat. Cook chopped onion for 3-4 minutes until soft, then add minced garlic for 1 minute. Add ground turkey, breaking it apart, and cook until browned, 5-7 minutes.
2. Add diced red bell pepper, shredded carrot, and chopped water chestnuts. Cook for 3-4 minutes until tender.
3. Whisk together soy sauce, hoisin sauce, rice vinegar, sesame oil, and grated ginger in a small bowl. Pour over turkey mixture and cook for 2 minutes.
4. Remove from heat and stir in chopped green onions. Serve turkey mixture in lettuce leaves, garnished with cilantro and sesame seeds if desired. Serve immediately, allowing diners to wrap their own.

Nutritional Information (per serving): Calories: 240 / Protein: 23g / Carbohydrates: 10g / Fats: 12g / Fiber: 2g / Cholesterol: 60mg / Sodium: 420mg / Potassium: 400mg

Slow-Cooked and Braised Meat Dishes

Slow-cooked and braised meat dishes offer a wonderful way to enjoy tender, flavorful meals that are also heart-healthy. These cooking techniques allow for the use of lean cuts of meat, which are ideal for maintaining cardiovascular health. By slowly cooking meats with vegetables and herbs, you can create dishes that are rich in nutrients, high in fiber, and low in unhealthy fats. This method also helps to retain the natural flavors and nutrients, ensuring every bite is as nutritious as it is delicious. Dive into this subchapter to discover how slow cooking and braising can enhance your heart-healthy diet while providing comfort and satisfaction.

Braised Lamb Shanks with Root Vegetables

Yield: 4 servings / **Preparation Time:** 20 minutes / **Cooking Time:** 2 hours 30 minutes

Ingredients:

- 4 lamb shanks (about 3 pounds total)
- 1 can (14.5 ounces) diced tomatoes
- 1 large onion, chopped
- 3 cloves garlic, minced
- 2 large carrots, peeled and cut into 1-inch pieces
- 2 parsnips, peeled and cut into 1-inch pieces
- 2 turnips, peeled and cut into 1-inch pieces

- 2 cups low-sodium beef broth
- 1 cup dry red wine (optional)
- 2 tablespoons tomato paste
- 2 tablespoons olive oil
- 1 teaspoon dried rosemary
- 1 teaspoon dried thyme
- 1 bay leaf

- Salt and pepper to taste (minimal)
- Fresh parsley, chopped (optional for garnish)

Instructions:

1. Preheat the oven to 325°F (165°C). Season the lamb shanks lightly with salt and pepper.
2. Heat the olive oil in a large Dutch oven over medium-high heat. Add the lamb shanks and sear on all sides until browned, about 8-10 minutes. Remove the shanks and set aside.
3. In the same pot, add the chopped onion and cook until softened, about 5 minutes. Add the garlic and cook for an additional minute.
4. Add the carrots, parsnips, and turnips to the pot. Stir in the beef broth, red wine (if using), diced tomatoes, tomato paste, rosemary, thyme, and bay leaf. Bring the mixture to a simmer.
5. Return the lamb shanks to the pot, nestling them among the vegetables. Cover the pot with a lid and transfer it to the preheated oven. Braise for 2 to 2.5 hours, or until the lamb is tender and falls off the bone.
6. Remove the lamb shanks and vegetables from the pot and place them on a serving platter. Discard the bay leaf. Skim any excess fat from the sauce and adjust the seasoning if needed. Pour the sauce over the lamb and vegetables. Garnish with fresh parsley if desired.

Nutritional Information (per serving): Calories: 450 / Protein: 30g / Carbohydrates: 25g / Fats: 25g / Fiber: 5g / Cholesterol: 90mg / Sodium: 400mg / Potassium: 900mg

---

Slow-Cooked Balsamic Beef

Yield: 6 servings / **Preparation Time:** 15 minutes / **Cooking Time:** 6-8 hours (slow cooker)

Ingredients:

- 2 pounds beef chuck roast, trimmed of visible fat
- 1 cup low-sodium beef broth
- 2 cups baby carrots
- 2 cups green beans, trimmed
- 1 large onion, sliced
- 3 cloves garlic, minced
- 1/2 cup balsamic vinegar
- 1/4 cup tomato paste (no added salt)
- 2 tablespoons Dijon mustard
- 1 tablespoon honey
- 1 tablespoon olive oil
- 2 cups baby carrots
- 2 cups green beans, trimmed

Instructions:

1. Trim any visible fat from the beef chuck roast. Season with black pepper. Heat the olive oil in a large skillet over medium-high heat. Sear the beef on all sides until browned, about 3-4 minutes per side. Transfer the beef to the slow cooker.
2. In the same skillet, add the sliced onion and minced garlic. Sauté for 2-3 minutes until the onion is softened. Add the balsamic vinegar, beef broth, tomato paste, Dijon mustard, honey, dried rosemary, and dried thyme to the skillet. Stir well to combine and bring to a simmer.
3. Pour the sauce over the beef in the slow cooker. Add the baby carrots around the beef. Cover and cook on low for 6-8 hours or until the beef is tender and easily shredded.
4. In the last 30 minutes of cooking, add the green beans to the slow cooker. This ensures they remain tender-crisp.
5. Remove the beef from the slow cooker and let it rest for a few minutes before shredding it with two forks. Return the shredded beef to the slow cooker and mix with the sauce and vegetables. Serve warm.

Nutritional Information (per serving): Calories: 350 / Protein: 30g / Carbohydrates: 15g / Fats: 18g / Fiber: 3g / Cholesterol: 80mg / Sodium: 250mg / Potassium: 800mg

Slow-Cooked Beef and Vegetable Stew

Yield: 6 servings / **Preparation Time:** 20 minutes / **Cooking Time:** 6-8 hours (slow cooker);

Ingredients:
- 1 1/2 pounds lean beef stew meat, trimmed of fat
- 4 cups low-sodium beef broth
- 1 cup water
- 2 tablespoons olive oil
- 1 large onion, diced
- 3 cloves garlic, minced
- 4 carrots, peeled and sliced
- 3 celery stalks, sliced
- 2 medium potatoes, diced
- 1 cup green beans, trimmed and cut into 1-inch pieces
- 1 can (14.5 ounces) diced tomatoes; no salt added
- 2 teaspoons dried thyme
- 1 teaspoon dried rosemary
- 2 bay leaves; salt and pepper to taste (optional and minimal)
- 1/4 cup fresh parsley, chopped (optional for garnish)

Instructions:
1. Heat the olive oil in a large skillet over medium-high heat. Add the beef stew meat and cook until browned on all sides, about 5-7 minutes. Transfer the browned beef to a slow cooker.
2. In the same skillet, add the diced onion and cook until translucent, about 3-4 minutes. Add the minced garlic and cook for another 1 minute until fragrant. Transfer the onion and garlic to the slow cooker.
3. Add the beef broth, water, carrots, celery, potatoes, green beans, diced tomatoes, dried thyme, dried rosemary, and bay leaves to the slow cooker. Stir to combine.
4. Cover and cook on low heat for 6-8 hours or on high heat for 3-4 hours, until the beef is tender, and the vegetables are cooked through.
5. Remove the bay leaves and season the stew with salt and pepper to taste, if desired.
6. Stir in the chopped fresh parsley for garnish before serving.

Nutritional Information (per serving): Calories: 290 / Protein: 25g / Carbohydrates: 22g / Fats: 10g / Fiber: 5g / Cholesterol: 70mg / Sodium: 280mg / Potassium: 800mg

Braised Turkey Legs with Mushrooms

Yield: 4 servings / **Preparation Time:** 20 minutes / **Cooking Time:** 1 hour 30 minutes

Ingredients:
- 4 turkey legs (skin removed)
- 1 cup low-sodium chicken broth
- 1 cup water
- 2 tablespoons olive oil
- 1 large onion, chopped
- 3 cloves garlic, minced
- 2 carrots, diced
- 2 celery stalks, diced
- 2 cups mushrooms, sliced
- 1 cup diced tomatoes (no salt added)
- 1 teaspoon dried thyme
- 1 teaspoon dried rosemary
- 1/2 teaspoon black pepper
- 1/2 teaspoon salt

Instructions:

1. Preheat your oven to 350°F (175°C). Remove the skin from the turkey legs to reduce fat content.
2. In a large oven-safe pot or Dutch oven, heat 1 tablespoon of olive oil over medium-high heat. Add the turkey legs and brown them on all sides, about 5-7 minutes.
3. Remove the turkey legs from the pot and set them aside.
4. In the same pot, add the remaining tablespoon of olive oil. Add the chopped onion, garlic, mushrooms, carrots, and celery. Sauté for about 5-7 minutes, until the vegetables are softened, and the mushrooms are browned.
5. Add the low-sodium chicken broth, water, and diced tomatoes to the pot, stirring to combine. Return the turkey legs to the pot. Add the dried thyme, rosemary, black pepper, and salt. Stir to mix well.
6. Cover the pot with a lid and transfer it to the preheated oven. Braise the turkey legs for 1 hour and 30 minutes, or until the turkey is tender and fully cooked. Remove the pot from the oven and place it on the stovetop.
7. Serve the braised turkey legs with the mushroom and vegetable mixture over whole grains like quinoa, brown rice, or whole wheat couscous for a complete meal.

Nutritional Information (per serving): Calories: 400 kcal / Protein: 36g / Carbohydrates: 18g / Fats: 20g / Fiber: 4g / Cholesterol: 130mg / Sodium: 450mg / Potassium: 800mg

---

Slow-Cooked Turkey with Vegetables

Yield: 6 servings / **Preparation Time:** 15 minutes / **Cooking Time:** 6-8 hours (on low) or 3-4 hours (on high)

Ingredients:

- 1 ½ lb. turkey breast, skinless and boneless
- 2 tablespoons olive oil
- 1 large onion, thinly sliced
- cloves garlic, minced
- 3 carrots, peeled and cut into 1-inch pieces
- 2 celery stalks, chopped
- 2 cups low-sodium chicken or turkey broth
- 1 cup diced tomatoes (no added salt)

- 1 tablespoon tomato paste
- 1 teaspoon dried thyme
- 1 teaspoon dried rosemary
- 1/2 teaspoon ground black pepper
- 1/2 teaspoon sea salt (optional)
- 2 cups baby spinach or kale leaves, chopped
- 1/2 cup pearl barley or brown rice (optional)

Instructions:

1. Pat the turkey breast dry and season with black pepper and salt (if using). In a skillet, heat olive oil over medium heat. Sear the turkey for 2-3 minutes on each side until browned. Remove from the skillet.
2. Place onion, garlic, carrots, and celery in the bottom of the slow cooker. Add the turkey on top of the vegetables. Pour in broth, then add diced tomatoes, tomato paste, thyme, rosemary, and black pepper.
3. Cover and cook on low for 6-8 hours or on high for 3-4 hours until the turkey is fully cooked (165°F or 75°C).
4. In the last 30 minutes of cooking, stir in spinach or kale and barley or rice if using. Cook until greens are wilted, and grains are tender.
5. Slice the turkey and serve with the vegetables and broth. Garnish with fresh herbs if desired.

Nutritional Information (per serving): Calories: 300 Protein: 28g Carbohydrates: 20g Fat: 10g Fiber: 4g Cholesterol: 60-70mg Potassium: 600-700mg Sodium: 250mg

Chapter 8: Vegetable Recipes

Vegetables are a cornerstone of a heart-healthy diet, offering a wealth of nutrients that are essential for maintaining cardiovascular health. Packed with vitamins, minerals, antioxidants, and fiber, vegetables help reduce blood pressure, lower cholesterol levels, and improve overall heart function. In this chapter, you will discover a variety of delicious and nutritious vegetable recipes that are easy to prepare and perfect for incorporating into your daily meals. These recipes will inspire you to embrace the vibrant flavors and heart-boosting benefits of a plant-based diet. Enjoy the journey to better heart health with these wholesome vegetable creations!

Vegetable Main Dishes

Embracing vegetable-based meals is a powerful way to support your heart health. These dishes are rich in fiber, vitamins, minerals, and antioxidants, all of which are essential for maintaining a healthy cardiovascular system. Vegetarian main dishes can help reduce cholesterol levels, lower blood pressure, and promote overall heart function. They are also a fantastic way to add variety and creativity to your diet. Dive into these delicious, plant-based recipes and discover how enjoyable and beneficial a heart-healthy vegetarian lifestyle can be!

Lentil and Vegetable Shepherd's Pie

Yield: 6 servings / **Preparation Time:** 30 minutes / **Cooking Time:** 1 hour

Ingredients:

- 1 cup dried green or brown lentils, rinsed and drained
- 2 cups low-sodium vegetable broth
- 1/2 cup low-fat milk or unsweetened almond milk
- 1 medium onion, finely chopped
- 2 carrots, diced
- 1 celery stalk, diced
- 4 large potatoes, peeled and cubed
- 2 cloves garlic, minced
- 1/2 teaspoon garlic powder
- 1 cup frozen peas
- 1 cup diced tomatoes (canned, no salt added)
- 2 tablespoons olive oil
- 1 tablespoon tomato paste
- 1 tablespoon low-sodium soy sauce
- 1 teaspoon dried thyme
- teaspoon dried rosemary
- 1 teaspoon smoked paprika
- 1/2 teaspoon black pepper
- Fresh parsley, chopped (optional for garnish)

Instructions:

1. Combine lentils and vegetable broth in a saucepan. Boil, then simmer for 20-25 minutes until tender. Drain and set aside.
2. Heat olive oil in a skillet over medium heat. Sauté onion and garlic until translucent. Add carrots and celery, cook for 5-7 minutes until softened. Stir in cooked lentils, peas, diced tomatoes, tomato paste, thyme, rosemary, smoked paprika, black pepper, and soy sauce. Cook for 10 minutes.
3. Boil potatoes until tender, about 15-20 minutes. Drain and mash with milk, olive oil, garlic powder, and black pepper until smooth.
4. Preheat oven to 375°F (190°C). Transfer lentil filling to a baking dish. Spread mashed potatoes over filling. Use a fork to create a pattern if desired.
5. Bake for 25-30 minutes until top is golden and filling is bubbly. Let cool before serving. Garnish with parsley if desired.

Nutritional Information (per serving): Calories: 320 / Protein: 11g / Carbohydrates: 55g / Fats: 7g / Fiber: 10g / Cholesterol: 0mg / Sodium: 220mg / Potassium: 1000mg

Stuffed Bell Peppers with Quinoa and Black Beans

Yield: 4 servings / **Preparation Time:** 15 minutes / **Cooking Time:** 40 minutes

Ingredients:

- 4 large bell peppers (any color), tops cut off and seeds removed
- 1 cup quinoa, rinsed
- 1 3/4 cups low-sodium vegetable broth
- 1 can (15 oz) black beans, drained and rinsed
- 1 cup corn kernels (fresh, frozen, or canned, drained)
- 1 cup diced tomatoes
- 1 small red onion, finely chopped
- 2 cloves garlic, minced
- 1 teaspoon ground cumin
- 1 teaspoon chili powder
- 1/2 teaspoon smoked paprika
- 1/4 teaspoon black pepper
- 1/4 cup fresh cilantro, chopped
- 1 tablespoon olive oil

Instructions:

1. Preheat your oven to 375°F (190°C).
2. In a medium saucepan, bring the vegetable broth to a boil. Add the quinoa, reduce the heat to low, cover, and simmer for about 15 minutes, or until the quinoa is cooked and the liquid is absorbed. Fluff with a fork and set aside.
3. In a large skillet, heat the olive oil over medium heat. Add the chopped onion and garlic, and sauté until the onion is translucent, about 5 minutes. Add the black beans, corn, diced tomatoes, cooked quinoa, cumin, chili powder, smoked paprika, and black pepper.
4. Stir well to combine and cook for another 5 minutes, allowing the flavors to meld together. Remove from heat and stir in the chopped cilantro (if using).
5. Place the bell peppers in a baking dish, cut side up. Spoon the quinoa and black bean mixture into each pepper, packing it down lightly. If using, sprinkle a little shredded cheese on top of each stuffed pepper.
6. Pour about 1/4 cup of water into the bottom of the baking dish to help steam the peppers. Cover the dish with aluminum foil and bake for 30 minutes. Remove the foil and bake for an additional 10 minutes, or until the peppers are tender. Allow the stuffed peppers to cool for a few minutes before serving. Garnish with additional fresh cilantro.

Nutritional Information (per serving): Calories: 280 / Protein: 10g / Carbohydrates: 48g / Fats: 6g / Fiber: 10g / Cholesterol: 0mg / Sodium: 350mg / Potassium: 800mg

Eggplant Parmesan

Yield: 4 servings / **Preparation Time:** 20 minutes / **Cooking Time:** 40 minutes

Ingredients:

- 2 medium eggplants, sliced into 1/4-inch rounds
- 1/2 cup whole wheat flour
- 1 cup whole wheat breadcrumbs
- 2 large eggs, beaten
- 1/4 cup grated Parmesan cheese
- 1 cup shredded part-skim mozzarella cheese
- 1 teaspoon garlic powder
- 1 teaspoon onion powder
- 1 teaspoon dried oregano
- 1 teaspoon dried basil
- 2 cups low-sodium marinara sauce
- 1/4 cup fresh basil, chopped
- 1 tablespoon olive oil

Instructions:

1. Preheat your oven to 375°F (190°C). Line a baking sheet with parchment paper or lightly grease it with olive oil.
2. Lay the eggplant slices on a clean kitchen towel or paper towels. Sprinkle both sides lightly with salt and let sit for 15 minutes to draw out excess moisture. Pat dry with paper towels.

3. In one shallow dish, combine whole wheat flour, garlic powder, and onion powder. In a second shallow dish, beat the eggs. In a third shallow dish, mix whole wheat breadcrumbs, grated Parmesan cheese, dried oregano, and dried basil.
4. Dredge each eggplant slice in the flour mixture, shaking off any excess. Dip in the beaten eggs, then coat with the breadcrumb mixture, pressing gently to adhere.
5. Arrange the breaded eggplant slices on the prepared baking sheet in a single layer. Drizzle lightly with olive oil. Bake for 20 minutes, flipping halfway through, until golden brown and tender.
6. In a baking dish, spread 1/2 cup of the marinara sauce. Layer half of the baked eggplant slices over the sauce. Top with another 1/2 cup of marinara sauce and sprinkle with 1/2 cup of shredded mozzarella cheese. Repeat with the remaining eggplant slices, marinara sauce, and mozzarella cheese.
7. Cover the baking dish with foil and bake for 15 minutes. Remove the foil and bake for an additional 10 minutes, or until the cheese is bubbly and golden.
8. Let the Eggplant Parmesan cool for a few minutes before serving. Garnish with fresh basil.

Nutritional Information (per serving): Calories: 320 / Protein: 15g / Carbohydrates: 42g / Fats: 12g / Fiber: 10g / Cholesterol: 60mg / Sodium: 400mg / Potassium: 850mg

---

Portobello Mushroom Burgers

Yield: 4 servings / **Preparation Time:** 15 minutes / **Cooking Time:** 15 minutes

Ingredients:
- 4 large Portobello mushroom caps
- 4 whole-grain burger buns
- 1 avocado, sliced
- 1 large tomato, sliced
- 1 red onion, thinly sliced
- 4 leaves of lettuce
- 2 tablespoons balsamic vinegar
- 2 tablespoons olive oil
- 1 tablespoon low-sodium soy sauce
- 1 teaspoon garlic powder
- 1 teaspoon dried oregano

Instructions:
1. In a small bowl, whisk together balsamic vinegar, olive oil, low-sodium soy sauce, garlic powder, and dried oregano.
2. Clean the Portobello mushroom caps and remove the stems. Place them in a large resealable plastic bag or a shallow dish. Pour the marinade over the mushrooms, ensuring they are evenly coated. Let them marinate for at least 15 minutes, turning occasionally.
3. Preheat a grill or grill pan over medium-high heat. Grill the marinated mushrooms for about 5-7 minutes on each side, or until tender and slightly charred.
4. Toast the whole-grain burger buns on the grill for about 1-2 minutes. Place a grilled Portobello mushroom cap on the bottom half of each bun.
5. Top with avocado slices, tomato slices, red onion, and lettuce. Cover with the top half of the bun. Serve immediately.

Nutritional Information (per serving): Calories: 300 / Protein: 8g / Carbohydrates: 36g / Fats: 16g / Fiber: 8g / Cholesterol: 0mg / Sodium: 300mg / Potassium: 700mg

Spinach and Ricotta Stuffed Shells

Yield: 6 servings / **Preparation Time:** 20 minutes / **Cooking Time:** 40 minutes

Ingredients:

- 20 jumbo pasta shells
- 3 cups fresh spinach, chopped
- 1 cup part-skim ricotta cheese
- 1 cup part-skim mozzarella cheese, shredded
- 1/4 cup grated Parmesan cheese
- 1 large egg, beaten
- 2 cloves garlic, minced

- 1 tablespoon olive oil
- 1 teaspoon dried basil]
- 1 teaspoon dried oregano
- 1/4 teaspoon ground black pepper
- 1/4 teaspoon salt (optional)
- 2 cups low-sodium marinara sauce
- Fresh basil leaves for garnish (optional)

Instructions:

1. Boil water and cook jumbo pasta shells until al dente. Drain and set aside.
2. Heat olive oil in a skillet over medium heat. Sauté minced garlic for 1 minute. Add chopped spinach and cook until wilted, 3-4 minutes. Let cool slightly.
3. In a bowl, mix cooked spinach, ricotta, 1/2 cup mozzarella, Parmesan, beaten egg, basil, oregano, black pepper, and salt. Preheat oven to 375°F (190°C). Spread 1 cup marinara sauce in a 9x13 inch baking dish.
4. Fill pasta shells with the spinach mixture and place in the dish. Pour remaining marinara sauce over shells and sprinkle with remaining mozzarella.
5. Cover with foil and bake for 20 minutes. Remove foil and bake for an additional 10 minutes until cheese is bubbly and golden. Let cool before serving. Garnish with fresh basil if desired.

Nutritional Information (per serving): Calories: 280 / Protein: 16g / Carbohydrates: 34g / Fats: 10g / Fiber: 4g / Cholesterol: 50mg / Sodium: 400mg / Potassium: 500mg

Nourishing Vegan Entrees

Incorporating vegan meals into your heart-healthy diet is a fantastic way to boost your cardiovascular health. Vegan entrees are packed with nutrient-dense ingredients that are naturally low in saturated fats and cholesterol. These meals are rich in fiber, antioxidants, and essential vitamins and minerals, which help reduce inflammation, improve blood circulation, and support overall heart function. Enjoy these delicious, plant-based recipes that not only benefit your heart but also add vibrant flavors and variety to your daily meals. Embrace the power of plants for a healthier heart!

Chickpea and Spinach Curry

Yield: 4 servings / **Preparation Time:** 10 minutes / **Cooking Time:** 20 minutes

Ingredients:

- 1 can (14.5 oz) diced tomatoes; no salt added
- 1 can (15 oz) chickpeas, drained and rinsed
- 1/2 cup vegetable broth, low sodium
- 1/4 cup coconut milk, light
- 4 cups fresh spinach, chopped
- 1 large onion, finely chopped
- 3 cloves garlic, minced
- 1 tablespoon fresh ginger, grated

- 1 tablespoon curry powder
- 1 teaspoon ground cumin
- 1 teaspoon ground coriander
- 1 teaspoon turmeric
- Salt and pepper to taste
- 1 tablespoon fresh lemon juice
- 1 tablespoon olive oil
- Fresh cilantro for garnish

Instructions:
1. Heat olive oil in a large skillet over medium heat. Add chopped onion and sauté for about 5 minutes until translucent. Add minced garlic and grated ginger, cooking for another 1-2 minutes until fragrant.
2. Stir in curry powder, ground cumin, ground coriander, and turmeric. Cook for another 1 minute to toast the spices.
3. Add the diced tomatoes and vegetable broth to the skillet, stirring to combine. Bring the mixture to a simmer. Stir in the chickpeas, and let it simmer for about 10 minutes until the flavors meld together.
4. Stir in the chopped spinach, allowing it to wilt into the curry. Add the light coconut milk and stir to combine, cooking for another 2-3 minutes until heated through.
5. Stir in the fresh lemon juice and season with salt and pepper to taste.
6. Remove from heat and garnish with fresh cilantro. Serve over brown rice or quinoa for a complete meal.

Nutritional Information (per serving): Calories: 250 / Protein: 10g / Carbohydrates: 38g / Fats: 8g / Fiber: 10g / Cholesterol: 0mg / Sodium: 350mg / Potassium: 700mg

---

Sweet Potato and Black Bean Enchiladas

Yield: 4 servings / **Preparation Time:** 15 minutes / **Cooking Time:** 40 minutes

Ingredients:
- 2 medium sweet potatoes, peeled and diced (about 4 cups)
- 8 small whole wheat tortillas
- 1 small onion, finely chopped
- 2 cloves garlic, minced
- 1 (15-ounce) can black beans, drained and rinsed
- 1/2 cup low-sodium vegetable broth
- 1/4 cup chopped fresh cilantro
- 1 1/2 cups enchilada sauce (low-sodium store-bought or homemade)
- 1/2 cup shredded low-fat cheddar cheese (optional)
- 1 teaspoon ground cumin
- 1 teaspoon smoked paprika
- 1/2 teaspoon chili powder
- 1/2 teaspoon ground coriander
- 1/4 teaspoon salt; 1/4 teaspoon black pepper
- 1 tablespoon olive oil
- Optional toppings: chopped fresh cilantro; sliced avocado; low-fat Greek yogurt or sour cream

Instructions:
1. Preheat oven to 400°F (200°C). Toss diced sweet potatoes with 1 tbsp olive oil on a baking sheet and roast for 20 minutes, stirring halfway. In a skillet, heat 1 tbsp olive oil over medium heat. Cook chopped onion until translucent, about 5 minutes.
2. Add minced garlic and cook for 1 minute. Stir in black beans, cumin, smoked paprika, chili powder, ground coriander, salt, and pepper. Cook for 2 minutes. Add roasted sweet potatoes and vegetable broth. Cook for 5 minutes. Stir in chopped cilantro and remove from heat.
3. Reduce oven to 375°F (190°C). Spread 1/2 cup enchilada sauce in a 9x13-inch baking dish. Place 1/2 cup sweet potato mixture in each tortilla, roll up, and place seam-side down in the dish. Pour remaining enchilada sauce over tortillas and sprinkle with cheese, if using.
4. Cover with foil and bake for 20 minutes. Remove foil and bake for another 10 minutes until cheese is melted and bubbly. Cool for a few minutes before serving. Garnish with cilantro, avocado, and a dollop of Greek yogurt or sour cream, if desired.

Nutritional Information (per serving): Calories: 350 / Protein: 12g / Carbohydrates: 55g / Fats: 10g / Fiber: 13g / Cholesterol: 10mg / Sodium: 420mg / Potassium: 1000mg

Vegan Mushroom Stroganoff

Yield: 4 servings / **Preparation Time:** 10 minutes / **Cooking Time:** 20 minutes

Ingredients:

- 1 lb. mushrooms (cremini, button, or mixed), sliced
- 2 cups vegetable broth, low sodium
- 1/2 cup unsweetened almond milk or other plant-based milk
- 1 tablespoon Dijon mustard
- 2 tablespoons nutritional yeast
- 1 large onion, finely chopped
- 3 cloves garlic, minced
- 2 tablespoons olive oil
- 1 teaspoon dried thyme
- 1 teaspoon smoked paprika
- Salt and pepper to taste
- 1/4 cup white wine (optional)
- 1 tablespoon cornstarch mixed with 2 tablespoons water
- 1/4 cup fresh parsley, chopped
- Whole grain pasta or brown rice, cooked, for serving

Instructions:

1. Heat the olive oil in a large skillet over medium heat. Add the chopped onion and sauté for about 5 minutes until translucent. Add the minced garlic and cook for another 1-2 minutes until fragrant.
2. Add the sliced mushrooms to the skillet and cook for about 8-10 minutes until they release their juices and begin to brown. Stir in the dried thyme and smoked paprika, cooking for another minute.
3. If using, pour in the white wine to deglaze the pan, stirring to scrape up any browned bits from the bottom. Cook until the wine is reduced by half. Add the vegetable broth and bring the mixture to a simmer.
4. Stir in the almond milk, Dijon mustard, and nutritional yeast. Mix the cornstarch with water to form a slurry, then slowly add it to the skillet, stirring constantly until the sauce thickens.
5. Season the stroganoff with salt and pepper to taste. Stir in the chopped fresh parsley just before serving.
6. Serve the mushroom stroganoff over whole grain pasta or brown rice for a complete meal.

Nutritional Information (per serving): Calories: 210 / Protein: 6g / Carbohydrates: 20g / Fats: 10g / Fiber: 4g / Cholesterol: 0mg / Sodium: 300mg / Potassium: 700mg

Vegan Stuffed Acorn Squash

Yield: 4 servings / **Preparation Time:** 20 minutes / **Cooking Time:** 45 minutes

Ingredients:

- 2 medium acorn squashes, halved and seeds removed
- 1 cup quinoa, rinsed
- 2 cups low-sodium vegetable broth
- 1 small onion, finely chopped
- 2 cloves garlic, minced
- 1 medium apple, diced
- 1/2 cup dried cranberries (unsweetened)
- 1/4 cup chopped pecans or walnuts
- 2 tablespoons olive oil
- 1 teaspoon ground cinnamon
- 1/2 teaspoon ground cumin
- 1/4 teaspoon ground nutmeg
- Salt and pepper to taste
- Fresh parsley, chopped (optional, for garnish)

Instructions:

1. Preheat the oven to 400°F (200°C). Brush the cut sides of the acorn squash halves with 1 tablespoon of olive oil and place them cut side down on a baking sheet. Roast in the preheated oven for about 30-35 minutes or until tender.

2. While the squash is roasting, bring the vegetable broth to a boil in a medium saucepan. Add the rinsed quinoa, reduce the heat to low, cover, and simmer for about 15 minutes until the quinoa is cooked and the broth is absorbed. Fluff with a fork and set aside.
3. In a large skillet, heat the remaining 1 tablespoon of olive oil over medium heat. Add the chopped onion and garlic, and sauté for about 5 minutes until the onion is translucent. Stir in the diced apple, dried cranberries, chopped pecans or walnuts, cooked quinoa, cinnamon, cumin, and nutmeg. Cook for an additional 3-5 minutes, stirring occasionally. Season with salt and pepper to taste.
4. Remove the roasted acorn squash from the oven and turn them cut side up. Spoon the quinoa mixture into each squash half, packing it in firmly. Return the stuffed squashes to the oven and bake for an additional 10 minutes.
5. Garnish with fresh chopped parsley, if desired, and serve warm.

Nutritional Information (per serving): Calories: 350 / Protein: 7g / Carbohydrates: 60g / Fats: 12g / Fiber: 8g / Cholesterol: 0mg / Sodium: 250mg / Potassium: 1000mg

---

Lentil and Sweet Potato Stew

Yield: 4 servings / **Preparation Time:** 15 minutes / **Cooking Time:** 40 minutes

Ingredients:
- 1 cup dried green or brown lentils, rinsed
- 4 cups low-sodium vegetable broth
- 1 (14.5-ounce) can diced tomatoes, no salt added
- 2 cups chopped kale or spinach
- 1 large onion, finely chopped
- 2 cloves garlic, minced
- 2 medium sweet potatoes, peeled and diced (about 4 cups)
- 2 large carrots, peeled and sliced
- 1 teaspoon ground cumin
- 1 teaspoon ground turmeric
- 1 teaspoon smoked paprika
- 1/2 teaspoon ground coriander
- 1/4 teaspoon black pepper
- 1/4 teaspoon cayenne pepper (optional, for spice)
- 1 tablespoon olive oil
- Juice of 1 lemon
- Fresh cilantro, chopped (optional, for garnish)

Instructions:
1. Rinse and dice the sweet potatoes and carrots. Rinse the lentils thoroughly.
2. In a large pot, heat the olive oil over medium heat. Add the chopped onion and cook for about 5 minutes until translucent. Add the minced garlic and cook for another 1 minute until fragrant.
3. Add the diced sweet potatoes and sliced carrots to the pot. Stir well to combine. Add the rinsed lentils, diced tomatoes, and vegetable broth.
4. Stir in the ground cumin, ground turmeric, smoked paprika, ground coriander, black pepper, and cayenne pepper (if using). Bring the mixture to a boil, then reduce the heat to low and let it simmer, covered, for about 25-30 minutes, or until the lentils and vegetables are tender.
5. Stir in the chopped kale or spinach and cook for another 5 minutes until the greens are wilted. Add the lemon juice and stir well. Taste the stew and adjust the seasoning if necessary. Ladle the stew into bowls and garnish with fresh chopped cilantro, if desired.

Nutritional Information (per serving): Calories: 320 / Protein: 14g / Carbohydrates: 60g / Fats: 5g / Fiber: 16g / Cholesterol: 0mg / Sodium: 200mg / Potassium: 1200mg

Vegetarian and Vegan Sides and Salads

Including these nutrient-rich dishes in your heart-healthy diet provides a wealth of benefits. Vegetarian and vegan sides and salads are brimming with fiber, antioxidants, and essential nutrients that help lower cholesterol, reduce blood pressure, and promote overall cardiovascular health. These dishes are naturally low in saturated fats and free of cholesterol, making them perfect complements to your meals. Enjoy these vibrant, delicious recipes that not only support your heart but also add variety and excitement to your dining experience. Embrace the goodness of plant-based sides and salads for a healthier heart!

Quinoa and Kale Salad

Yield: 4 servings / **Preparation Time:** 15 minutes / **Cooking Time:** 15 minutes

Ingredients:

- 1 cup quinoa, rinsed
- 2 cups low-sodium vegetable broth or water
- 4 cups kale, finely chopped (stems removed)
- 1 cup cherry tomatoes, halved
- 1/2 cup red bell pepper, diced
- 1/4 cup red onion, finely chopped
- 1/4 cup feta cheese, crumbled (optional)
- 1/4 cup almonds, sliced or slivered
- 1/4 cup dried cranberries (unsweetened)
- 1 tablespoon olive oil
- 2 tablespoons lemon juice
- 1 tablespoon apple cider vinegar
- 1 teaspoon Dijon mustard
- Salt and pepper to taste

Instructions:

1. In a medium saucepan, bring the vegetable broth or water to a boil. Add the rinsed quinoa, reduce the heat to low, cover, and simmer for about 15 minutes, or until the quinoa is cooked and the liquid is absorbed. Remove from heat and let it cool.
2. While the quinoa is cooking, place the chopped kale in a large bowl. Add a drizzle of olive oil and a pinch of salt, then massage the kale with your hands for 2-3 minutes until it softens and becomes a darker green.
3. In a large mixing bowl, combine the cooked quinoa, massaged kale, cherry tomatoes, red bell pepper, red onion, feta cheese (if using), almonds, and dried cranberries.
4. In a small bowl or jar, whisk together the olive oil, lemon juice, apple cider vinegar, Dijon mustard, salt, and pepper until well combined. Pour the dressing over the quinoa and kale mixture and toss to combine, ensuring everything is evenly coated. Serve immediately or refrigerate for 30 minutes to allow the flavors to meld.

Nutritional Information (per serving): Calories: 290 / Protein: 9g / Carbohydrates: 38g / Fats: 12g / Fiber: 6g / Cholesterol: 0mg (with feta: 10mg) / Sodium: 150mg / Potassium: 610mg

Roasted Brussels Sprouts with Balsamic Glaze

Yield: 4 servings / **Preparation Time:** 10 minutes / **Cooking Time:** 25-30 minutes

Ingredients:

- 1 pound Brussels sprouts, trimmed and halved
- 1/4 cup balsamic vinegar
- 2 tablespoons olive oil
- 1/4 teaspoon salt
- 1/4 teaspoon black pepper
- 1 tablespoon honey or maple syrup (optional for added sweetness)
- 1/4 cup sliced almonds (optional for added crunch and nutrition)

Instructions:

1. Preheat oven to 400°F (200°C). Toss halved Brussels sprouts with olive oil, salt, and pepper in a large bowl.
2. Spread Brussels sprouts on a baking sheet. Roast for 20-25 minutes, turning halfway, until golden brown and crispy.
3. In a small saucepan, heat balsamic vinegar over medium heat. Boil, then simmer for 10 minutes until syrupy. Add honey or maple syrup if desired.
4. Transfer roasted Brussels sprouts to a serving dish. Drizzle with balsamic glaze and sprinkle with sliced almonds if using. Serve immediately as a side dish or part of a main course.

Nutritional Information (per serving): Calories: 120 / Protein: 3g / Carbohydrates: 12g / Fats: 7g / Fiber: 4g / Cholesterol: 0mg / Sodium: 160mg / Potassium: 400mg

---

Vegan Coleslaw with Tangy Dressing

Yield: 6 servings / **Preparation Time:** 15 minutes / **Cooking Time:** None

Ingredients:

- 4 cups shredded green cabbage
- 2 cups shredded red cabbage
- 2 large carrots, grated
- 1/2 cup thinly sliced red onion
- 1/2 cup chopped fresh parsley (optional)
- 1/4 cup apple cider vinegar

- 2 tablespoons Dijon mustard
- 2 tablespoons maple syrup
- 3 tablespoons olive oil
- 1/2 teaspoon salt
- 1/4 teaspoon black pepper

Instructions:

1. In a large mixing bowl, combine the shredded green cabbage, shredded red cabbage, grated carrots, and sliced red onion. Add the chopped parsley if using.
2. In a small bowl, whisk together the apple cider vinegar, Dijon mustard, and maple syrup. Slowly drizzle in the olive oil while continuing to whisk until the dressing is well emulsified. Season with salt and black pepper to taste.
3. Pour the tangy dressing over the shredded vegetables. Toss everything together until the vegetables are evenly coated with the dressing. Let the coleslaw sit for at least 10 minutes to allow the flavors to meld. Serve chilled or at room temperature as a side dish.

Nutritional Information (per serving): Calories: 110 / Protein: 2g / Carbohydrates: 10g / Fats: 7g / Fiber: 3g / Cholesterol: 0mg / Sodium: 180mg / Potassium: 250mg

---

Grilled Vegetable Platter with Hummus

Yield: 4 servings / **Preparation Time:** 15 minutes / **Cooking Time:** 15-20 minutes

Ingredients:

- 1 large zucchini, sliced lengthwise
- 1 large yellow squash, sliced lengthwise
- 1 red bell pepper, cut into strips
- 1 yellow bell pepper, cut into strips
- 1 red onion, sliced into rounds
- 1 garlic clove, minced
- 1 cup cherry tomatoes
- 1 can (15 oz) chickpeas, drained and rinsed

- 1/4 cup tahini
- 1 teaspoon dried oregano
- 1 teaspoon dried thyme
- 2 tablespoons olive oil
- 2 tablespoons lemon juice
- 1/2 teaspoon ground cumin
- 1/2 teaspoon paprika (optional)
- Water, as needed for desired consistency

Instructions:
1. Preheat the grill to medium-high heat. In a large bowl, toss the zucchini, yellow squash, bell peppers, red onion, and cherry tomatoes with olive oil, dried oregano, dried thyme, salt, and black pepper.
2. Place the prepared vegetables directly on the grill grates. Grill for 5-7 minutes per side, or until the vegetables are tender and have nice grill marks. Cherry tomatoes may require less time, so monitor them closely.
3. While the vegetables are grilling, prepare the hummus. In a food processor, combine the chickpeas, tahini, olive oil, lemon juice, garlic, cumin, paprika (if using), and salt. Blend until smooth, adding water as necessary to reach the desired consistency. Adjust the seasoning to taste.
4. Arrange the grilled vegetables on a large serving platter. Serve with a generous bowl of hummus in the center.

Nutritional Information (per serving): Calories: 250 / Protein: 6g / Carbohydrates: 20g / Fats: 17g / Fiber: 6g / Cholesterol: 0mg / Sodium: 220mg / Potassium: 500mg

---

Moroccan Carrot Salad

Yield: 4 servings / **Preparation Time:** 15 minutes / **Cooking Time:** 0 minutes

Ingredients:
- 4 large carrots, peeled and grated
- 1/4 cup fresh cilantro, chopped
- 1/4 cup fresh parsley, chopped
- 1/4 cup raisins or currants
- 1/4 cup slivered almonds, toasted
- 1/4 cup freshly squeezed lemon juice
- 2 tablespoons olive oil
- 1 teaspoon ground cumin
- 1 teaspoon ground cinnamon
- 1/2 teaspoon ground coriander
- 1/4 teaspoon ground ginger
- 1/4 teaspoon paprika
- 1/4 teaspoon cayenne pepper (optional, for a bit of heat)
- 1 tablespoon honey or maple syrup (optional, for a touch of sweetness)
- 1 small garlic clove, minced (optional, for added flavor)

Instructions:
1. Peel and grate the carrots using a box grater or food processor.
2. In a large mixing bowl, combine the grated carrots, chopped cilantro, chopped parsley, raisins or currants, and toasted slivered almonds.
3. In a small bowl, whisk together the lemon juice, olive oil, ground cumin, ground cinnamon, ground coriander, ground ginger, paprika, salt, and black pepper. If using, add honey or maple syrup, minced garlic, and cayenne pepper.
4. Pour the dressing over the carrot mixture and toss well to combine, ensuring that all the ingredients are evenly coated with the dressing.
5. Serve immediately or refrigerate for at least 30 minutes to allow the flavors to meld together.

Nutritional Information (per serving): Calories: 180 / Protein: 3g / Carbohydrates: 18g / Fats: 12g / Fiber: 4g / Cholesterol: 0mg / Sodium: 150mg / Potassium: 450mg

Chapter 9: Soups

Incorporating soups into your heart-healthy diet offers numerous benefits that go beyond their comforting and calming effects. Soups are a fantastic way to pack in a variety of vegetables, lean proteins, and whole grains, making them nutrient-dense and satisfying. They can help control portions, manage weight, and ensure you get essential vitamins and minerals while being naturally low in saturated fats and sodium. Enjoy these delicious and nourishing soup recipes to support your cardiovascular health and bring warmth and comfort to your meals.

Vegetable-Based Soups

Vegetable-based soups are fundamental to a heart-healthy diet, providing a flavorful and convenient way to boost your intake of vital nutrients. Packed with vitamins, minerals, and fiber, these soups support cardiovascular health by promoting healthy blood pressure, reducing cholesterol levels, and aiding in weight management. Additionally, they have a beneficial effect on the digestive system, helping to maintain regularity and gut health. Naturally low in calories and saturated fats, vegetable-based soups are an ideal choice for those looking to nourish their heart and enjoy a flavorful, satisfying meal. Dive into these recipes to discover how tasty heart-healthy eating can be!

Classic Minestrone Soup

Yield: 6 servings / **Preparation Time:** 15 minutes / **Cooking Time:** 40 minutes

Ingredients:

- 1 cup whole wheat pasta (such as small shells or elbows)
- 1 (14.5 oz) can diced tomatoes, no salt added
- 1 (15 oz) can cannellini beans, drained and rinsed
- 1 cup water
- 4 cups low-sodium vegetable broth
- 1 medium onion, chopped
- 2 cloves garlic, minced
- 2 medium carrots, diced
- 2 celery stalks, diced
- 1 medium zucchini, diced
- 1 cup green beans, trimmed and cut into 1-inch pieces
- 1 cup baby spinach leaves
- 1 teaspoon dried basil
- 1 teaspoon dried oregano
- 1/2 teaspoon dried thyme
- 1/4 teaspoon red pepper flakes (optional)
- Salt and pepper to taste
- 2 tablespoons fresh parsley, chopped
- 1 tablespoon fresh lemon juice
- 2 tablespoons olive oil
- Optional: 1/4 cup grated Parmesan cheese (for serving)
- Optional: 1 tablespoon balsamic vinegar (for added depth of flavor)

Instructions:

1. Heat olive oil in a large pot over medium heat. Add the chopped onion, minced garlic, diced carrots, and diced celery. Cook for about 5 minutes, until vegetables are tender. Stir in the diced zucchini and green beans. Cook for another 3-4 minutes until they start to soften. Pour in the low-sodium vegetable broth, water, and the can of diced tomatoes. Stir to combine.
2. Add the dried basil, dried oregano, dried thyme, and red pepper flakes (if using). Bring the mixture to a boil.
3. Reduce the heat to low and let the soup simmer for about 15 minutes. Stir in the whole wheat pasta and the cannellini beans. Continue to simmer for another 10 minutes, or until the pasta is al dente.
4. Add the baby spinach leaves and cook for another 2-3 minutes until wilted. Stir in the fresh parsley and lemon juice. Season with salt and pepper to taste. Serve the minestrone soup hot. Optionally, top each bowl with a sprinkle of grated Parmesan cheese and a dash of balsamic vinegar for extra flavor.

Nutritional Information (per serving): Calories: 210 / Protein: 8g / Carbohydrates: 35g / Fats: 6g / Fiber: 8g / Cholesterol: 0mg / Sodium: 300mg / Potassium: 600mg

Roasted Tomato and Basil Soup

Yield: 4 servings / **Preparation Time:** 15 minutes / **Cooking Time:** 45 minutes

Ingredients:

- 2 pounds ripe tomatoes, halved
- 4 cups low-sodium vegetable broth
- 1/2 cup fresh basil leaves, packed
- 1 medium onion, quartered
- 4 cloves garlic, peeled
- 2 tablespoons olive oil
- 1 tablespoon balsamic vinegar
- 1 teaspoon dried oregano
- 1/2 teaspoon red pepper flakes (optional)
- salt and pepper to taste
- 1/4 cup plain Greek yogurt (optional, for creaminess)
- 1/4 cup grated Parmesan cheese (optional for serving)
- Optional for garnish: 1 tablespoon fresh thyme leaves
- Optional for garnish: 1 tablespoon chopped fresh parsley

Instructions:

1. Preheat your oven to 400°F (200°C). Place the halved tomatoes, quartered onion, and garlic cloves on a baking sheet. Drizzle with olive oil and season with salt and pepper. Toss to coat evenly.
2. Roast in the preheated oven for 30-35 minutes, until the tomatoes are soft and slightly caramelized. Transfer the roasted tomatoes, onion, and garlic to a blender. Add the fresh basil leaves and blend until smooth.
3. Pour the blended mixture into a large pot. Add the low-sodium vegetable broth, balsamic vinegar, dried oregano, and red pepper flakes (if using). Stir to combine. Bring the mixture to a boil, then reduce the heat and simmer for 10 minutes. For a creamy texture, stir in the plain Greek yogurt and blend again until smooth.
4. Taste and adjust the seasoning with additional salt and pepper if needed. Ladle the soup into bowls. Optionally, top each serving with a sprinkle of grated Parmesan cheese, fresh thyme leaves, and chopped fresh parsley.

Nutritional Information (per serving): Calories: 140 / Protein: 4g / Carbohydrates: 18g / Fats: 7g / Fiber: 4g / Cholesterol: 0mg / Sodium: 280mg / Potassium: 600mg

Creamy Broccoli Soup (Without Cream)

Yield: 4 servings / **Preparation Time:** 10 minutes / **Cooking Time:** 25 minutes

Ingredients:

- 4 cups broccoli florets (about 2 heads of broccoli)
- 1 large potato, peeled and diced
- 4 cups low-sodium vegetable broth
- 1 cup unsweetened almond milk (or other plant-based milk)
- 1/4 cup nutritional yeast (optional for a cheesy flavor)
- 1 tablespoon olive oil
- 1 medium onion, chopped
- 2 cloves garlic, minced
- 1 teaspoon dried thyme
- 1/2 teaspoon ground nutmeg (optional for added flavor)
- Salt and pepper to taste

Instructions:

1. Chop onion and mince garlic. Cut broccoli into florets and dice the potato.
2. Heat olive oil in a large pot over medium heat. Cook onion until soft, about 5 minutes. Add garlic and cook for 2 minutes.
3. Add broccoli and potato to the pot. Stir, then pour in vegetable broth. Bring to a boil, reduce to a simmer, and cook until tender, about 15 minutes.

4. Puree the soup with an immersion blender or in batches in a regular blender. Stir in almond milk and thyme. Heat through without boiling. Season with salt, pepper, and lemon juice. Add nutmeg and nutritional yeast for extra flavor, if desired.
5. Adjust thickness with more broth or almond milk. Serve in bowls and garnish with fresh herbs if desired.

Nutritional Information (per serving): Calories: 150 / Protein: 5g / Carbohydrates: 22g / Fats: 5g / Fiber: 6g / Cholesterol: 0mg / Sodium: 180mg / Potassium: 650mg

---

Pumpkin Zucchini Ginger Cream Soup

Yield: 4 servings / **Preparation Time:** 10 minutes / **Cooking Time:** 25 minutes

Ingredients:

- 2 cups pumpkin, peeled and diced
- 1 cup zucchini, diced
- 4 cups water
- 1 cup unsweetened almond milk (or other plant-based milk)
- 2 tablespoons olive oil
- 1 medium onion, chopped
- 2 cloves garlic, minced
- 1 tablespoon fresh ginger, grated
- 1 teaspoon ground cumin
- 1/2 teaspoon ground cinnamon
- Salt and pepper to taste

Instructions:

1. Chop onion, mince garlic, grate ginger, and dice pumpkin and zucchini.
2. Heat olive oil in a large pot over medium heat. Cook onion for 5 minutes until soft. Add garlic and ginger, cook for 2 minutes. Add pumpkin and zucchini, stir to combine.
3. Add water and bring to a boil. Reduce heat and simmer for 15 minutes until tender.
4. Puree the soup with an immersion blender or in batches in a regular blender.
5. Stir in almond milk, cumin, and cinnamon. Heat through without boiling. Season with salt and pepper, adjusting thickness with more water or almond milk if needed. Serve in bowls, garnished with cilantro or parsley if desired.

Nutritional Information (per serving): Calories: 110 / Protein: 2g / Carbohydrates: 18g / Fats: 4g / Fiber: 3g / Cholesterol: 0mg / Sodium: 120mg / Potassium: 580mg

---

Carrot and Ginger Soup

Yield: 4 servings / **Preparation Time:** 15 minutes / **Cooking Time:** 30 minutes

Ingredients:

- 1 lb. carrots, peeled and sliced
- 1 tablespoon fresh ginger, grated
- 4 cups low-sodium vegetable broth
- 1/4 cup light coconut milk (optional for creaminess)
- 1 medium onion, chopped
- 2 cloves garlic, minced
- 1 tablespoon olive oil
- 1 tablespoon lemon juice (optional for added flavor)
- 1/2 teaspoon ground turmeric
- Salt and pepper to taste
- 1 teaspoon ground cumin
- 1/2 teaspoon ground coriander

Instructions:

1. Chop onion, mince garlic, grate ginger, and slice carrots. Heat olive oil in a large pot over medium heat. Cook onion for 5 minutes until soft. Add garlic and ginger, cook for 2 minutes.

2. Add carrots and optional spices (turmeric, cumin, coriander). Cook for 2-3 minutes. Add vegetable broth, bring to a boil, then simmer for 20 minutes until carrots are tender.
3. Puree soup with an immersion blender or in batches in a regular blender. Stir in light coconut milk if desired and heat through without boiling. Adjust seasoning with salt, pepper, and lemon juice if using. Serve in bowls, garnished with cilantro if desired.

Nutritional Information (per serving): Calories: 120 / Protein: 2g / Carbohydrates: 18g / Fats: 5g / Fiber: 4g / Cholesterol: 0mg / Sodium: 150mg / Potassium: 500mg

Protein-Rich Soups

Protein-rich soups are a vital addition to a heart-healthy diet, offering a delicious and satisfying way to meet your daily protein needs. Perfect for both lunches and dinners, these soups provide essential amino acids that support muscle maintenance, boost metabolism, and keep you feeling full longer. Incorporating protein-rich soups into your meals can help stabilize blood sugar levels, promote healthy weight management, and support cardiovascular health. Explore this subchapter to discover a variety of flavorful, nutritious soup recipes that will keep your heart and body strong.

Chicken and Vegetable Soup

Yield: 6 servings / **Preparation Time:** 15 minutes / **Cooking Time:** 30 minutes

Ingredients:
- 1 lb. boneless, skinless chicken breast, cut into bite-sized pieces
- 6 cups low-sodium chicken broth
- 2 medium carrots, diced
- 2 celery stalks, diced
- 1 medium zucchini, diced
- 1 medium onion, chopped
- 2 cloves garlic, minced
- 1 cup green beans, chopped
- 1 cup baby spinach leaves
- 1 tablespoon olive oil
- 1 teaspoon dried thyme
- 1 teaspoon dried oregano
- 1 bay leaf; salt and pepper to taste
- Fresh parsley, chopped (optional, for garnish)

Instructions:
1. Chop the onion, mince the garlic, and dice the carrots, celery, zucchini, and green beans. Cut the chicken breast into bite-sized pieces.
2. In a large pot, heat the olive oil over medium heat. Add the chopped onion and cook until soft and translucent, about 5 minutes. Add the minced garlic and cook for another 2 minutes until fragrant. Add the diced carrots, celery, zucchini, and green beans to the pot. Stir to combine with the aromatics and cook for 5 minutes until slightly softened.
3. Add the chicken pieces to the pot and cook until they are no longer pink, about 5 minutes. Pour in the low-sodium chicken broth and bring the mixture to a boil.
4. Add the dried thyme, dried oregano, and bay leaf. Reduce the heat to a simmer and cook for 20 minutes until the vegetables are tender and the chicken is cooked through. Stir in the baby spinach leaves and cook for another 2 minutes until wilted.
5. Season the soup with salt and pepper to taste. Remove the bay leaf before serving. Ladle the soup into bowls and garnish with fresh parsley if desired.

Nutritional Information (per serving): Calories: 190 / Protein: 22g / Carbohydrates: 15g / Fats: 6g / Fiber: 3g / Cholesterol: 55mg / Sodium: 250mg / Potassium: 700mg

Lentil and Spinach Soup

Yield: 6 servings / **Preparation Time:** 15 minutes / **Cooking Time:** 30 minutes

Ingredients:

- 1 cup dried green or brown lentils, rinsed
- 2 cups fresh spinach leaves
- 6 cups low-sodium vegetable broth
- 2 medium carrots, diced
- 2 celery stalks, diced
- 1 medium onion, chopped
- 2 cloves garlic, minced
- 1 can (14.5 oz) diced tomatoes, no added salt
- 1 tablespoon olive oil
- 1 teaspoon ground cumin
- 1 teaspoon paprika
- 1/2 teaspoon dried thyme
- 1 bay leaf
- Salt and black pepper to taste
- Fresh parsley, chopped (optional, for garnish)

Instructions:

1. Chop onion, mince garlic, dice carrots and celery. Rinse lentils.
2. Heat olive oil in a large pot over medium heat. Cook onion for 5 minutes until soft. Add garlic and cook for 1-2 minutes. Add carrots and celery, stir and cook for 5 minutes until softened.
3. Stir in lentils, vegetable broth, diced tomatoes, cumin, paprika, thyme, and bay leaf. Bring to a boil.
4. Reduce heat, cover, and simmer for 25 minutes until lentils and vegetables are tender.
5. Remove bay leaf, stir in spinach, and cook for 2 minutes until wilted. Season with salt, pepper, and lemon juice if using. Serve and garnish with parsley if desired.

Nutritional Information (per serving): Calories: 180 / Protein: 10g / Carbohydrates: 30g / Fats: 4g / Fiber: 10g / Cholesterol: 0mg / Sodium: 290mg / Potassium: 700mg

Seafood Stew with Tomatoes and Herbs

Yield: 4 servings / **Preparation Time:** 20 minutes / **Cooking Time:** 40 minutes

Ingredients:

- 1 lb. mixed seafood (shrimp, scallops, and firm white cod or halibut)
- 4 cups low-sodium vegetable broth
- 1 cup cherry tomatoes, halved
- 1 red bell pepper, diced
- 1 yellow bell pepper, diced
- 1 zucchini, sliced
- 1 medium onion, chopped
- 2 cloves garlic, minced
- 1 can (14.5 oz) diced tomatoes; no salt added
- 1 cup green beans, trimmed and cut into 1-inch pieces
- 1 tablespoon olive oil
- 1/2 teaspoon dried thyme
- 1/2 teaspoon dried oregano
- 1/2 teaspoon dried basil
- 1/4 teaspoon black pepper
- Juice of 1 lemon

Instructions:

1. Chop onion, mince garlic, dice bell peppers, slice zucchini, and halve cherry tomatoes.
2. Heat olive oil in a large pot over medium heat. Cook onion for 5 minutes until softened.
3. Add garlic and cook for 1-2 minutes. Add diced tomatoes, cherry tomatoes, bell peppers, zucchini, and green beans. Cook for 5 minutes.
4. Pour in vegetable broth, add thyme, oregano, basil, and black pepper. Bring to a boil, then simmer for 20 minutes. Add mixed seafood and cook for 5-7 minutes until opaque.
5. Stir in lemon juice, adjust seasoning, and serve in bowls garnished with parsley.

Nutritional Information (per serving): Calories: 280 / Protein: 28g / Carbohydrates: 20g / Fats: 8g / Fiber: 5g / Cholesterol: 110mg / Sodium: 420mg / Potassium: 900mg

---

Chicken Tortilla Soup

Yield: 6 servings / **Preparation Time:** 15 minutes / **Cooking Time:** 30 minutes

Ingredients:

- 2 cups cooked, shredded chicken breast
- 4 cups homemade chicken broth
- 1 can (14.5 oz) no-salt-added diced tomatoes
- 1 can (14.5 oz) black beans, rinsed and drained
- 1 cup frozen corn
- 1/4 cup fresh cilantro, chopped
- 1 medium onion, diced
- 2 cloves garlic, minced
- 1 jalapeño, seeded and diced
- 1 teaspoon ground cumin
- 1 teaspoon chili powder
- 1/2 teaspoon smoked paprika
- Salt and pepper to taste
- 1 tablespoon olive oil
- 1 lime, juiced
- Optional for garnish: baked tortilla strips
- Optional for garnish: diced avocado
- Optional for garnish: sliced radishes
- Optional for garnish: fresh cilantro leaves
- Optional for garnish: lime wedges

Instructions:

1. Heat olive oil in a large pot over medium heat. Add diced onion and cook until softened, about 5 minutes. Add minced garlic and diced jalapeño, cooking for an additional 1-2 minutes until fragrant.
2. Stir in ground cumin, chili powder, and smoked paprika, cooking for another minute to toast the spices.
3. Pour in the low-sodium chicken broth, diced tomatoes, black beans, and corn. Bring the mixture to a boil, then reduce heat and simmer for 15 minutes. Stir in the shredded chicken breast and cook until heated through, about 5 minutes. Add lime juice and chopped cilantro. Season with salt and pepper to taste.
4. Ladle the soup into bowls and garnish with optional toppings like baked tortilla strips, diced avocado, sliced radishes, fresh cilantro leaves, and lime wedges.

Nutritional Information (per serving): Calories: 220 / Protein: 18g / Carbohydrates: 24g / Fats: 6g / Fiber: 7g / Cholesterol: 40mg / Sodium: 380mg / Potassium: 550mg

---

Turkey and White Bean Chili

Yield: 6 servings / **Preparation Time:** 15 minutes / **Cooking Time:** 45 minutes

Ingredients:

- 1 pound ground turkey (lean)
- 2 cups low-sodium chicken broth
- 1 can (15 oz) white beans, drained and rinsed
- 1 can (15 oz) diced tomatoes, no added salt
- 1 can (6 oz) tomato paste, no added salt
- 1 cup corn kernels (fresh or frozen)
- 1 medium onion, chopped
- 2 cloves garlic, minced
- 1 red bell pepper, diced
- 1 green bell pepper, diced
- 1 tablespoon olive oil
- 1 teaspoon ground cumin
- 1 teaspoon chili powder
- 1/2 teaspoon paprika
- 1/2 teaspoon dried oregano
- 1/2 teaspoon black pepper
- 1/4 teaspoon cayenne pepper (optional for heat)
- Juice of 1 lime; fresh cilantro, chopped (optional, for garnish)

Instructions:

1. Chop the onion, mince the garlic, and dice the bell peppers.
2. In a large pot, heat the olive oil over medium heat. Add the chopped onion and cook until soft and translucent, about 5 minutes. Add the minced garlic and cook for another 1-2 minutes until fragrant. Add the ground turkey to the pot. Cook until browned and no longer pink, breaking it up with a spoon as it cooks, about 5-7 minutes.
3. Stir in the diced bell peppers, cumin, chili powder, paprika, oregano, black pepper, and cayenne pepper (if using). Cook for another 3-4 minutes until the vegetables start to soften.
4. Add the white beans, diced tomatoes, tomato paste, and low-sodium chicken broth. Stir to combine. Bring the chili to a boil, then reduce the heat to low and let it simmer for 30 minutes, stirring occasionally.
5. Stir in the corn kernels and lime juice. Cook for another 5 minutes until the corn is heated through.
6. Ladle the chili into bowls and garnish with fresh chopped cilantro if desired.

Nutritional Information (per serving): Calories: 220 / Protein: 25g / Carbohydrates: 25g / Fats: 5g / Fiber: 6g / Cholesterol: 50mg / Sodium: 320mg / Potassium: 700mg

Grain and Legume Soups

Grain and legume soups are an excellent choice for those seeking to combine a heart-healthy diet with stomach-calming meal solutions. These soups provide a perfect blend of fiber, protein, and essential nutrients, helping to regulate cholesterol levels, stabilize blood sugar, and support digestive health. By incorporating wholesome grains and legumes, you'll enjoy hearty, satisfying meals that nourish your body and promote cardiovascular well-being. Dive into this subchapter to discover delicious and nutritious soup recipes that will keep your heart and taste buds happy.

Bulgur Wheat and Tomato Soup

Yield: 6 servings / **Preparation Time:** 10 minutes / **Cooking Time:** 25 minutes

Ingredients:

- 3/4 cup bulgur wheat, rinsed
- 4 cups low-sodium vegetable broth
- 1 can (14.5 oz) no-salt-added diced tomatoes
- 1 medium onion, diced
- 2 cloves garlic, minced
- 1 carrot, diced
- 1 celery stalk, diced
- 1 teaspoon ground cumin
- 1/2 teaspoon smoked paprika
- 1 teaspoon dried oregano
- 1/2 teaspoon dried thyme
- 1 tablespoon olive oil
- 1/4 cup fresh parsley, chopped (optional)
- Salt and pepper to taste

Instructions:

1. Heat olive oil in a large pot over medium heat. Add the diced onion, carrot, and celery. Cook until softened, about 5 minutes. Add the minced garlic and cook for an additional 1-2 minutes until fragrant.
2. Stir in the ground cumin and smoked paprika, cooking for another minute to toast the spices.
3. Pour in the low-sodium vegetable broth and diced tomatoes. Bring to a boil.
4. Add the rinsed bulgur wheat, dried oregano, and dried thyme. Reduce the heat and simmer for 15-20 minutes, or until the bulgur is tender.
5. Season with salt and pepper to taste. Stir in fresh parsley, if using. Ladle the soup into bowls and serve hot.

Nutritional Information (per serving): Calories: 160 / Protein: 4g / Carbohydrates: 26g / Fats: 5g / Fiber: 5g / Cholesterol: 0mg / Sodium: 220mg / Potassium: 460mg

Farro and White Bean Soup

Yield: 6 servings / **Preparation Time:** 10 minutes / **Cooking Time:** 40 minutes

Ingredients:

- 1 can (15 oz) no-salt-added white beans, drained and rinsed
- 1 can (14.5 oz) no-salt-added diced tomatoes
- 1 cup farro, rinsed
- 6 cups low-sodium vegetable broth
- 2 cups fresh spinach, chopped
- 1 medium onion, diced
- 2 cloves garlic, minced
- 2 medium carrots, diced
- 2 celery stalks, diced
- 1 teaspoon dried thyme
- 1 teaspoon dried oregano
- 1 bay leaf; salt and pepper to taste
- 1 tablespoon olive oil

Instructions:

1. Heat olive oil in a large pot over medium heat. Cook diced onion, carrots, and celery for 5 minutes. Add minced garlic and cook for 1-2 minutes.
2. Stir in thyme and oregano for 1 minute. Add rinsed farro and combine with vegetables and spices.
3. Pour in vegetable broth and diced tomatoes. Add bay leaf and bring to a boil. Simmer for 20-25 minutes until farro is tender.
4. Add white beans and chopped spinach. Simmer for 5-10 minutes until spinach is wilted and beans are heated. Remove bay leaf. Season with salt, pepper. Serve hot.

Nutritional Information (per serving): Calories: 220 / Protein: 8g / Carbohydrates: 38g / Fats: 4g / Fiber: 8g / Cholesterol: 0mg / Sodium: 220mg / Potassium: 500mg

Wild Rice and Vegetable Soup

Yield: 6 servings / **Preparation Time:** 15 minutes / **Cooking Time:** 45 minutes

Ingredients:

- 1 cup wild rice, rinsed
- 6 cups low-sodium vegetable broth
- 1 cup mushrooms, sliced
- 1 can (14.5 oz) no-salt-added diced tomatoes
- 2 cups fresh spinach, chopped
- 1 medium onion, diced
- 2 cloves garlic, minced
- 2 medium carrots, diced
- 2 celery stalks, diced
- 1 red bell pepper, diced
- 1 zucchini, diced
- 1 teaspoon dried thyme
- 1 teaspoon dried oregano
- 1 bay leaf
- Salt and pepper to taste
- 2 tablespoons olive oil

Instructions:

1. Boil 4 cups of water in a medium pot. Add rinsed wild rice, simmer for 35-40 minutes until tender. Drain and set aside.
2. Heat olive oil in a large pot over medium heat. Cook diced onion, carrots, and celery for 5 minutes. Add minced garlic and cook for 1-2 minutes. Add red bell pepper, zucchini, and mushrooms. Cook for 5 minutes until tender.
3. Pour in vegetable broth and diced tomatoes. Add thyme, oregano, and bay leaf. Bring to a boil, then simmer for 15-20 minutes. Add cooked wild rice and chopped spinach. Cook for 5 minutes until spinach is wilted. Remove bay leaf, season with salt and pepper. Serve hot.

Nutritional Information (per serving): Calories: 200 / Protein: 6g / Carbohydrates: 36g / Fats: 5g / Fiber: 6g / Cholesterol: 0mg / Sodium: 220mg / Potassium: 600mg

Quinoa and Kale Soup

Yield: 6 servings / **Preparation Time:** 15 minutes / **Cooking Time:** 30 minutes

Ingredients:
- 1 cup quinoa, rinsed
- 4 cups chopped kale; stems removed
- 6 cups low-sodium vegetable broth
- 1 can (14.5 oz) diced tomatoes; no salt added
- 1 medium onion, diced
- 3 cloves garlic, minced
- 2 medium carrots, diced
- 2 celery stalks, diced
- 1 teaspoon dried thyme
- 1 teaspoon dried oregano
- 1 bay leaf
- Salt and pepper to taste
- 1 tablespoon olive oil
- 1/4 cup fresh parsley, chopped (optional)

Instructions:
1. Heat olive oil in a large pot over medium heat. Cook diced onion, carrots, and celery for 5-7 minutes. Add minced garlic and cook for 1-2 minutes. Stir in rinsed quinoa.
2. Add vegetable broth, diced tomatoes, thyme, oregano, and bay leaf. Bring to a boil, then simmer for 15-20 minutes until quinoa is tender.
3. Add chopped kale and cook for 5 minutes until wilted. Remove bay leaf. Season with salt, pepper, and parsley if desired. Serve hot.

Nutritional Information (per serving): Calories: 180 / Protein: 6g / Carbohydrates: 32g / Fats: 3g / Fiber: 5g / Cholesterol: 0mg / Sodium: 150mg / Potassium: 500mg

Barley and Mushroom Soup

Yield: 6 servings / **Preparation Time:** 15 minutes / **Cooking Time:** 45 minutes

Ingredients:
- 8 oz mushrooms, sliced (such as cremini or button mushrooms)
- 6 cups low-sodium vegetable broth
- 1 cup pearl barley, rinsed
- 1 medium onion, diced
- 3 cloves garlic, minced
- 2 medium carrots, diced
- 2 celery stalks, diced
- 1 teaspoon dried thyme
- 1 teaspoon dried oregano
- 1 bay leaf
- Salt and pepper to taste
- 2 tablespoons olive oil
- 2 cups fresh spinach, chopped (optional)
- 1/4 cup fresh parsley, chopped (optional)

Instructions:
1. Boil 4 cups of water in a medium pot. Add rinsed barley, simmer for 30-35 minutes until tender. Drain and set aside.
2. Heat olive oil in a large pot over medium heat. Cook diced onion, carrots, and celery for 5 minutes. Add minced garlic and cook for 1-2 minutes.
3. Stir in sliced mushrooms and cook for 5-7 minutes until browned. Pour in vegetable broth. Add thyme, oregano, and bay leaf. Bring to a boil, then simmer for 15-20 minutes.
4. Add cooked barley to the pot. Stir in chopped spinach and cook for 5 minutes until wilted. Remove bay leaf. Season with salt, pepper, and parsley if desired. Serve hot.

Nutritional Information (per serving): Calories: 220 / Protein: 6g / Carbohydrates: 38g / Fats: 5g / Fiber: 7g / Cholesterol: 0mg / Sodium: 200mg / Potassium: 550mg

Chapter 10: Desserts

Embarking on a heart-healthy diet doesn't mean you have to exclude sweets from your life. In fact, making the right choices when it comes to desserts can be both delicious and beneficial for your cardiovascular health. Well-balanced desserts, crafted with wholesome ingredients, can satisfy your sweet tooth while providing essential nutrients and promoting overall well-being. In this chapter, you'll discover delightful recipes that allow you to indulge mindfully, proving that heart-healthy eating can be both enjoyable and nourishing. Dive in and explore these tasty treats designed to support your heart health.

Guilt-Free Desserts for Heart Health

Who says desserts have to be a guilty pleasure? In this subchapter, you'll find the best-balanced dessert recipes that not only satisfy your sweet cravings but also support your heart health. Discover how you can indulge without compromising your well-being. Dive into these delicious, guilt-free treats and enjoy desserts that are as good for your heart as they are for your taste buds.

Almond Flour Brownies

Yield: 12 servings / **Preparation Time:** 10 minutes / **Cooking Time:** 25-30 minutes

Ingredients:
- 1 cup almond flour
- 1/4 cup unsweetened cocoa powder
- 2 large eggs
- 1/2 teaspoon baking powder
- 1/4 teaspoon salt
- 1/2 cup dark chocolate chips or chopped dark chocolate (70% cocoa or higher)
- 1/3 cup coconut oil or olive oil
- 1/4 cup honey or pure maple syrup
- 1 teaspoon vanilla extract
- 1/4 cup chopped walnuts or almonds (optional, for added texture and nutritional benefits)

Instructions:
1. Preheat your oven to 350°F (175°C). Line an 8x8-inch baking pan with parchment paper or lightly grease it.
2. In a medium bowl, whisk together the almond flour, unsweetened cocoa powder, baking powder, and salt until well combined.
3. In a small saucepan over low heat, melt the dark chocolate and coconut oil together, stirring until smooth. Remove from heat and let cool slightly.
4. In a large bowl, whisk together the eggs, honey (or maple syrup), and vanilla extract until well combined.
5. Gradually add the melted chocolate mixture to the wet ingredients, stirring continuously to prevent the eggs from cooking. Add the dry ingredients to the wet mixture and stir until just combined.
6. If using, fold in the chopped walnuts or almonds. Pour the batter into the prepared baking pan, spreading it evenly.
7. Bake in the preheated oven for 25-30 minutes, or until a toothpick inserted into the center comes out clean or with a few moist crumbs.
8. Allow the brownies to cool completely in the pan on a wire rack before cutting into squares.

Nutritional Information (per serving): Calories: 170 / Protein: 4g / Carbohydrates: 17g / Fats: 11g / Fiber: 3g / Cholesterol: 30mg / Sodium: 60mg / Potassium: 160mg

Dark Chocolate Avocado Mousse

Yield: 4 servings / **Preparation Time:** 10 minutes / **Cooking (or Setting) Time:** 30 minutes (chilling time)

Ingredients:
- 2 ripe avocados
- 1/4 cup unsweetened cocoa powder
- 1/4 cup dark chocolate chips, melted and slightly cooled
- 1/4 cup maple syrup or honey
- 1/4 cup unsweetened almond milk
- 1 teaspoon vanilla extract
- A pinch of salt
- 1 tablespoon chia seeds (for extra fiber) - optional
- Fresh berries for garnish (optional for extra nutritional benefits)

Instructions:
1. Slice the avocados in half, remove the pits, and scoop the flesh into a blender or food processor.
2. Melt the dark chocolate chips in a microwave or a double boiler until smooth. Allow to cool slightly.
3. Add the avocado, cocoa powder, melted dark chocolate, maple syrup (or honey), almond milk, vanilla extract, and a pinch of salt to the blender. Blend all the ingredients until smooth and creamy.
4. You may need to scrape down the sides of the blender to ensure everything is well combined.
5. Spoon the mousse into individual serving dishes or ramekins. Refrigerate for at least 30 minutes to allow the flavors to meld and the mousse to firm up. Garnish with fresh berries and a few chia seeds if desired. Serve chilled.

Nutritional Information (per serving): Calories: 210 / Protein: 3g / Carbohydrates: 22g / Fats: 14g / Fiber: 7g / Cholesterol: 0mg / Sodium: 20mg / Potassium: 500mg

---

Baked Apples with Cinnamon

Yield: 4 servings / **Preparation Time:** 10 minutes / **Cooking Time:** 25-30 minutes

Ingredients:
- 4 medium apples (such as Honeycrisp, Granny Smith, or Fuji)
- 1/4 cup rolled oats
- 1 tablespoon raisins (optional)
- 1 teaspoon ground cinnamon
- 1/4 teaspoon ground nutmeg
- 1 tablespoon honey or maple syrup
- 1 tablespoon unsweetened applesauce or water
- 2 tablespoons chopped walnuts or pecans (optional for added nutritional benefits)

Instructions:
1. Preheat your oven to 350°F (175°C). Core the apples using an apple corer or a paring knife, ensuring to remove all the seeds and create a hollow center while leaving the bottom intact.
2. In a small bowl, combine the rolled oats, chopped walnuts or pecans (if using), raisins (if using), ground cinnamon, ground nutmeg, honey or maple syrup, and unsweetened applesauce or water. Mix well until combined. Evenly divide the filling mixture among the cored apples, pressing it into the center of each apple.
3. Place the stuffed apples in a baking dish and cover with aluminum foil. Bake in the preheated oven for 25-30 minutes, or until the apples are tender and the filling is golden brown. Allow the apples to cool slightly before serving. They can be enjoyed warm or at room temperature.

Nutritional Information (per serving): Calories: 120 / Protein: 1.5g / Carbohydrates: 28g / Fats: 2.5g / Fiber: 4g / Cholesterol: 0mg / Sodium: 0mg / Potassium: 200mg

Mango Sorbet

Yield: 4 servings / **Preparation Time:** 10 minutes / **Freezing Time:** 4 hours

Ingredients:
- 4 ripe mangoes (about 4 cups of mango chunks)
- 1/4 cup fresh lime juice (about 2 limes)
- 1/2 cup water
- 1/4 cup honey or agave syrup (optional, for added sweetness)

Instructions:
1. Peel the mangoes and cut the flesh away from the pit. Chop the mango flesh into chunks.
2. In a blender or food processor, combine the mango chunks, lime juice, honey or agave syrup (if using), and water. Blend until smooth and creamy. If desired, strain the mixture through a fine-mesh sieve to remove any fibrous bits for a smoother texture.
3. Pour the mango mixture into a shallow, freezer-safe container. Cover and freeze for about 4 hours, or until the sorbet is firm. For a smoother consistency, you can break up the frozen sorbet into chunks and blend it again until smooth. Return to the container and freeze until firm. Scoop the sorbet into bowls or cones and enjoy!

Nutritional Information (per serving): Calories: 110 / Protein: 1g / Carbohydrates: 28g / Fats: 0g / Fiber: 3g / Cholesterol: 0mg / Sodium: 2mg / Potassium: 180mg

Chilled Citrus Fruit Salad

Yield: 4 servings / **Preparation Time:** 15 minutes / **Chilling Time:** 1 hour

Ingredients:
- 2 large oranges, peeled and segmented
- 2 large grapefruits, peeled and segmented
- 2 kiwis, peeled and sliced
- 1 cup strawberries, hulled and sliced
- 1 cup pineapple chunks
- 1/4 cup fresh mint leaves, chopped
- 1 tablespoon lime juice
- 1 tablespoon lemon juice
- 2 tablespoons honey (optional, for added sweetness)

Instructions:
1. Peel and segment the oranges and grapefruits, ensuring all pith is removed. Peel and slice the kiwis. Hull and slice the strawberries. Cut the pineapple into chunks.
2. In a large bowl, combine the orange segments, grapefruit segments, kiwi slices, strawberry slices, and pineapple chunks. In a small bowl, mix the lime juice, lemon juice, and honey (if using) until well combined. Pour the dressing over the fruit mixture. Gently toss to coat all the fruit with the dressing. Sprinkle the chopped mint leaves over the fruit salad and give it a gentle toss.
3. Cover the bowl with plastic wrap and refrigerate for at least 1 hour before serving to allow the flavors to meld.

Nutritional Information (per serving): Calories: 120 / Protein: 1.5g / Carbohydrates: 30g / Fats: 0.5g / Fiber: 5g / Cholesterol: 0mg / Sodium: 10mg / Potassium: 350mg

Nutrient-Dense Desserts

In this subchapter, we present a collection of nutrient-dense desserts that are both delicious and heart-friendly. These recipes are designed to satisfy your sweet tooth while providing essential nutrients that support cardiovascular well-being. Packed with wholesome ingredients, these treats ensure you enjoy your desserts guilt-free, knowing you're making choices that benefit your heart. Dive in and discover how delightful and nutritious desserts can go hand in hand.

Blueberry Almond Tart

Yield: 8 servings / **Preparation Time:** 20 minutes / **Cooking Time:** 30 minutes

Ingredients:
- 1 cup almond flour
- 1/2 cup rolled oats
- 2 tablespoons coconut oil, melted
- 2 tablespoons honey or maple syrup
- 2 cups fresh blueberries
- 1/4 cup sliced almonds
- 2 tablespoons cornstarch
- 1 teaspoon lemon zest
- 1 teaspoon vanilla extract
- 1/4 teaspoon salt

Instructions:
1. Preheat your oven to 350°F (175°C). In a food processor, combine almond flour, rolled oats, melted coconut oil, honey or maple syrup, and salt. Pulse until the mixture is well combined and holds together when pressed.
2. Press the mixture evenly into the bottom of a tart pan. Bake for 10-12 minutes or until lightly golden. Remove from the oven and let it cool.
3. In a medium saucepan, combine the blueberries, honey or maple syrup, cornstarch, lemon zest, and vanilla extract. Cook over medium heat, stirring constantly, until the mixture thickens, and the blueberries start to burst, about 5-7 minutes. Remove from heat and let it cool slightly.
4. Pour the blueberry filling into the cooled crust. Sprinkle sliced almonds over the top. Drizzle with honey or maple syrup. Bake the tart for 20 minutes or until the almonds are lightly toasted. Remove from the oven and let it cool completely before serving.

Nutritional Information (per serving): Calories: 180 / Protein: 3g / Carbohydrates: 22g / Fats: 10g / Fiber: 3g / Cholesterol: 0mg / Sodium: 40mg / Potassium: 80mg

---

Mixed Berry Crumble

Yield: 8 servings / **Preparation Time:** 15 minutes / **Cooking Time:** 30 minutes

Ingredients:
- 2 cups fresh or frozen mixed berries (e.g., strawberries, blueberries, raspberries)
- 1/4 cup chopped almonds
- 1/2 cup almond flour
- 1 cup rolled oats
- 1/4 cup coconut oil, melted
- 2 tablespoons honey or maple syrup
- 1 tablespoon lemon juice
- 1 tablespoon cornstarch
- 1 teaspoon ground cinnamon
- 1/4 teaspoon salt

Instructions:

1. Preheat your oven to 350°F (175°C). In a large bowl, combine the mixed berries, honey or maple syrup, lemon juice, and cornstarch. Mix well until the berries are evenly coated.
2. Transfer the berry mixture to a baking dish and spread it out evenly. In another bowl, combine the rolled oats, almond flour, chopped almonds, melted coconut oil, honey or maple syrup, ground cinnamon, and salt.
3. Mix until the ingredients are well combined and form a crumbly texture.
4. Sprinkle the crumble topping evenly over the berry mixture in the baking dish.
5. Bake in the preheated oven for 25-30 minutes or until the topping is golden brown and the berries are bubbly.
6. Allow the crumble to cool slightly before serving. Serve warm, optionally with a dollop of Greek yogurt or a scoop of low-fat ice cream.

Nutritional Information (per serving): Calories: 220 / Protein: 3g / Carbohydrates: 30g / Fats: 11g / Fiber: 5g / Cholesterol: 0mg / Sodium: 50mg / Potassium: 150mg

---

Pineapple Coconut Bars

Yield: 16 servings / **Preparation Time:** 15 minutes / **Cooking Time:** 25 minutes

Ingredients:

- 1 cup almond flour
- 1/2 cup rolled oats
- 1/4 cup coconut oil, melted
- 2 cups fresh or canned pineapple chunks (drained if using canned)
- 1/4 cup unsweetened shredded coconut
- 2 tablespoons honey or maple syrup
- 2 tablespoons chia seeds
- 1 teaspoon lemon juice
- 1/2 teaspoon vanilla extract
- 1/4 teaspoon salt
- 1/4 ground cinnamon (optional for added flavor)

Instructions:

1. Preheat your oven to 350°F (175°C). Line an 8x8 inch baking dish with parchment paper.
2. In a medium bowl, combine almond flour, rolled oats, melted coconut oil, honey or maple syrup, vanilla extract, and salt. Mix until well combined.
3. Press the mixture firmly into the bottom of the prepared baking dish to form an even layer. Bake in the preheated oven for 10 minutes or until lightly golden.
4. Remove from the oven and let it cool slightly while preparing the pineapple layer.
5. In a food processor, blend the pineapple chunks until smooth. Add the unsweetened shredded coconut, chia seeds, honey or maple syrup (if using), and lemon juice. Blend until well combined and thickened slightly.
6. Spread the pineapple mixture evenly over the baked base layer. Sprinkle the 1/4 cup of shredded coconut evenly over the top.
7. Return to the oven and bake for an additional 15 minutes or until the topping is lightly toasted and the filling is set. Allow the bars to cool completely in the baking dish.
8. Once cooled, remove from the dish and cut into 16 squares.

Nutritional Information (per serving): Calories: 140 / Protein: 2g / Carbohydrates: 12g / Fats: 10g / Fiber: 3g / Cholesterol: 0mg / Sodium: 45mg Potassium: 100mg

European Berry Bliss

Yield: 6 servings / **Preparation Time:** 10 minutes / **Cooking Time:** 20 minutes

Ingredients:
- 2 cups fresh strawberries, hulled and halved
- 1/4 cup fresh basil leaves, chopped
- 4 tablespoons honey or maple syrup
- 1 tablespoon fresh lemon juice
- 1/2 teaspoon vanilla extract (optional)
- 1 teaspoon cornstarch
- tablespoon water (to dissolve cornstarch)

Instructions:
1. Hull and halve the strawberries. Chop the fresh basil leaves. In a medium saucepan, combine the strawberries, honey (or maple syrup), lemon juice, and a pinch of salt. Stir to combine and bring to a simmer over medium heat. Reduce the heat to low and let the mixture simmer for about 10 minutes, stirring occasionally. Cook until the strawberries are soft.
2. In a small bowl, dissolve the cornstarch in 1 tablespoon of water. Stir the cornstarch slurry into the simmering strawberry mixture. Continue to cook for another 5-10 minutes until the bliss has thickened to your desired consistency. Stir in the chopped basil and vanilla extract (if using). Simmer for an additional 2 minutes.
3. Remove the saucepan from the heat and let the bliss cool to room temperature. The bliss will continue to thicken as it cools. Serve warm or chilled. Store any leftovers in an airtight container in the refrigerator for up to one week.

Nutritional Information (per serving): Calories: 45 / Protein: 0.5g / Carbohydrates: 12g / Fats: 0g / Fiber: 1.5g / Cholesterol: 0mg / Sodium: 5mg / Potassium: 95mg

Grilled Peaches with Honey

Yield: 4 servings / **Preparation Time:** 10 minutes / **Cooking Time:** 10 minutes

Ingredients:
- 4 ripe peaches, halved and pitted
- 2 tablespoons honey
- 1 tablespoon olive oil
- Optional: 1 teaspoon ground cinnamon
- 1 teaspoon vanilla extract
- Fresh mint leaves for garnish (optional)

Instructions:
1. Preheat the grill to medium-high heat. Brush the cut sides of the peach halves with olive oil.
2. Place the peach halves cut side down on the grill. Grill for 3-4 minutes, until grill marks appear, and peaches are slightly softened. Flip the peaches and grill for another 2-3 minutes on the other side.
3. Remove the peaches from the grill and drizzle each half with honey. If using, sprinkle ground cinnamon and vanilla extract over the peaches for added flavor. Garnish with fresh mint leaves if desired. Serve warm.

Nutritional Information (per serving): Calories: 120 / Protein: 1g / Carbohydrates: 30g / Fats: 2g / Fiber: 2g / Cholesterol: 0mg / Sodium: 0mg / Potassium: 300mg

Healthy Alternatives to Traditional Sweets

Finding healthy alternatives to traditional sweets is essential when following a heart-healthy diet. In this subchapter, we explore creative and delicious ways to enjoy sweet treats without compromising your cardiovascular health. These recipes replace high-sugar, high-fat ingredients with wholesome, nutrient-rich options that satisfy your cravings while supporting your heart. Embrace these alternatives to indulge guilt-free and maintain a balanced, heart-healthy lifestyle. Discover how simple swaps can make a big difference in your diet and overall well-being.

Oatmeal Raisin Cookies

Yield: 24 cookies / **Preparation Time:** 15 minutes / **Cooking Time:** 12-15 minutes

Ingredients:

- 1 cup rolled oats
- 1/2 cup whole wheat flour
- 1/4 cup unsweetened applesauce
- 1/4 cup honey or pure maple syrup
- 1/4 cup coconut oil, melted
- 1/2 cup raisins
- 1 large egg
- 1/2 teaspoon baking soda
- 1/2 teaspoon ground cinnamon
- 1/4 teaspoon salt
- 1 teaspoon vanilla extract

Instructions:

1. Preheat your oven to 350°F (175°C). Line a baking sheet with parchment paper or a silicone baking mat.
2. In a medium bowl, whisk together the rolled oats, whole wheat flour, baking soda, cinnamon, and salt.
3. In a large bowl, mix the unsweetened applesauce, honey or maple syrup, melted coconut oil, egg, and vanilla extract until well combined. Gradually add the dry ingredients to the wet ingredients, stirring until just combined.
4. Drop spoonful of dough onto the prepared baking sheet, spacing them about 2 inches apart. Gently flatten each cookie with the back of a spoon or your fingers.
5. Bake in the preheated oven for 12-15 minutes, or until the cookies are golden brown and set. Remove from the oven and allow the cookies to cool on the baking sheet for 5 minutes before transferring them to a wire rack to cool completely.

Nutritional Information (per serving, 1 cookie): Calories: 90 / Protein: 2g / Carbohydrates: 14g / Fats: 3g / Fiber: 1.5g / Cholesterol: 10mg / Sodium: 55mg / Potassium: 70mg

Pumpkin Spice Energy Balls

Yield: 12 energy balls / **Preparation Time:** 10 minutes / **Cooking Time:** None (setting time: 30 minutes in the fridge)

Ingredients:

- 1 cup rolled oats
- 1/4 cup ground flaxseed
- 1/2 cup canned pumpkin puree
- 1/4 cup almond butter
- 1/4 cup honey or maple syrup
- 1/2 teaspoon pumpkin pie spice
- 1/2 teaspoon ground cinnamon
- 1/4 cup chopped walnuts or pecans (optional)
- 1/4 cup dark chocolate chips (optional for added flavor)

Instructions:

1. In a large bowl, combine the rolled oats, ground flaxseed, pumpkin pie spice, and ground cinnamon. Mix well.
2. Add the canned pumpkin puree, almond butter, and honey or maple syrup to the bowl. Stir until the mixture is well combined and forms a dough-like consistency.
3. If using, fold in the chopped walnuts or pecans and dark chocolate chips until evenly distributed. Using your hands, roll the mixture into 12 small balls, about 1 inch in diameter.
4. Place the energy balls on a baking sheet or plate lined with parchment paper.
5. Refrigerate for at least 30 minutes to firm up.
6. Once set, enjoy the energy balls immediately or store them in an airtight container in the fridge for up to one week.

Nutritional Information (per serving, 1 energy ball): Calories: 90 / Protein: 2g / Carbohydrates: 11g / Fats: 4g / Fiber: 2g / Cholesterol: 0mg / Sodium: 10mg / Potassium: 90mg

---

Chia Seed Banana Bread

Yield: 10 servings / **Preparation Time:** 15 minutes / **Cooking Time:** 50-60 minutes

Ingredients:

- 1 ½ cups whole wheat flour
- 1/2 cup rolled oats
- 3 ripe bananas, mashed
- 1/4 cup honey or maple syrup
- 4 cup olive oil or melted coconut oil
- 2 large eggs
- 1 teaspoon vanilla extract
- 1 teaspoon baking soda
- 1/2 teaspoon salt
- 1 teaspoon ground cinnamon
- 2 tablespoons chia seeds
- 1/2 cup chopped walnuts or pecans (optional for added nutritional benefits)

Instructions:

1. Preheat your oven to 350°F (175°C). Grease a 9x5 inch loaf pan or line it with parchment paper.
2. In a large bowl, combine the mashed bananas, honey or maple syrup, olive oil or melted coconut oil, eggs, and vanilla extract. Mix until well combined.
3. In another bowl, whisk together the whole wheat flour, rolled oats, chia seeds, baking soda, salt, and ground cinnamon. Gradually add the dry ingredients to the wet ingredients, stirring until just combined.
4. If using, fold in the chopped walnuts or pecans.
5. Pour the batter into the prepared loaf pan and smooth the top.
6. Bake in the preheated oven for 50-60 minutes, or until a toothpick inserted into the center comes out clean. If the top starts to brown too quickly, cover with aluminum foil for the last 10-15 minutes of baking.
7. Remove from the oven and let the banana bread cool in the pan for 10 minutes. Then transfer to a wire rack to cool completely before slicing.

Nutritional Information (per serving): Calories: 190 / Protein: 4g / Carbohydrates: 27g / Fats: 7g / Fiber: 3g / Cholesterol: 35mg / Sodium: 180mg / Potassium: 220mg

Apple Walnut Bread

Yield: 12 servings / **Preparation Time:** 15 minutes / **Cooking Time:** 50-60 minutes

Ingredients:

- 1 1/2 cups whole wheat flour
- 1/2 cup rolled oats
- 1/2 cup chopped walnuts
- 2 medium apples, peeled, cored, and chopped
- 1/4 cup honey or maple syrup
- 1/4 cup unsweetened applesauce
- 1/4 cup plain Greek yogurt
- 2 large eggs
- 1/2 cup unsweetened almond milk (or any low-fat milk)
- 1 teaspoon baking powder
- 1/2 teaspoon baking soda
- 1/2 teaspoon salt
- 1 teaspoon ground cinnamon
- 1/4 teaspoon ground nutmeg
- 1 teaspoon vanilla extract
- Optional: 1/4 cup raisins or dried cranberries for added flavor

Instructions:

1. Preheat your oven to 350°F (175°C). Grease a 9x5 inch loaf pan or line it with parchment paper.
2. In a large bowl, combine the whole wheat flour, rolled oats, baking powder, baking soda, salt, ground cinnamon, and ground nutmeg. Stir well to ensure even distribution.
3. In another bowl, whisk together the honey or maple syrup, unsweetened applesauce, Greek yogurt, eggs, and vanilla extract until well combined. Then, stir in the almond milk. Pour the wet ingredients into the dry ingredients and mix until just combined. Do not overmix. Gently fold in the chopped apples, walnuts, and optional raisins or dried cranberries if using.
4. Pour the batter into the prepared loaf pan and spread it evenly. Bake in the preheated oven for 50-60 minutes, or until a toothpick inserted into the center comes out clean.
5. Allow the bread to cool in the pan for about 10 minutes before transferring it to a wire rack to cool completely.

Nutritional Information (per serving): Calories: 160 / Protein: 4g / Carbohydrates: 25g / Fats: 6g / Fiber: 3g / Cholesterol: 30mg / Sodium: 150mg / Potassium: 150mg

Greek Yogurt Popsicles

Yield: 8 servings / **Preparation Time:** 10 minutes / **Freezing Time:** 4-6 hours

Ingredients:

- 2 cups Greek yogurt (plain or vanilla)
- 1 cup fresh berries (strawberries, blueberries, raspberries, or a mix)
- 1/4 cup honey or maple syrup
- 1 teaspoon vanilla extract
- Optional: 1 tablespoon chia seeds or ground flaxseeds for added fiber

Instructions:

1. Combine Greek yogurt, honey/maple syrup, and vanilla extract in a bowl until smooth. Fold in fresh berries. For a smoother texture, blend the berries with the yogurt mixture.
2. Stir in chia or flaxseeds if using. Spoon mixture into popsicle molds, tapping to remove air bubbles. Insert popsicle sticks and freeze for 4-6 hours until set. To remove, run warm water over the molds and gently pull out the popsicles.

Nutritional Information (per serving): Calories: 100 / Protein: 6g / Carbohydrates: 15g / Fats: 1.5g / Fiber: 1g / Cholesterol: 5mg / Sodium: 25mg / Potassium: 150mg

BONUS Chapter: Heart Healthy Beverages

In this bonus chapter, we delve into the world of delicious drinks that do more than just quench your thirst — they actively support your cardiovascular health. Well-balanced drinks, packed with essential nutrients and antioxidants, can play a crucial role in maintaining and improving heart health. We've gathered the best recipes to ensure your beverages are as heart friendly as they are refreshing. Enjoy exploring these wonderful drink options that will help you maintain a healthy heart while delighting your taste buds.

Energizing Protein Shakes

Well-balanced shakes are a fantastic addition to a heart-healthy diet, offering a delicious and convenient way to pack in essential nutrients. These shakes are designed to support cardiovascular health while satisfying your cravings for something sweet and refreshing. Each recipe combines heart-friendly ingredients that provide a perfect blend of fiber, protein, and antioxidants. Dive into these tasty shake recipes and discover how easy and enjoyable it can be to nourish your heart.

Here are some revised tips:
- You can replace unsweetened almond milk with any plant-based or low-fat milk to reduce saturated fat intake and promote heart health.
- Consider adding turmeric powder, which contains anti-inflammatory curcumin to help lower the risk of heart disease.
- Ground cinnamon can be added for flavor enhancement and blood sugar regulation, benefiting heart health.
- Using honey or maple syrup as natural sweeteners provides antioxidants that protect the heart but be sure to use them in moderation.
- Consider adding whey or plant-based protein powder to your smoothies or shakes for a heart-healthy boost of protein and essential nutrients

These tips include heart-healthy ingredients that not only improve the taste of your dishes but also support cardiovascular well-being.

Spinach and Pineapple Shake

Yield: 2 servings / **Preparation Time:** 10 minutes / **Cooking Time:** none

Ingredients:
- 2 cups fresh spinach leaves, packed
- 1 cup fresh pineapple chunks
- 1 medium banana, sliced
- 1 cup unsweetened almond milk
- 1/2 cup plain Greek yogurt
- 1 tablespoon chia seeds
- 1 teaspoon honey or maple syrup

Instructions:
1. Wash the spinach leaves thoroughly. Peel and chop the pineapple and banana.
2. In a blender, combine the spinach, pineapple chunks, and banana slices. Add the almond milk and Greek yogurt.
3. Sprinkle in the chia seeds and add honey or maple syrup and grated ginger if using.
4. Blend on high until smooth and creamy, ensuring there are no chunks of spinach or fruit left.
5. Pour the shake into two glasses and serve immediately.

Nutritional Information (per serving): Calories: 180 / Protein: 7g / Carbohydrates: 32g / Fats: 4g / Fiber: 6g / Cholesterol: 2mg / Sodium: 80mg / Potassium: 550mg

---

Mango Protein Shake

Yield: 2 servings / **Preparation Time:** 10 minutes / **Cooking Time:** none

Ingredients:
- 1 cup fresh or frozen mango chunks
- 1 cup unsweetened almond milk
- 1/2 cup plain low-fat Greek yogurt
- 1 tablespoon chia seeds
- 1 tablespoon ground flaxseeds
- 1/2 teaspoon turmeric powder
- 1/2 teaspoon ground cinnamon
- 1 teaspoon honey or maple syrup
- 1 scoop vanilla protein powder
- 1/2 cup ice cubes (optional, for a thicker shake)

Instructions:
1. If using fresh mango, peel and chop the mango into chunks. In a blender, combine the mango chunks, unsweetened almond milk, Greek yogurt, and protein powder. Blend on high until smooth and creamy.
2. Add the chia seeds, ground flaxseeds, turmeric powder, and ground cinnamon to the blender. Blend again until all ingredients are well incorporated.
3. Taste the shake and add honey or maple syrup if a sweeter flavor is desired. Add ice cubes if a thicker consistency is preferred, and blend until smooth. Pour the shake into two glasses and serve immediately.

Nutritional Information (per serving): Calories: 220 / Protein: 20g / Carbohydrates: 25g / Fats: 6g / Fiber: 6g / Cholesterol: 5mg / Sodium: 90mg / Potassium: 500mg

Pumpkin Spice Protein Shake

Yield: 2 servings / **Preparation Time:** 10 minutes / **Cooking Time:** none

Ingredients:
- 1 cup unsweetened almond milk
- 1/2 cup pure pumpkin puree (not pumpkin pie filling)
- 1/2 cup plain low-fat Greek yogurt
- 1 scoop vanilla protein powder
- 1 tablespoon chia seeds
- 1 tablespoon ground flaxseeds
- 1 teaspoon pumpkin pie spice
- 1/2 teaspoon vanilla extract
- 1/2 teaspoon ground cinnamon
- 1 teaspoon honey or maple syrup
- 1/2 cup ice cubes (optional, for a thicker shake)

Instructions:
1. Measure out the pure pumpkin puree, ensuring it is not sweetened or spiced as pumpkin pie filling.
2. In a blender, combine the unsweetened almond milk, pumpkin puree, Greek yogurt, and protein powder. Blend on high until smooth and creamy.
3. Add the chia seeds, ground flaxseeds, pumpkin pie spice, ground cinnamon (if using), and vanilla extract to the blender. Blend again until all ingredients are well incorporated.
4. Taste the shake and add honey or maple syrup if a sweeter flavor is desired. Add ice cubes if a thicker consistency is preferred, and blend until smooth. Pour the shake into two glasses and serve immediately.

Nutritional Information (per serving): Calories: 210 / Protein: 22g / Carbohydrates: 24g / Fats: 5g / Fiber: 7g / Cholesterol: 5mg / Sodium: 85mg / Potassium: 550mg

Apple Cinnamon Shake

Yield: 2 servings **Preparation Time:** 10 minutes **Cooking Time:** none

Ingredients:
- large apple, cored and chopped (leave the skin on for added fiber)
- 1 cup unsweetened almond milk
- 1/2 cup plain low-fat Greek yogurt
- 1 scoop vanilla protein powder
- 1 tablespoon chia seeds
- 1 tablespoon ground flaxseeds
- 1/2 teaspoon ground cinnamon
- 1/4 teaspoon ground nutmeg (optional)
- 1 teaspoon honey or maple syrup
- 1/2 cup ice cubes (optional, for a thicker shake)

Instructions:
1. Core and chop the apple, leaving the skin on for extra fiber. In a blender, combine the chopped apple, unsweetened almond milk, Greek yogurt, and protein powder. Blend on high until smooth and creamy.
2. Add the chia seeds, ground flaxseeds, ground cinnamon, and ground nutmeg (if using) to the blender. Blend again until all ingredients are well incorporated.
3. Taste the shake and add honey or maple syrup if a sweeter flavor is desired. Add ice cubes if a thicker consistency is preferred, and blend until smooth. Pour the shake into two glasses and serve immediately.

Nutritional Information (per serving): Calories: 210 / Protein: 18g / Carbohydrates: 30g / Fats: 6g / Fiber: 7g / Cholesterol: 5mg / Sodium: 70mg / Potassium: 450mg

---

Blueberry Coconut Shake

Yield: 2 servings / **Preparation Time:** 10 minutes / **Cooking Time:** none

Ingredients:
- 1 cup fresh or frozen blueberries
- 1 cup unsweetened coconut milk
- 1/2 cup plain low-fat Greek yogurt
- 1 scoop vanilla protein powder
- 1 tablespoon chia seeds
- 1 tablespoon ground flaxseeds
- 1/2 teaspoon vanilla extract
- 1 teaspoon honey or maple syrup (optional)
- 1/2 cup ice cubes (optional, for a thicker shake)

Instructions:
1. If using fresh blueberries, rinse them thoroughly. If using frozen blueberries, ensure they are free from added sugars.
2. In a blender, combine the blueberries, unsweetened coconut milk, Greek yogurt, and protein powder. Blend on high until smooth and creamy. Add the chia seeds, ground flaxseeds, and vanilla extract to the blender. Blend again until all ingredients are well incorporated.
3. Taste the shake and add honey or maple syrup if a sweeter flavor is desired. Add ice cubes if a thicker consistency is preferred, and blend until smooth. Pour the shake into two glasses and serve immediately.

Nutritional Information (per serving): Calories: 180 / Protein: 18g / Carbohydrates: 23g / Fats: 6g / Fiber: 6g / Cholesterol: 5mg / Sodium: 60mg / Potassium: 400mg

Refreshing Juices and Mocktails

In this subchapter you'll find a collection of invigorating beverages, each thoughtfully crafted to enhance your cardiovascular health. These recipes blend nutrient-packed ingredients into delicious drinks that are perfect for any time of day. From zesty morning juices to sophisticated evening mocktails, enjoy a burst of freshness that nourishes your body and delights your taste buds. Cheers to a healthier heart with every sip!

Tropical Mango Mocktail

Yield: 2 servings / **Preparation Time:** 10 minutes / **Cooking Time:** none

Ingredients:
- 1 cup fresh or frozen mango chunks
- 1/2 cup pineapple juice (unsweetened)
- 1/2 cup coconut water
- 1 tablespoon fresh lime juice
- 1 teaspoon honey or maple syrup
- 1/2 cup ice cubes (optional, for a chilled drink)
- Optional for garnish: fresh mint leaves; lime slices

Instructions:
1. If using fresh mango, peel and chop the mango into chunks. If using frozen mango, ensure it is free from added sugars.
2. In a blender, combine the mango chunks, pineapple juice, coconut water, fresh lime juice, and honey or maple syrup (if using). Blend on high until smooth and creamy.
3. Add the ice cubes to the blender if a chilled drink is preferred, and blend until the ice is well incorporated. Pour the mocktail into two glasses and serve immediately.

Nutritional Information (per serving): Calories: 90 / Protein: 1g / Carbohydrates: 22g / Fats: 0g / Fiber: 2g / Cholesterol: 0mg / Sodium: 25mg / Potassium: 180mg

---

Cucumber and Mint Cooler

Yield: 2 servings / **Preparation Time:** 10 minutes / **Cooking Time:** none

Ingredients:
- large cucumber, peeled and chopped
- 1/4 cup fresh mint leaves
- 1 tablespoon fresh lime juice
- 1 teaspoon honey or maple syrup
- 2 cups cold water
- Ice cubes (optional, for serving)
- Optional for garnish: mint sprigs; lime slices

Instructions:
1. Peel and chop the cucumber. Rinse the fresh mint leaves. In a blender, combine the chopped cucumber, fresh mint leaves, fresh lime juice, and honey or maple syrup (if using). Add the cold water and blend on high until smooth and well combined.
2. If a smoother drink is preferred, strain the mixture through a fine mesh strainer into a pitcher, pressing down on the solids to extract as much liquid as possible. Pour the cooler into two glasses over ice cubes if a chilled drink is preferred.

Nutritional Information (per serving): Calories: 25 / Protein: 1g / Carbohydrates: 6g / Fats: 0g / Fiber: 1g / Cholesterol: 0mg / Sodium: 5mg / Potassium: 150mg

Radiant Pomegranate-Orange Bliss

Yield: 2 servings / **Preparation Time:** 10 minutes / **Cooking Time:** none

Ingredients:
- cup fresh pomegranate seeds (from about 1 large pomegranate)
- 1 cup fresh orange juice (juice from about 2-3 oranges)
- 1/2 cup water
- 1 teaspoon honey or maple syrup
- Ice cubes (optional, for serving)
- Pomegranate seeds and orange slices (optional, for garnish)

Instructions:
1. Extract the seeds from the pomegranate and juice the oranges. In a blender, combine the pomegranate seeds, fresh orange juice, water, and honey or maple syrup (if using). Blend on high until smooth and well combined.
2. f a smoother juice is preferred, strain the mixture through a fine mesh strainer into a pitcher, pressing down on the solids to extract as much liquid as possible. Pour the juice into two glasses over ice cubes if a chilled drink is preferred.

Nutritional Information (per serving): Calories: 90 / Protein: 1g / Carbohydrates: 22g / Fats: 0.5g / Fiber: 3g / Cholesterol: 0mg / Sodium: 5mg / Potassium: 350mg

Watermelon Basil Mocktail

Yield: 2 servings / **Preparation Time:** 10 minutes / **Cooking Time:** none

Ingredients:
- 2 cups fresh watermelon chunks (seedless)
- 1/4 cup fresh basil leaves
- 1 cup cold water
- 1 tablespoon fresh lime juice
- 1 teaspoon honey or maple syrup
- Ice cubes (optional, for serving)
- basil sprigs and lime slices (optional, for garnish)

Instructions:
1. Cut the watermelon into chunks and rinse the fresh basil leaves. In a blender, combine the watermelon chunks, fresh basil leaves, fresh lime juice, and honey or maple syrup (if using). Add the cold water and blend on high until smooth and well combined.
2. If a smoother drink is preferred, strain the mixture through a fine mesh strainer into a pitcher, pressing down on the solids to extract as much liquid as possible.
3. Pour the mocktail into two glasses over ice cubes if a chilled drink is preferred. Garnish with a sprig of basil and a slice of lime for an extra touch of flavor and visual appeal.

Nutritional Information (per serving): Calories: 35 / Protein: 1g / Carbohydrates: 9g / Fats: 0g / Fiber: 1g / Cholesterol: 0mg / Sodium: 5mg / Potassium: 150mg

Pineapple and Ginger Juice

Yield: 2 servings / **Preparation Time:** 10 minutes / **Cooking Time:** none

Ingredients:

- 2 cups fresh pineapple chunks
- 1 cup water
- 1-inch piece of fresh ginger, peeled and slice
- 1 tablespoon fresh lime juice
- 1 teaspoon honey or maple syrup (optional)
- Fresh mint leaves (optional, for garnish)
- ice cubes (optional, for serving)

Instructions:

1. Peel and chop the pineapple into chunks. Peel and slice the ginger. In a blender, combine the pineapple chunks, ginger, water, and fresh lime juice. Blend on high until smooth and well combined.
2. If a smoother juice is preferred, strain the mixture through a fine mesh strainer into a pitcher, pressing down on the solids to extract as much liquid as possible. Stir in the honey or maple syrup (if using) until well dissolved.
3. Pour the juice into two glasses over ice cubes if a chilled drink is preferred.

Nutritional Information (per serving): Calories: 70 / Protein: 0g / Carbohydrates: 18g / Fats: 0g / Fiber: 1g / Cholesterol: 0mg / Sodium: 5mg / Potassium: 150mg

Cozy Warm Drinks

These comforting beverages are designed to soothe you on chilly days while supporting your heart health with nutrient-rich ingredients. From spiced elixirs to soothing teas, each recipe is crafted to be low in sodium and saturated fats, yet rich in antioxidants and other heart-healthy nutrients. Embrace the cozy flavors and savor the heartwarming benefits of each delicious drink!

Hibiscus Tea with Rose Hips

Yield: 4 servings / **Preparation Time:** 5 minutes / **Cooking Time:** 10 minutes

Ingredients:

- 4 cups water
- 1/2 cup dried hibiscus flowers
- 1/4 cup dried rose hips
- Cinnamon stick
- 1 teaspoon grated fresh ginger (optional)
- 1 tablespoon honey or maple syrup (optional)
- lemon slices (optional, for garnish)

Instructions:

1. Measure out the dried hibiscus flowers and rose hips. If using fresh ginger, peel and grate it. In a medium saucepan, bring 4 cups of water to a boil. Once the water is boiling, add the dried hibiscus flowers, dried rose hips, cinnamon stick, and grated ginger (if using). Reduce the heat and let the mixture simmer for 5-7 minutes.
2. Remove the saucepan from heat. Stir in the honey or maple syrup (if using) until dissolved. Strain the mixture through a fine mesh strainer into a heatproof pitcher or another saucepan. Pour the tea into mugs and serve warm. Garnish with lemon slices if desired.

Nutritional Information (per serving): Calories: 30 / Protein: 0g / Carbohydrates: 8g / Fats: 0g / Fiber: 0g / Cholesterol: 0mg / Sodium: 5mg / Potassium: 20mg

Warm Spiced Cranberry Elixir

Yield: 4 servings / **Preparation Time:** 10 minutes / **Cooking Time:** 20 minutes

Ingredients:
- 4 cups fresh or frozen cranberries
- 6 cups water
- 1 cinnamon stick
- 3 whole cloves
- 1 teaspoon vanilla extract
- 1/2 teaspoon ground ginger (optional)
- Zest of 1 orange (optional, for a citrusy note)
- 1/4 cup honey or maple syrup (optional)

Instructions:
1. Rinse the cranberries thoroughly. If using fresh cranberries, discard any that are bruised or soft.
2. In a large saucepan, combine the cranberries and water. Bring to a boil over medium-high heat. Reduce the heat and simmer for about 10 minutes, or until the cranberries have burst and softened. Add the honey or maple syrup (if using), cinnamon stick, cloves, vanilla extract, ground ginger (if using), and orange zest (if using). Stir to combine.
3. Continue to simmer the mixture for another 10 minutes, allowing the flavors to meld together.
4. Remove the saucepan from the heat. Using a fine mesh strainer, strain the mixture into a heatproof pitcher or another saucepan, pressing down on the solids to extract as much liquid as possible.
5. Pour the warm elixir into mugs and serve immediately.

Nutritional Information (per serving): Calories: 60 / Protein: 0.5g / Carbohydrates: 16g / Fats: 0g / Fiber: 2g / Cholesterol: 0mg / Sodium: 5mg / Potassium: 60mg

Warm Pumpkin Orange Spice Elixir

Yield: 4 servings / **Preparation Time:** 10 minutes / **Cooking Time:** 20 minutes

Ingredients:
- 4 cups water
- 1 cup pure pumpkin puree (not pumpkin pie filling)
- 1/2 cup fresh orange juice (juice from about 2 oranges)
- zest of 1 orange
- 1/4 cup honey or maple syrup (optional)
- 1 cinnamon stick
- 3 whole cloves
- 1/2 teaspoon ground cinnamon
- 1/4 teaspoon ground nutmeg
- 1/2 teaspoon ground ginger

Instructions:
1. Juice the oranges and zest one of them, ensuring the zest is finely grated.
2. In a large saucepan, combine the water, pumpkin puree, fresh orange juice, and orange zest. Stir well to mix. Add the honey or maple syrup (if using), cinnamon stick, cloves, ground ginger (if using), ground cinnamon, and ground nutmeg to the saucepan. Stir to combine.
3. Bring the mixture to a boil over medium-high heat. Once it reaches a boil, reduce the heat and let it simmer for about 15 minutes, allowing the flavors to meld together.
4. Remove the saucepan from the heat. Using a fine mesh strainer, strain the mixture into a heatproof pitcher or another saucepan, pressing down on the solids to extract as much liquid as possible. Pour the warm elixir into mugs and serve immediately.

Nutritional Information (per serving): Calories: 70 / Protein: 1g / Carbohydrates: 18g / Fats: 0.5g / Fiber: 2g / Cholesterol: 0mg / Sodium: 5mg / Potassium: 160mg

Warm Pomegranate Citrus Delight

Yield: 4 servings / **Preparation Time:** 10 minutes / **Cooking Time:** 20 minutes

Ingredients:

- 4 cups water; 2 cups pure pomegranate juice (unsweetened)
- 1/2 cup fresh orange juice (juice from about 2 oranges)
- zest of 1 orange
- 1/4 cup honey or maple syrup (optional)

- 1 cinnamon stick
- 3 whole cloves
- 1/2 teaspoon ground cinnamon
- 1/4 teaspoon ground nutmeg
- 1/2 teaspoon ground ginger
- Seeds from 1 pomegranate (optional, for garnish)

Instructions:

1. Juice the oranges and zest one of them, ensuring the zest is finely grated. In a large saucepan, combine the water, pomegranate juice, fresh orange juice, and orange zest. Stir well to mix.
2. Add the honey or maple syrup (if using), cinnamon stick, cloves, ground ginger (if using), ground cinnamon, and ground nutmeg to the saucepan. Stir to combine. Bring the mixture to a boil over medium-high heat. Once it reaches a boil, reduce the heat and let it simmer for about 15 minutes, allowing the flavors to meld together.
3. Remove the saucepan from the heat. Using a fine mesh strainer, strain the mixture into a heatproof pitcher or another saucepan, pressing down on the solids to extract as much liquid as possible.
4. Pour the warm drink into mugs and serve immediately. Optionally, garnish with pomegranate seeds.

Nutritional Information (per serving): Calories: 80 / Protein: 1g / Carbohydrates: 21g / Fats: 0.5g / Fiber: 2g / Cholesterol: 0mg / Sodium: 5mg / Potassium: 200mg

---

Green Tea with Lemon and Ginger

Yield: 4 servings / **Preparation Time:** 5 minutes / **Cooking Time:** 10 minutes

Ingredients:

- 4 cups water
- 4 green tea bags (decaffeinated if desired)
- 1-inch piece of fresh ginger, peeled and thinly sliced

- 1 lemon, juiced
- 1 tablespoon honey or maple syrup (optional)
- Optional for garnish: lemon slices
- Optional for garnish: fresh mint leaves

Instructions:

1. Peel and thinly slice the ginger. Juice the lemon and set the juice aside.
2. In a medium saucepan, bring 4 cups of water to a boil. Once the water is boiling, add the sliced ginger. Reduce the heat and let it simmer for 5 minutes to infuse the flavor.
3. Remove the saucepan from heat. Add the green tea bags to the water and let them steep for 3-4 minutes, or according to the package instructions.
4. Remove the tea bags and ginger slices from the saucepan. Stir in the lemon juice and honey or maple syrup (if using) until well combined. Pour the tea into mugs and serve warm. Garnish with lemon slices and fresh mint leaves if desired.

Nutritional Information (per serving): Calories: 20 / Protein: 0g / Carbohydrates: 6g / Fats: 0g / Fiber: 0g / Cholesterol: 0mg / Sodium: 5mg / Potassium: 30mg

Conclusion

Embarking on a journey towards better heart health begins with the choices you make in your kitchen. This Heart Healthy Cookbook for Beginners has provided you with the tools and recipes to nourish your body with delicious, nutritious meals. By embracing heart-friendly ingredients and cooking methods, you can enjoy flavorful dishes that support your cardiovascular wellness. Remember, every meal is an opportunity to invest in your health. Here's to a heart-healthy future, filled with vibrant flavors and a happier, healthier you.

Eating Out and Social Events Made Healthy

Maintaining a heart-healthy diet doesn't mean you have to miss out on social activities. When dining out, choose menu items that are grilled, baked, steamed, or poached, and avoid fried or heavily sauced options. Don't hesitate to ask for healthier modifications, such as dressing on the side, whole grain substitutions, or extra vegetables. Opt for water or unsweetened beverages, and practice mindful eating by savoring each bite and paying attention to your hunger cues.

At social events, bring a heart-healthy dish to share, ensuring there's at least one nutritious option available. Focus on portion control, and fill your plate with fruits, vegetables, lean proteins, and whole grains. Engaging in conversation and activities can help you avoid mindless snacking. By making thoughtful choices, you can enjoy social gatherings without compromising your heart health.

Conquering Challenges and Boosting Motivation

Adopting a heart-healthy lifestyle can present challenges, but with the right mindset and strategies, you can overcome them. Planning and preparation are essential—keep your kitchen stocked with heart-healthy staples, and prep meals and snacks in advance to avoid unhealthy choices when you're pressed for time. Set realistic goals and celebrate your progress, no matter how small.

Boost your motivation by finding support from friends, family, or a health community. Share your journey, exchange recipes, and encourage each other to stay on track. Incorporate variety into your meals to keep things exciting and prevent dietary boredom. Remember, setbacks are a natural part of the process; don't be discouraged by occasional slip-ups. Instead, focus on your long-term goals and get back on track with your next meal.

Regular physical activity complements a heart-healthy diet, so find exercises you enjoy and make them a part of your routine. Whether it's walking, swimming, or dancing, staying active helps manage weight, reduce stress, and improve overall heart health.

Final Thoughts

Your journey towards better heart health is a lifelong commitment that begins with daily choices. With the recipes and knowledge provided in this cookbook, you are well-equipped to create meals that are both delicious and beneficial for your heart. Embrace the joy of cooking and eating wholesome foods, and let this be the foundation for a healthier, more vibrant life. Here's to a future filled with flavorful, heart-healthy meals and a stronger, happier you. Relish each step on your path to heart wellness!

60-Day Heart Healthy Meal Plan

Day	Breakfast	Lunch	Snack	Dinner
1 Sun	High-Fiber Breakfast Muffins, 11	Lentil and Vegetable Stew, 33 Herb-Roasted Turkey Breast, 51	Carrot Sticks with Hummus, 16	Chicken and Vegetable Soup, 83
2	Spinach and Feta Omelet, 9	Lentil and Vegetable Stew, 33 Lean Beef and Spinach Lasagna, 64	Smoked Salmon and Cream Cheese Cucumber Bites, 18	Ground Turley Lettuce Wraps, 70
3	Oat and Flaxseed Smoothie, 13	Mediterranean Chickpea Salad, 26	Apple Slices with Almond Butter, 16	Gound Beef and Vegetable Stuffed Peppers, 64
4	Chia Seed Pudding with Fresh Fruit, 9	Lemon Herb Rice with Grilled Vegetables, 39 Turkey Meatballs with Marinara Sauce, 65	Baked Kale Chips, 20	Turkey and Quinoa Stew, 55
5	Tomato and Basil Breakfast Sandwich,10	Spelt and Roasted Butternut Squash Salad, 33	Greek Yogurt with Honey and Walnuts, 17	Braised Turkey Legs with Mushrooms, 68
6	Berry Antioxidant Smoothie, 14	One-Pot Pesto Pasta with Peas, 35	Bruschetta with Tomato and Basil, 18	Shrimp and Mango Salad, 42
7 Sat	Pumpkin Flaxseed Pancakes, 11	Spinach and Ricotta Stuffed Shells, 73	Veggie Sticks with Greek Yogurt Dip, 15	Seafood Stew with Tomatoes and Herbs, 84
8 Sun	Avocado and Egg Toast, 8	Farro and White Bean Soup, 87 Lean Beef Tacos with Fresh Salsa, 63	Air-Popped Popcorn with Nutritional Yeast, 21	Moroccan Carrot Salad, 79 Lean Beef and Vegetable Stir-Fry, 61
9	Whole-Grain Overnight Oats, 11	Farro and White Bean Soup, 87 Seared Venison with Berry Sauce, 61	Caprese Skewers with Balsamic Glaze, 19	Roasted Brussels Sprouts with Balsamic Glaze, 77
10	Green Detox Smoothie, 13	Mediterranean Quinoa Salad, 32	Plain Greek Yogurt with Fresh Berries, 22	Scallop and Citrus Salad, 43
11	Banana Nut Smoothie Bowl, 14	Portobello Mushroom Burgers, 72	Stuffed Mini Bell Peppers with Quinoa, 20	Baked Honey Mustard Chicken, 51
12	Avocado and Black Bean Breakfast Wrap, 12	Balsamic Glazed Portobello Mushrooms with Wild Rice, 37	Rice Cakes with Avocado and Cherry Tomatoes, 21	Slow-Cooked Balsamic Beef, 67
13	Apple Cinnamon Quinoa Bowl, 10	Spaghetti Squash with Marinara, 34	Grilled Vegetable Platter with Hummus, 78	Flaxseed-Crusted Mackerel, 46
14 Sat	Berry Oatmeal Bake, 12	Sweet Potato and Black Bean Enchiladas, 80	Whole-Grain Crackers with Avocado Spread, 17	Slow-Cooked Beef and Vegetable Stew, 68
15 Sun	Spinach and Feta Omelet, 9	Classic Minestrone Soup, 80 Quick Teriyaki Chicken Stir-Fry, 57	Baked Kale Chips, 20	Citrus-Marinated Shrimp Salad, 43
16	Chia Seed Pudding with Fresh Fruit, 9	Classic Minestrone Soup, 80 Spicy Chicken Wraps, 58	Smoked Salmon and Cream Cheese Cucumber Bites, 18	Baked Cod with Mediterranean Vegetables, 44
17	Oat and Flaxseed Smoothie, 13	Farro and Vegetable Medley, 32 Lemon Garlic Chicken Tenders, 57	Pumpkin Spice Energy Balls, 95	Lemon Pepper Baked Turkey, 52 Creamy Broccoli Soup (Without Cream), 81

18	Tomato and Basil Breakfast Sandwich,10	Barley and Mushroom Stew, 31 Baked Lemon Rosemary Chicken Thighs, 52	Stuffed Mini Bell Peppers with Quinoa, 20	Grilled Sirloin with Chimichurri Sauce, 60
19	Berry Antioxidant Smoothie, 14	Chickpea Pasta with Spinach and Garlic, 35	Grilled Vegetable Platter with Hummus, 78	Mediterranean Chickpea Salad, 26
20	Avocado and Egg Toast, 8	Tuna and White Bean Salad, 42	Tropical Fruit and Spinach Salad, 34	Eggplant Parmesan, 77
21 Sat	High-Fiber Breakfast Muffins, 11	Lentil and Vegetable Shepherd's Pie, 70	Veggie Sticks with Greek Yogurt Dip, 15	Slow-Cooked Beef and Vegetable Stew, 68
22 Sun	Spinach and Feta Omelet, 9	Bulgur Wheat and Tomato Soup, 86 Rosemary Garlic Lamb Chops, 62	Caprese Skewers with Balsamic Glaze, 19	Quick Teriyaki Chicken Stir-Fry, 57 Vegan Coleslaw with Tangy Dressing, 78
23	Whole-Grain Overnight Oats, 11	Bulgur Wheat and Tomato Soup, 86 Rosemary Garlic Lamb Chops, 62	Greek Yogurt with Honey and Walnuts, 17	Sardine and Tomato Pasta, 45
24	Green Detox Smoothie, 13	Vegan Mushroom Stroganoff, 75 Roasted Beet and Arugula Salad, 24	Carrot Sticks with Hummus, 16	Baked Chicken Parmesan, 50
25	Banana Nut Smoothie Bowl, 14	Whole Grain Penne with Broccoli and Olive Oil, 36	Plain Greek Yogurt with Fresh Berries, 22	Citrus-Marinated Shrimp Salad, 43
26	Avocado and Black Bean Breakfast Wrap, 12	Wild Rice and Cranberry Pilaf, 38 Flaxseed-Crusted Mackerel, 46	Whole-Grain Crackers with Avocado Spread, 17	Baked Lemon Rosemary Chicken Thighs, 52
27	Apple Cinnamon Quinoa Bowl, 10	Lentil Pasta with Roasted Red Pepper Sauce, 36	Tropical Fruit and Spinach Salad, 34	Pan-Seared Scallops with Garlic Butter, 47
28 Sat	Pumpkin Flaxseed Pancakes, 11	Stuffed Bell Peppers with Quinoa and Black Beans, 71	Orange and Pomegranate Salad, 30	Herb-Roasted Turkey Breast, 51
29 Sun	Berry Oatmeal Bake, 12	Brown Rice and Vegetable Stir-Fry, 38 Miso-Glazed Sea Bass, 46	Greek Yogurt with Honey and Walnuts, 17	Tuna and White Bean Salad, 42
30	Spinach and Feta Omelet, 9	Chickpea and Spinach Curry, 73	Veggie Sticks with Greek Yogurt Dip, 15	Baked Honey Mustard Chicken, 51
31	High-Fiber Breakfast Muffins, 11	Creamy Chicken and Mushroom Casserole, 54 Quinoa and Kale Salad, 77	Apple Chips with Cinnamon, 22	Sardine and Tomato Pasta, 45
32	Tomato and Basil Breakfast Sandwich,10	Turkey and White Bean Chili, 85 Strawberry Spinach Salad with Poppy Seed Dressing, 23	Caprese Skewers with Balsamic Glaze, 19	Moroccan Chicken Stew, 53
33	Oat and Flaxseed Smoothie, 13	Turkey and White Bean Chili, 85 Citrus and Fennel Salad, 25	Carrot Sticks with Hummus, 16	Shrimp and Mango Salad, 42
34	Chia Seed Pudding with Fresh Fruit, 9	Sweet Potato and Black Bean Enchiladas, 80 Kale and Radish Salad with Lemon-Tahini Dressing, 25	Bruschetta with Tomato and Basil, 18	Lemon Pepper Baked Turkey, 52 Eggplant Parmesan, 71
35 Sat	Spinach and Feta Omelet, 9	Spinach and Feta Stuffed Peppers, 45	Plain Greek Yogurt with Fresh Berries, 22	Herb-Crusted Salmon with Quinoa, 44

		Ceviche with Fresh Lime and Cilantro, 41		
36 Sun	Berry Antioxidant Smoothie, 14	Wild Rice and Vegetable Soup, 87 Baked Herb-Crusted Pork Tenderloin, 62	Pear and Pecan Salad, 30	Turkey Meatballs with Marinara Sauce, 65
37	Avocado and Black Bean Breakfast Wrap, 12	Wild Rice and Vegetable Soup, 87 Baked Herb-Crusted Pork Tenderloin, 62	Greek Yogurt with Honey and Walnuts, 17	Scallop and Citrus Salad, 43
38	Avocado and Egg Toast, 8	Mediterranean Chickpea Salad, 26 Fish Fillet Sandwiches with Tartar Sauce, 48	Whole-Grain Crackers with Avocado Spread, 17	Creamy Chicken and Mushroom Casserole, 54
39	Whole-Grain Overnight Oats, 11	Lemon Herb Rice with Grilled Vegetables, 39 Quick Lemon Pepper Baked Fish, 47	Air-Popped Popcorn with Nutritional Yeast, 21	Ground Turkey Lettuce Wraps, 66
40	Green Detox Smoothie, 13	Spelt and Roasted Butternut Squash Salad, 33 Pan-Seared Scallops with Garlic Butter, 47	Cucumber Avocado Rolls, 19	Lemon Garlic Chicken Tenders, 57
41	Banana Nut Smoothie Bowl, 14	Baked Chicken Parmesan, 50 Avocado and Black Bean Salad, 28	Apple Chips with Cinnamon, 22	Simple Tuna Steak with Soy Sauce and Ginger, 48
42 Sat	Pumpkin Flaxseed Pancakes, 11	Turkey and Quinoa Stew, 55 Vegan Stuffed Acorn Squash, 75	Pear and Pecan Salad, 30	Turkey and Spinach Quesadillas, 58
43 Sun	Apple Cinnamon Quinoa Bowl, 10	Turkey and Quinoa Stew, 55	Bruschetta with Tomato and Basil, 18	Baked Cod with Mediterranean Vegetables, 44
44	Berry Antioxidant Smoothie, 14	Chicken and Vegetable Stew, 56	Carrot Sticks with Hummus, 16	Grilled Sirloin with Chimichurri Sauce, 60
45	Spinach and Feta Omelet, 9	Chicken and Vegetable Stew, 56	Apple Slices with Almond Butter, 16	Turkey Chili, 54
46	Chia Seed Pudding with Fresh Fruit, 9	Chicken Tortilla Soup, 85	Greek Yogurt with Honey and Walnuts, 17	Braised Lamb Shanks with Root Vegetables, 66
47	Oat and Flaxseed Smoothie, 13	Sweet Potato and Black Bean Enchiladas, 74	Veggie Sticks with Greek Yogurt Dip, 15	Miso-Glazed Sea Bass, 46
48	Tomato and Basil Breakfast Sandwich,10	Whole Grain Penne with Broccoli and Olive Oil, 36 Lean Beef and Vegetable Stir-Fry, 61	Apple Chips with Cinnamon, 22	Chicken and Vegetable Soup, 83
49 Sat	Berry Oatmeal Bake, 12	Easy Fish Curry with Coconut Milk, 49 Cucumber and Dill Salad, 24	Bruschetta with Tomato and Basil, 18	Seafood Stew with Tomatoes and Herbs, 84
50 Sun	High-Fiber Breakfast Muffins, 11	Lentil and Sweet Potato Stew, 76 Seared Venison with Berry Sauce, 61	Whole-Grain Crackers with Avocado Spread, 17	Lean Beef and Vegetable Stir-Fry, 61
51	Avocado and Egg Toast, 8	Lentil and Sweet Potato Stew, 76 Salmon and Mixed Greens Salad, 26	Plain Greek Yogurt with Fresh Berries, 22	Braised Turkey Legs with Mushrooms, 68

52	Spinach and Feta Omelet, 9	Easy Chicken Fajitas, 59 Pumpkin Zucchini Ginger Cream Soup, 82	Air-Popped Popcorn with Nutritional Yeast, 21	Egg and Spinach Salad, 28
53	Whole-Grain Overnight Oats, 11	Herb-Crusted Salmon with Quinoa, 44	Carrot Sticks with Hummus, 16	Turkey and Quinoa Stew, 55
54	Green Detox Smoothie, 13	Turkey Chili, 54	Pumpkin Spice Energy Balls, 95	Ground Turley Lettuce Wraps, 70
55	Banana Nut Smoothie Bowl, 14	Turkey Chili, 54	Veggie Sticks with Greek Yogurt Dip, 15	Quick Lemon Pepper Baked Fish, 47
56 Sat	Pumpkin Flaxseed Pancakes, 11	Lean Beef Tacos with Fresh Salsa, 63	Greek Yogurt with Honey and Walnuts, 17	Easy Fish Curry with Coconut Milk, 49
57 Sun	Berry Oatmeal Bake, 12	Barley and Mushroom Soup, 88	Cucumber Avocado Rolls, 19	Turkey and Cranberry Salad, 27
58	Avocado and Black Bean Breakfast Wrap, 12	Barley and Mushroom Soup, 88	Apple Chips with Cinnamon, 22	Fish Fillet Sandwiches with Tartar Sauce, 48
59	Apple Cinnamon Quinoa Bowl, 10	Turkey and Spinach Quesadillas, 58	Bruschetta with Tomato and Basil, 18	Turkey and Quinoa Stew, 55
60	Spinach and Feta Omelet, 9	Moroccan Chicken Stew, 53	Plain Greek Yogurt with Fresh Berries, 22	Simple Tuna Steak with Soy Sauce and Ginger, 48

Nutritionist's Explanation for the 60-Day Meal Plan

Feeling satiated is a crucial factor for daily productivity. By nourishing our bodies with a variety of nutrients, we lay a long-term foundation for our health and longevity. Diverse nutrition is essential for the health of all internal organs, including the heart. We have meticulously designed this meal plan to be diverse, ensuring that your body receives a wide array of nutrients daily. Variety in your diet is key to maintaining overall health and preventing nutritional deficiencies.

To save time during busy mornings, we have scheduled the most time-consuming recipes for the weekends. Additionally, we have included a practical tip: prepare a lunch dish on Sunday that can also be enjoyed for lunch on Monday. This approach helps streamline your meal preparation routine and ensures you have nutritious meals ready to go.

If you still feel hungry between meals, we recommend incorporating an additional snack between breakfast and lunch from any of the following chapters: Guilt-Free Desserts for Heart Health, Healthy Alternatives, or Leafy Green and Vegetable Salads, Fruit Salads. For an afternoon snack between lunch and dinner, refer to Heart Healthy Beverages.

Carbohydrates are an important nutrient that should not be eliminated, even if you are trying to lose weight. They fuel our bodies with energy, which is why we have included meals containing sufficient carbohydrates for lunch. As the day progresses, your body's need for carbohydrates decreases as it prepares for rest and sleep. Therefore, we have planned protein-rich, light meals for the evening. If you go to bed late or find the portion planned for dinner insufficient to satisfy your hunger, please select any salad from the chapters Leafy Green and Vegetable Salads, Vegetable-Based Soups, or Vegetarian and Vegan Sides and Salads.

This thoughtful approach ensures that your diet remains balanced, nutritious, and convenient, helping you to maintain your health and well-being over the 60-day period.

Index of Recipes

A

acorn squashes
Vegan Stuffed Acorn Squash, 75
almond butter
Apple Slices with Almond Butter, 16
Pumpkin Spice Energy Balls, 95
almond flour
Almond Flour Brownies, 89
Blueberry Almond Tart, 92
Mixed Berry Crumble, 92
Pineapple Coconut Bars, 93
almond milk
Apple Cinnamon Quinoa Bowl, 10
High-Fiber Breakfast Muffins, 11
Lentil and Vegetable Shepherd's Pie, 70
Creamy Broccoli Soup (Without Cream), 81
Pumpkin Zucchini Ginger Cream Soup (Without Cream), 82
Dark Chocolate Avocado Mousse, 90
Apple Walnut Bread, 97
Spinach and Pineapple Shake, 98
Mango Protein Shake, 99
Pumpkin Spice Protein Shake, 99
Apple Cinnamon Shake, 100
Berry Oatmeal Bake, 12
Oat and Flaxseed Smoothie, 13
Green Detox Smoothie, 13
Berry Antioxidant Smoothie, 14
Banana Nut Smoothie Bowl, 14
Lentil Pasta with Roasted Red Pepper Sauce, 36
Creamy Chicken and Mushroom Casserole, 54
Vegan Mushroom Stroganoff, 75
Whole-Grain Overnight Oats, 11
Pumpkin Flaxseed Pancakes, 11
High-Fiber Breakfast Muffins, 11
almonds
High-Fiber Breakfast Muffins, 11
Berry Oatmeal Bake, 12
Banana Nut Smoothie Bowl, 14
Strawberry Spinach Salad with Poppy Seed Dressing, 23
Kale and Radish Salad with Lemon-Tahini Dressing, 25
Mixed Berry and Almond Salad, 29
Quinoa and Kale Salad, 77
Roasted Brussels Sprouts with Balsamic Glaze, 77
Moroccan Carrot Salad, 79
Blueberry Almond Tart, 92

Mixed Berry Crumble, 92
apples
Apple Cinnamon Quinoa Bowl, 10
Green Detox Smoothie, 13
Apple Slices with Almond Butter, 16
Apple Chips with Cinnamon, 22
Baked Apples with Cinnamon, 90
Apple Walnut Bread, 97
Apple Cinnamon Shake, 100
applesauce
Oatmeal Raisin Cookies, 95
Apple Walnut Bread, 97
Mango Protein Shake, 99
arugula
Roasted Beet and Arugula Salad, 24
Salmon and Mixed Greens Salad, 26
Turkey and Cranberry Salad, 27
Mixed Berry and Almond Salad, 29
Pear and Pecan Salad, 30
Orange and Pomegranate Salad, 30
Scallop and Citrus Salad, 43
Citrus-Marinated Shrimp Salad, 45
avocado
Avocado and Black Bean Breakfast Wrap, 12
Green Detox Smoothie, 13
Greek Yogurt with Honey and Walnuts, 17
Whole-Grain Crackers with Avocado Spread, 17
Cucumber Avocado Rolls, 19
Rice Cakes with Avocado and Cherry Tomatoes, 21
Kale and Radish Salad with Lemon-Tahini Dressing, 25
Salmon and Mixed Greens Salad, 26
Egg and Spinach Salad, 28
Avocado and Black Bean Salad, 28
Ceviche with Fresh Lime and Cilantro, 41
Shrimp and Mango Salad, 42
Scallop and Citrus Salad, 43
Easy Chicken Fajitas, 59
Lean Beef Tacos with Fresh Salsa, 63
Portobello Mushroom Burgers, 72
Dark Chocolate Avocado Mousse, 90

B

baby kale
Salmon and Mixed Greens Salad, 26
Mixed Berry and Almond Salad, 29
baby spinach

Egg and Spinach Salad, 28
Tropical Fruit and Spinach Salad, 29
Herb-Crusted Salmon with Quinoa, 44
Turkey and Quinoa Stew, 55
Classic Minestrone Soup, 80
Chicken and Vegetable Soup, 83

banana
Chia Seed Pudding with Fresh Fruit, 9
Oat and Flaxseed Smoothie, 13
Berry Antioxidant Smoothie, 14
Banana Nut Smoothie Bowl, 14
Chia Seed Banana Bread, 96
Spinach and Pineapple Shake, 98

basil leaves
Bruschetta with Tomato and Basil, 18
Caprese Skewers with Balsamic Glaze, 19
Farro and Vegetable Medley, 32
Spaghetti Squash with Marinara, 34
One-Pot Pesto Pasta with Peas, 35
Roasted Tomato and Basil Soup, 81
European Berry Bliss, 94
Watermelon Basil Mocktail, 102

beef broth
Braised Lamb Shanks with Root Vegetables, 66
Slow-Cooked Balsamic Beef, 67
Slow-Cooked Beef and Vegetable Stew, 68

beef
Slow-Cooked Balsamic Beef, 67
Grilled Sirloin with Chimichurri Sauce, 60
Lean Beef and Vegetable Stir-Fry, 61
Slow-Cooked Beef and Vegetable Stew, 68

beets
Roasted Beet and Arugula Salad, 24

bell pepper
Veggie Sticks with Greek Yogurt Dip, 15
Mediterranean Chickpea Salad, 26
Avocado and Black Bean Salad, 28
Farro and Vegetable Medley, 32
Lentil and Vegetable Stew, 33
Lentil Pasta with Roasted Red Pepper Sauce, 36
Brown Rice and Vegetable Stir-Fry, 38
Lemon Herb Rice with Grilled Vegetables, 39
Spinach and Feta Stuffed Peppers, 40
Shrimp and Mango Salad, 42
Baked Cod with Mediterranean Vegetables, 44
Easy Fish Curry with Coconut Milk, 49
Moroccan Chicken Stew, 53
Turkey Chili, 54

Turkey and Quinoa Stew, 55
Chicken and Vegetable Stew, 56
Quick Teriyaki Chicken Stir-Fry, 57
Spicy Chicken Wraps, 58
Easy Chicken Fajitas, 59
Lean Beef and Vegetable Stir-Fry, 61
Gound Beef and Vegetable Stuffed Peppers, 64
Turkey Meatballs with Marinara Sauce, 65
Turkey and Quinoa Stew, 55
Stuffed Bell Peppers with Quinoa and Black Beans, 71
Quinoa and Kale Salad, 77
Grilled Vegetable Platter with Hummus, 78
Seafood Stew with Tomatoes and Herbs, 84
Turkey and White Bean Chili, 85
Wild Rice and Vegetable Soup, 87

black beans
Stuffed Mini Bell Peppers with Quinoa, 20

black beans (canned)
Avocado and Black Bean Salad, 28
Turkey Chili, 54
Stuffed Bell Peppers with Quinoa and Black Beans, 71
Sweet Potato and Black Bean Enchiladas, 74
Chicken Tortilla Soup, 85
Avocado and Black Bean Breakfast Wrap, 12

blackberries
Seared Venison with Berry Sauce, 61
High-Fiber Breakfast Muffins, 11
Berry Oatmeal Bake, 12
Berry Antioxidant Smoothie, 14
Banana Nut Smoothie Bowl, 14
Plain Greek Yogurt with Fresh Berries, 22
Mixed Berry and Almond Salad, 29
Blueberry Almond Tart, 92
Mixed Berry Crumble, 92
Greek Yogurt Popsicles, 97
Blueberry Coconut Shake, 100

broccoli florets
Whole Grain Penne with Broccoli and Olive Oil, 36
Brown Rice and Vegetable Stir-Fry, 38
Quick Teriyaki Chicken Stir-Fry, 57
Lean Beef and Vegetable Stir-Fry, 61
Creamy Broccoli Soup (Without Cream), 81

brown lentils
Lentil and Vegetable Stew, 33
Lentil and Vegetable Shepherd's Pie, 70
Lentil and Sweet Potato Stew, 76
Lentil and Spinach Soup, 84

brown rice

Brown Rice and Vegetable Stir-Fry, 38
Lemon Herb Rice with Grilled Vegetables, 39
Spinach and Feta Stuffed Peppers, 40
Moroccan Chicken Stew, 53
Vegan Mushroom Stroganoff, 75

Brussels sprouts
Roasted Brussels Sprouts with Balsamic Glaze, 77

bulgur wheat
Bulgur Wheat and Tomato Soup, 86

butternut squash
Spelt and Roasted Butternut Squash Salad, 33

C

cannellini beans
Classic Minestrone Soup, 80

capers
Fish Fillet Sandwiches with Tartar Sauce, 48

carrots
High-Fiber Breakfast Muffins, 11
Carrot Sticks with Hummus, 16
Veggie Sticks with Greek Yogurt Dip, 15
Barley and Mushroom Stew, 31
Lentil and Vegetable Stew, 33
Brown Rice and Vegetable Stir-Fry, 38
Moroccan Chicken Stew, 53
Turkey Chili, 54
Turkey and Quinoa Stew, 55
Chicken and Vegetable Stew, 56
Quick Teriyaki Chicken Stir-Fry, 57
Lean Beef and Vegetable Stir-Fry, 61
Braised Lamb Shanks with Root Vegetables, 66
Slow-Cooked Balsamic Beef, 67
Slow-Cooked Beef and Vegetable Stew, 68
Braised Turkey Legs with Mushrooms, 68
Turkey and Quinoa Stew, 55
Lentil and Vegetable Shepherd's Pie, 70
Vegan Coleslaw with Tangy Dressing, 78
Moroccan Carrot Salad, 79
Classic Minestrone Soup, 80
Carrot and Ginger Soup, 82
Chicken and Vegetable Soup, 83
Lentil and Spinach Soup, 84
Bulgur Wheat and Tomato Soup, 86
Farro and White Bean Soup, 87
Wild Rice and Vegetable Soup, 87
Quinoa and Kale Soup, 88
Barley and Mushroom Soup, 88

celery

Veggie Sticks with Greek Yogurt Dip, 15
Turkey and Cranberry Salad, 27
Barley and Mushroom Stew, 31
Lentil and Vegetable Stew, 33
Turkey and Quinoa Stew, 55
Chicken and Vegetable Stew, 56
Slow-Cooked Beef and Vegetable Stew, 68
Braised Turkey Legs with Mushrooms, 68
Lentil and Vegetable Shepherd's Pie, 70
Classic Minestrone Soup, 80
Chicken and Vegetable Soup, 83
Lentil and Spinach Soup, 84
Bulgur Wheat and Tomato Soup, 86
Farro and White Bean Soup, 87
Wild Rice and Vegetable Soup, 87
Quinoa and Kale Soup, 88
Barley and Mushroom Soup, 88

cheddar cheese
Turkey and Spinach Quesadillas, 58
Sweet Potato and Black Bean Enchiladas, 74

cherry tomatoes
Caprese Skewers with Balsamic Glaze, 19
Rice Cakes with Avocado and Cherry Tomatoes, 21
Mediterranean Chickpea Salad, 26
Salmon and Mixed Greens Salad, 26
Egg and Spinach Salad, 28
Avocado and Black Bean Salad, 28
Mediterranean Quinoa Salad, 32
Farro and Vegetable Medley, 32
Ceviche with Fresh Lime and Cilantro, 41
Tuna and White Bean Salad, 42
Citrus-Marinated Shrimp Salad, 45
Baked Cod with Mediterranean Vegetables, 44
Herb-Crusted Salmon with Quinoa, 44
Quinoa and Kale Salad, 77
Grilled Vegetable Platter with Hummus, 78
Seafood Stew with Tomatoes and Herbs, 84

chia seeds
Chia Seed Pudding with Fresh Fruit, 9
Whole-Grain Overnight Oats, 11
High-Fiber Breakfast Muffins, 11
Oat and Flaxseed Smoothie, 13
Green Detox Smoothie, 13
Berry Antioxidant Smoothie, 14
Banana Nut Smoothie Bowl, 14
Pineapple Coconut Bars, 93
Chia Seed Banana Bread, 96
Spinach and Pineapple Shake, 98

Mango Protein Shake, 99
Apple Cinnamon Shake, 100
Blueberry Coconut Shake, 100

chicken breast
Baked Chicken Parmesan, 50
Baked Honey Mustard Chicken, 51
Chicken and Vegetable Stew, 56
Quick Teriyaki Chicken Stir-Fry, 57
Spicy Chicken Wraps, 58
Easy Chicken Fajitas, 59
Chicken and Vegetable Soup, 83
Chicken Tortilla Soup, 85
Creamy Chicken and Mushroom Casserole, 54

chicken broth
Herb-Roasted Turkey Breast, 51
Moroccan Chicken Stew, 53
Turkey Chili, 54
Creamy Chicken and Mushroom Casserole, 54
Turkey and Quinoa Stew, 55
Chicken and Vegetable Stew, 56
Quick Teriyaki Chicken Stir-Fry, 57
Seared Venison with Berry Sauce, 61
Braised Turkey Legs with Mushrooms, 68
Chicken and Vegetable Soup, 83
Chicken Tortilla Soup, 85
Turkey and White Bean Chili, 85

chicken tenders
Lemon Garlic Chicken Tenders, 57

chicken thighs
Baked Lemon Rosemary Chicken Thighs, 52
Moroccan Chicken Stew, 53

chickpea pasta
Chickpea Pasta with Spinach and Garlic, 35

chickpeas (canned)
Mediterranean Chickpea Salad, 26
Chickpea Pasta with Spinach and Garlic, 35
Moroccan Chicken Stew, 53
Chickpea and Spinach Curry, 73
Grilled Vegetable Platter with Hummus, 78
Carrot Sticks with Hummus, 16

cocoa powder
Dark Chocolate Avocado Mousse, 90
Almond Flour Brownies, 89

coconut
Pineapple Coconut Bars, 93

coconut milk
Chickpea and Spinach Curry, 73
Carrot and Ginger Soup, 82

Blueberry Coconut Shake, 100

coconut oil
Almond Flour Brownies, 89
Blueberry Almond Tart, 92
Pineapple Coconut Bars, 93
Oatmeal Raisin Cookies, 95
Chia Seed Banana Bread, 96

coconut water
Tropical Mango Mocktail, 101

cod
Fish Fillet Sandwiches with Tartar Sauce, 48
Easy Fish Curry with Coconut Milk, 49
Seafood Stew with Tomatoes and Herbs, 84
Quick Lemon Pepper Baked Fish, 47
Baked Cod with Mediterranean Vegetables, 44

corn kernels
Stuffed Bell Peppers with Quinoa and Black Beans, 71
Turkey and White Bean Chili, 85
Stuffed Mini Bell Peppers with Quinoa, 20
Avocado and Black Bean Salad, 28
Turkey Chili, 54

cottage cheese
Lean Beef and Spinach Lasagna, 64

cranberries
Warm Spiced Cranberry Elixir, 104

cream cheese
Smoked Salmon and Cream Cheese Cucumber Bites, 18

cucumber
Green Detox Smoothie, 13
Veggie Sticks with Greek Yogurt Dip, 15
Smoked Salmon and Cream Cheese Cucumber Bites, 18
Cucumber Avocado Rolls, 19
Cucumber and Dill Salad, 24
Mediterranean Chickpea Salad, 26
Salmon and Mixed Greens Salad, 26
Egg and Spinach Salad, 28
Ceviche with Fresh Lime and Cilantro, 41
Tuna and White Bean Salad, 42
Cucumber and Mint Cooler, 101

currants
Moroccan Carrot Salad, 79

D

dark chocolate
Almond Flour Brownies, 89

dark chocolate chips
Dark Chocolate Avocado Mousse, 90
Almond Flour Brownies, 89

Pumpkin Spice Energy Balls, 95

dill

Smoked Salmon and Cream Cheese Cucumber Bites, 18

Cucumber and Dill Salad, 24

Fish Fillet Sandwiches with Tartar Sauce, 48

dried cranberries

Turkey and Cranberry Salad, 27

Pear and Pecan Salad, 30

Wild Rice and Cranberry Pilaf, 38

Vegan Stuffed Acorn Squash, 75

Quinoa and Kale Salad, 77

E

eggplant

Eggplant Parmesan, 71

eggs

Avocado and Egg Toast, 8

Spinach and Feta Omelet, 9

Pumpkin Flaxseed Pancakes, 11

High-Fiber Breakfast Muffins, 11

Avocado and Black Bean Breakfast Wrap, 12

Berry Oatmeal Bake, 12

Egg and Spinach Salad, 28

Baked Chicken Parmesan, 50

Lean Beef and Spinach Lasagna, 64

Eggplant Parmesan, 71

Spinach and Ricotta Stuffed Shells, 73

Almond Flour Brownies, 89

Oatmeal Raisin Cookies, 95

Chia Seed Banana Bread, 96

Apple Walnut Bread, 97

F

farro

Farro and Vegetable Medley, 32

Farro and White Bean Soup, 87

feta cheese

Spinach and Feta Omelet, 9

Strawberry Spinach Salad with Poppy Seed Dressing, 23

Kale and Radish Salad with Lemon-Tahini Dressing, 25

Mediterranean Chickpea Salad, 26

Salmon and Mixed Greens Salad, 26

Mediterranean Quinoa Salad, 32

Spinach and Feta Stuffed Peppers, 40

Quinoa and Kale Salad, 77

fish broth

Easy Fish Curry with Coconut Milk, 49

G

ginger (fresh)

Brown Rice and Vegetable Stir-Fry, 38

Chickpea and Spinach Curry, 73

Pumpkin Zucchini Ginger Cream Soup, 82

Carrot and Ginger Soup, 82

Pineapple and Ginger Juice, 103

Green Tea with Lemon and Ginger, 105

goat cheese

Roasted Beet and Arugula Salad, 24

Turkey and Cranberry Salad, 27

Mixed Berry and Almond Salad, 29

granola

Banana Nut Smoothie Bowl, 14

grapefruit

Citrus and Fennel Salad, 25

Scallop and Citrus Salad, 43

Chilled Citrus Fruit Salad, 91

Greek yogurt

Chia Seed Pudding with Fresh Fruit, 9

Whole-Grain Overnight Oats, 11

High-Fiber Breakfast Muffins, 11

Oat and Flaxseed Smoothie, 13

Berry Antioxidant Smoothie, 14

Banana Nut Smoothie Bowl, 14

Veggie Sticks with Greek Yogurt Dip, 15

Greek Yogurt with Honey and Walnuts, 17

Cucumber and Dill Salad, 24

Fish Fillet Sandwiches with Tartar Sauce, 48

Creamy Chicken and Mushroom Casserole, 54

Spicy Chicken Wraps, 58

Turkey and Spinach Quesadillas, 58

Easy Chicken Fajitas, 59

Lean Beef Tacos with Fresh Salsa, 63

Roasted Tomato and Basil Soup, 81

Apple Walnut Bread, 97

Greek Yogurt Popsicles, 97

Spinach and Pineapple Shake, 98

Mango Protein Shake, 99

Pumpkin Spice Protein Shake, 99

Apple Cinnamon Shake, 100

Blueberry Coconut Shake, 100

Chia Seed Pudding with Fresh Fruit, 9

green beans

Chicken and Vegetable Stew, 56

Slow-Cooked Balsamic Beef, 67

Slow-Cooked Beef and Vegetable Stew, 68

Classic Minestrone Soup, 80

Chicken and Vegetable Soup, 83

Seafood Stew with Tomatoes and Herbs, 84

green cabbage
Vegan Coleslaw with Tangy Dressing, 78
green lentils
Lentil and Vegetable Stew, 33
Lentil and Vegetable Shepherd's Pie, 70
Lentil and Sweet Potato Stew, 76
Lentil and Spinach Soup, 84
green onions
Miso-Glazed Sea Bass, 46
Lean Beef and Vegetable Stir-Fry , 61
Turkey Meatballs with Marinara Sauce, 65
ground beef
Gound Beef and Vegetable Stuffed Peppers, 64
Lean Beef and Spinach Lasagna, 64
Lean Beef Tacos with Fresh Salsa, 63
ground flaxseed
Whole-Grain Overnight Oats, 11
Pumpkin Flaxseed Pancakes, 11
Oat and Flaxseed Smoothie, 13
Green Detox Smoothie, 13
Berry Antioxidant Smoothie, 14
Banana Nut Smoothie Bowl, 14
Flaxseed-Crusted Mackerel, 46
Mango Protein Shake, 99
Apple Cinnamon Shake, 100
Blueberry Coconut Shake, 100
Pumpkin Spice Energy Balls, 95
ground turkey
Turkey Chili, 54
Turkey and Spinach Quesadillas, 58
Turkey and Quinoa Stew, 55
Turkey Meatballs with Marinara Sauce, 65
Ground Turkey Lettuce Wraps, 66
Turkey and White Bean Chili, 85

H

haddock
Quick Lemon Pepper Baked Fish, 47
halibut
Ceviche with Fresh Lime and Cilantro, 41
Seafood Stew with Tomatoes and Herbs, 84

K

Kalamata olives
Mediterranean Chickpea Salad, 26
Mediterranean Quinoa Salad, 32
Tuna and White Bean Salad, 42
kale
Kale and Radish Salad with Lemon-Tahini Dressing, 25

Lentil and Sweet Potato Stew, 76
Quinoa and Kale Salad, 77
Quinoa and Kale Soup, 88
Baked Kale Chips, 20
Green Detox Smoothie, 13
Turkey Chili, 54
kiwi
Chilled Citrus Fruit Salad, 91
Rosemary Garlic Lamb Chops, 62

L

lamb chops
Braised Lamb Shanks with Root Vegetables, 66
lamb shanks
Flaxseed-Crusted Mackerel, 46
lemon
Pan-Seared Scallops with Garlic Butter, 47
Herb-Roasted Turkey Breast, 51
Lemon Pepper Baked Turkey, 52
Baked Lemon Rosemary Chicken Thighs, 52
Lemon Garlic Chicken Tenders, 57
Grilled Sirloin with Chimichurri Sauce, 60
Rosemary Garlic Lamb Chops, 62
Baked Herb-Crusted Pork Tenderloin, 62
Lentil and Sweet Potato Stew, 76
Moroccan Carrot Salad, 79
Green Tea with Lemon and Ginger, 105
Sardine and Tomato Pasta, 45
Citrus-Marinated Shrimp Salad, 45
Portobello Mushroom Burgers, 72
lettuce
Lean Beef Tacos with Fresh Salsa, 63
Ceviche with Fresh Lime and Cilantro, 41
Citrus-Marinated Shrimp Salad, 45
Fish Fillet Sandwiches with Tartar Sauce, 48
Spicy Chicken Wraps, 58
Chicken Tortilla Soup, 85
lime
Mango Sorbet, 91
Citrus-Marinated Shrimp Salad, 45

M

mackerel fillets
Flaxseed-Crusted Mackerel, 46
mango
Tropical Fruit and Spinach Salad, 29
Shrimp and Mango Salad, 42
Mango Sorbet, 91
Mango Protein Shake, 99

Tropical Mango Mocktail, 101
Baked Chicken Parmesan, 50

milk
Creamy Chicken and Mushroom Casserole, 54
Apple Walnut Bread, 97
Spinach and Pineapple Shake, 98
Stuffed Mini Bell Peppers with Quinoa, 20

mini bell peppers
Stuffed Mini Bell Peppers with Quinoa, 20

mint leaves
Orange and Pomegranate Salad, 30
Mediterranean Quinoa Salad, 32
Scallop and Citrus Salad, 43
Chilled Citrus Fruit Salad, 91
Cucumber and Mint Cooler, 101
Pineapple and Ginger Juice, 103
Miso-Glazed Sea Bass, 46

mozzarella cheese
Lean Beef and Spinach Lasagna, 64
Eggplant Parmesan, 71
Spinach and Ricotta Stuffed Shells, 73
Caprese Skewers with Balsamic Glaze, 19
Creamy Chicken and Mushroom Casserole, 54

mushrooms
Braised Turkey Legs with Mushrooms, 68
Vegan Mushroom Stroganoff, 75
Wild Rice and Vegetable Soup, 87
Barley and Mushroom Soup, 88
Air-Popped Popcorn with Nutritional Yeast, 21

N

nutritional yeast
Vegan Mushroom Stroganoff, 75
Creamy Broccoli Soup (Without Cream), 81
High-Fiber Breakfast Muffins, 11

O

oranges
Orange and Pomegranate Salad, 30
Scallop and Citrus Salad, 43
Chilled Citrus Fruit Salad, 91
Radiant Pomegranate-Orange Bliss, 102
Warm Pumpkin Orange Spice Elixir, 104
Warm Pomegranate Citrus Delight, 105
Tropical Fruit and Spinach Salad, 29
Citrus-Marinated Shrimp Salad, 45

P

papaya
Tropical Fruit and Spinach Salad, 29

Parmesan cheese
Herb-Crusted Salmon with Quinoa, 44
Baked Chicken Parmesan, 50
Creamy Chicken and Mushroom Casserole, 54
Lean Beef and Spinach Lasagna, 64
Eggplant Parmesan, 71
Spinach and Ricotta Stuffed Shells, 73
Classic Minestrone Soup, 80
Roasted Tomato and Basil Soup, 81
Citrus and Fennel Salad, 25

parsnips
Classic Minestrone Soup, 80

peach
Grilled Peaches with Honey, 94

pearl barley
Barley and Mushroom Soup, 88
Barley and Mushroom Stew, 31

pears
Pear and Pecan Salad, 30

peas
One-Pot Pesto Pasta with Peas, 35
Lentil and Vegetable Shepherd's Pie, 70

pecans
Pear and Pecan Salad, 30
Wild Rice and Cranberry Pilaf, 38
Vegan Stuffed Acorn Squash, 75
Baked Apples with Cinnamon, 90
Chia Seed Banana Bread, 96
One-Pot Pesto Pasta with Peas, 35

penne
Whole Grain Penne with Broccoli and Olive Oil, 36
Fish Fillet Sandwiches with Tartar Sauce, 48

pickle relish
One-Pot Pesto Pasta with Peas, 35

pine nuts
Tropical Fruit and Spinach Salad, 29

pineapple
Tropical Fruit and Spinach Salad, 29
Chilled Citrus Fruit Salad, 91
Pineapple Coconut Bars, 93
Spinach and Pineapple Shake, 98
Pineapple and Ginger Juice, 103
Tropical Mango Mocktail, 101

pomegranate juice
Warm Pomegranate Citrus Delight, 105

pomegranate seeds
Orange and Pomegranate Salad, 30
Radiant Pomegranate-Orange Bliss, 102

poppy seeds

Strawberry Spinach Salad with Poppy Seed Dressing, 23

pork tenderloin

Baked Herb-Crusted Pork Tenderloin, 62

portobello mushroom

Balsamic Glazed Portobello Mushrooms with Wild Rice, 37

Portobello Mushroom Burgers, 72

potatoes

Slow-Cooked Beef and Vegetable Stew, 68

Lentil and Vegetable Shepherd's Pie, 70

Creamy Broccoli Soup (Without Cream), 81

pumpkin

Pumpkin Flaxseed Pancakes, 11

Pumpkin Zucchini Ginger Cream Soup, 82

pumpkin puree

Pumpkin Spice Energy Balls, 95

Pumpkin Spice Protein Shake, 99

Warm Pumpkin Orange Spice Elixir, 104

Apple Cinnamon Quinoa Bowl, 10

Q

quinoa

Stuffed Mini Bell Peppers with Quinoa, 20

Mediterranean Quinoa Salad, 32

Herb-Crusted Salmon with Quinoa, 44

Moroccan Chicken Stew, 53

Creamy Chicken and Mushroom Casserole, 54

Turkey and Quinoa Stew, 55

Stuffed Bell Peppers with Quinoa and Black Beans, 71

Vegan Stuffed Acorn Squash, 75

Quinoa and Kale Salad, 77

Quinoa and Kale Soup, 88

Kale and Radish Salad with Lemon-Tahini Dressing, 25

R

radish

Kale and Radish Salad with Lemon-Tahini Dressing, 25

raisins

Baked Apples with Cinnamon, 90

Oatmeal Raisin Cookies, 95

Berry Oatmeal Bake, 12

raspberries

Berry Antioxidant Smoothie, 14

Banana Nut Smoothie Bowl, 14

Plain Greek Yogurt with Fresh Berries, 22

Mixed Berry and Almond Salad, 29

Seared Venison with Berry Sauce, 61

Mixed Berry Crumble , 92

Greek Yogurt Popsicles, 97

Vegan Coleslaw with Tangy Dressing, 78

red cabbage

Avocado and Black Bean Breakfast Wrap, 12

ricotta cheese

Lean Beef and Spinach Lasagna, 64

Spinach and Ricotta Stuffed Shells, 73

Whole-Grain Overnight Oats, 11

rolled oats

High-Fiber Breakfast Muffins, 11

Berry Oatmeal Bake, 12

Oat and Flaxseed Smoothie, 13

Baked Apples with Cinnamon, 90

Blueberry Almond Tart, 92

Mixed Berry Crumble, 92

Pineapple Coconut Bars, 93

Oatmeal Raisin Cookies, 95

Pumpkin Spice Energy Balls, 95

Chia Seed Banana Bread, 96

Apple Walnut Bread, 97

Turkey and Cranberry Salad, 27

S

salad greens

Salmon and Mixed Greens Salad, 26

Herb-Crusted Salmon with Quinoa, 44

salmon fillets

Salmon and Mixed Greens Salad, 26

Turkey and Spinach Quesadillas, 58

sardines (canned)

Seafood Stew with Tomatoes and Herbs, 84

sea bass

Miso-Glazed Sea Bass, 46

Scallop and Citrus Salad, 43

sea scallops

Pan-Seared Scallops with Garlic Butter, 47

Seafood Stew with Tomatoes and Herbs, 84

Ceviche with Fresh Lime and Cilantro, 41

sesame seeds

Simple Tuna Steak with Soy Sauce and Ginger, 48

Lean Beef and Vegetable Stir-Fry, 61

Shrimp and Mango Salad, 42

shrimp

Citrus-Marinated Shrimp Salad, 45

Seafood Stew with Tomatoes and Herbs, 84

smoked salmon

Smoked Salmon and Cream Cheese Cucumber Bites, 18

spaghetti

Sardine and Tomato Pasta, 45

Spaghetti Squash with Marinara, 34

spelt

Avocado and Black Bean Breakfast Wrap, 12

spinach

Strawberry Spinach Salad with Poppy Seed Dressing, 23

Salmon and Mixed Greens Salad, 26

Turkey and Cranberry Salad, 27

Mixed Berry and Almond Salad, 29

Pear and Pecan Salad, 30

Orange and Pomegranate Salad, 30

Barley and Mushroom Stew, 31

Spelt and Roasted Butternut Squash Salad, 33

Chickpea Pasta with Spinach and Garlic, 35

Spinach and Feta Stuffed Peppers , 40

Scallop and Citrus Salad, 43

Citrus-Marinated Shrimp Salad, 45

Turkey and Spinach Quesadillas, 58

Spinach and Ricotta Stuffed Shells, 73

Chickpea and Spinach Curry, 73

Lentil and Sweet Potato Stew, 76

Lentil and Spinach Soup, 84

Farro and White Bean Soup, 87

Wild Rice and Vegetable Soup, 87

Spinach and Pineapple Shake, 98

Lean Beef and Spinach Lasagna, 64

Berry Oatmeal Bake, 12

Spinach and Feta Omelet, 9

Green Detox Smoothie, 13

strawberries

Berry Antioxidant Smoothie, 14

Banana Nut Smoothie Bowl, 14

Plain Greek Yogurt with Fresh Berries, 22

Strawberry Spinach Salad with Poppy Seed Dressing, 23

Mixed Berry and Almond Salad, 29

Tropical Fruit and Spinach Salad, 29

Chilled Citrus Fruit Salad, 91

Mixed Berry Crumble, 92

European Berry Bliss, 94

Greek Yogurt Popsicles, 97

Sweet Potato and Black Bean Enchiladas, 74

sweet potatoes

Carrot Sticks with Hummus, 16

T

tilapia

Quick Lemon Pepper Baked Fish, 47

Fish Fillet Sandwiches with Tartar Sauce, 48

Easy Fish Curry with Coconut Milk, 49

Lean Beef and Spinach Lasagna, 64

tomato paste

Braised Lamb Shanks with Root Vegetables, 66

Slow-Cooked Balsamic Beef, 67

Turkey and White Bean Chili, 85

Lean Beef and Spinach Lasagna, 64

tomatoes

Tomato and Basil Breakfast Sandwich, 10

Avocado and Black Bean Breakfast Wrap, 14

Bruschetta with Tomato and Basil, 18

Stuffed Mini Bell Peppers with Quinoa, 20

Fish Fillet Sandwiches with Tartar Sauce, 48

Spicy Chicken Wraps, 58

Lean Beef Tacos with Fresh Salsa, 63

Braised Turkey Legs with Mushrooms, 68

Stuffed Bell Peppers with Quinoa and Black Beans, 71

Portobello Mushroom Burgers, 72

Roasted Tomato and Basil Soup, 81

Barley and Mushroom Stew, 31

tuna (canned)

Simple Tuna Steak with Soy Sauce and Ginger, 48

tuna steaks

Turkey and Cranberry Salad, 27

turkey breast

Herb-Roasted Turkey Breast, 51

Lemon Pepper Baked Turkey, 52

Slow-Cooked Turkey with Vegetables, 69

turkey legs

Braised Turkey Legs with Mushrooms, 68

W

walnuts

Berry Oatmeal Bake, 12

Banana Nut Smoothie Bowl, 14

Greek Yogurt with Honey and Walnuts, 17

Roasted Beet and Arugula Salad, 24

One-Pot Pesto Pasta with Peas, 35

Vegan Stuffed Acorn Squash, 75

Baked Apples with Cinnamon, 90

Almond Flour Brownies, 89

Pumpkin Spice Energy Balls, 95

Chia Seed Banana Bread, 96

Apple Walnut Bread, 97

Turkey Meatballs with Marinara Sauce, 65

water chestnuts

Ground Turkey Lettuce Wraps, 66

watermelon

Watermelon Basil Mocktail, 102

white beans (canned)

Tuna and White Bean Salad, 42

Turkey and White Bean Chili, 85

Farro and White Bean Soup, 87

white fish

Seafood Stew with Tomatoes and Herbs, 84

Ceviche with Fresh Lime and Cilantro, 41

Quick Lemon Pepper Baked Fish, 47

Fish Fillet Sandwiches with Tartar Sauce, 48

Easy Fish Curry with Coconut Milk, 49

Miso-Glazed Sea Bass, 46

whole wheat flour

Pumpkin Flaxseed Pancakes, 11

High-Fiber Breakfast Muffins, 11

Fish Fillet Sandwiches with Tartar Sauce, 48

Eggplant Parmesan, 71

Chia Seed Banana Bread, 96

Apple Walnut Bread, 97

whole wheat tortillas

Easy Chicken Fajitas, 59

Lean Beef Tacos with Fresh Salsa, 63

Sweet Potato and Black Bean Enchiladas, 74

Turkey and Spinach Quesadillas, 58

wild rice

Balsamic Glazed Portobello Mushrooms with Wild Rice, 37

Wild Rice and Cranberry Pilaf, 38

Wild Rice and Vegetable Soup, 87

Z

zucchini

Lentil and Vegetable Stew, 33

Lemon Herb Rice with Grilled Vegetables, 39

Baked Cod with Mediterranean Vegetables, 44

Easy Fish Curry with Coconut Milk, 49

Moroccan Chicken Stew, 53

Turkey and Quinoa Stew, 55

Chicken and Vegetable Stew, 56

Grilled Vegetable Platter with Hummus, 78

Classic Minestrone Soup, 80

Pumpkin Zucchini Ginger Cream Soup, 82

Chicken and Vegetable Soup, 83

Seafood Stew with Tomatoes and Herbs, 84

Made in the USA
Las Vegas, NV
24 October 2024

10341726R00070